Undergraduate Topics in Computer Science

D1381681

Undergraduate Topics in Computer Science (UTiCS) delivers high-quality instructional content for undergraduates studying in all areas of computing and information science. From core foundational and theoretical material to final-year topics and applications, UTiCS books take a fresh, concise, and modern approach and are ideal for self-study or for a one- or two-semester course. The texts are all authored by established experts in their fields, reviewed by an international advisory board, and contain numerous examples and problems. Many include fully worked solutions.

For further volumes:
http://www.springer.com/series/7592

Maribel Fernández

Programming Languages and Operational Semantics

A Concise Overview

 Springer

Prof. Maribel Fernández
King's College London
London
UK

ISSN 1863-7310   ISSN 2197-1781   (electronic)
ISBN 978-1-4471-6367-1   ISBN 978-1-4471-6368-8   (eBook)
DOI 10.1007/978-1-4471-6368-8
Springer London Heidelberg New York Dordrecht

Library of Congress Control Number: 2014932000

Springer is part of Springer Science+Business Media (www.springer.com)

Preface

Aim

This book is addressed to undergraduate students as a complement to programming courses. The general aim of the book is to present and compare alternative programming language paradigms, and to provide the foundations and tools needed to design new programming languages and understand the existing ones. These are ambitious goals, and to achieve our aims, we have chosen to introduce and explain in a concise way the most significant constructs of modern imperative, functional and logic programming languages, and describe their operational semantics first in an informal way, and then using transition systems.

About this Book

This book provides a concise introduction to the essential concepts in programming languages, using operational semantics techniques. The book is for the most part self-contained, but we assume readers have some basic programming skills and have used at least one programming language. Knowledge of more programming languages will be helpful but is not necessary.

Each chapter includes exercises that provide an opportunity to apply the concepts and techniques presented. Doing exercises is an important part of the learning process: to understand how a programming language works and be able to use it, it is not sufficient to read about it. Of course, the same can be said about many other topics (learning to play a musical instrument or learning to ride a bicycle are familiar examples). Since practice is unavoidable, we have included not just exercises to be done on paper, but also some programming exercises that require checking on a computer. Although some of the exercises are just introductory, most of the questions are designed with the goal of testing the *understanding* of the subject (for instance, by requiring students to adapt a given technique to different contexts). Some challenging exercises for more advanced students are also included; these are marked with (†). Answers to selected exercises are given in the final chapter of the book.

The book is organised as follows:

Part I provides an introduction to programming languages and operational semantics in Chap. 1, followed by basic mathematical background for the rest of the book in Chap. 2.

In Part II we study the main components of imperative languages. We first give an informal description in Chap. 3, and then give a formal specification of the main constructs in imperative languages using transition systems in Chap. 4.

Part III is dedicated to functional languages and their type systems. In Chap. 5 we give an overview of functional programming (using Haskell for our examples), and then give some examples of semantic descriptions of functional languages in Chap. 6.

Finally, in Part IV (Chaps. 7 and 8) we briefly study logic programming languages and describe the operational semantics of Prolog.

The last chapter of the book (Chap. 9) contains answers to a selection of exercises.

We have not included chapters on object-oriented languages, but we do study aspects of these languages in Chaps. 1 and 3.

Each chapter includes a list of recommended further reading, a list of exercises, and a bibliographical section with references to relevant articles and books where the interested reader can find more information. In particular, for each programming language there is a reference to its definition, which is indicated the first time the language is mentioned.

Acknowledgments

The material presented in this book has been prepared using several different sources, including the references mentioned above and lecture notes for my courses at King's College London and in France. I would like to thank the editors of the UTiCS series for inviting me to write this book. I am very grateful to the students in the Department of Informatics at King's and the teaching assistants in my courses (in particular, Asad Ali, Christophe Calvès, Jesús Domínguez, Elliot Fairweather, Fabien Fleutot, François-Régis Sinot and Jeffrey Terrell) for their comments on previous versions of the book. Special thanks to Elliot Fairweather and Jeff Terrell for their careful reading and helpful suggestions. Last, but not least, I thank my family for their continuous support.

London, January 2014   Maribel Fernández

Contents

Part I
Preliminaries

Chapter 1
Introduction

This book is concerned with programming languages. Programming languages are tools for writing software; they enable the user to communicate with the computer.

There are hundreds of programming languages in use in the world today. Many of them have evolved from older languages, and are likely to continue evolving in the future. In order to understand this plethora of languages and adapt easily to changes in the languages we are familiar with, it is useful to study the concepts underlying programming languages in general. We will study the main components of programming languages, and some of the tools that are used to describe in a precise way the behaviour of their main constructs. Our goal will be not only to understand how programming language primitives work but also to be able to describe their behaviour in a detailed and precise way. This is important in order to:

- understand the differences between apparently similar constructs in different languages;
- be able to choose a suitable programming language for each application;
- increase our ability to learn new languages and our ability to adapt to changes in existing languages;
- design new languages (not just programming languages: the general concepts underlying programming language design can also be applied to the design of other kind of languages, for instance, software modelling languages, languages to specify security policies, or user-interfaces for software applications).

In this book, we focus on general purpose languages as opposed to domain specific languages. General purpose languages are programming languages that can be used to program a variety of applications, whereas domain specific languages are special purpose languages designed to be used in specific domains. Special purpose languages include specific constructs to facilitate programming particular kinds of applications. For example, one of the first domain specific languages was GPSS (General Purpose Simulation System [1]), designed in the 1960s for systems simulation. More modern examples of domain specific languages include eXtensible Stylesheet Language Transformations (XSLT [2]), a language defined by the World

M. Fernández, *Programming Languages and Operational Semantics*,
Undergraduate Topics in Computer Science, DOI: 10.1007/978-1-4471-6368-8_1,
© Springer-Verlag London 2014

Wide Web Consortium in the 1990s to transform XML documents, and JavaServer Pages Standard Tag Library (JSTL [3]), a markup language with programming capabilities. Domain specific languages usually have a narrow application domain, and have their own specific programming techniques and design methodologies, which cannot be easily compared with those of general purpose languages. Since our aim is to analyse the features of various programming languages in order to be able to understand their differences and make informed choices, in the rest of the book we will only consider general purpose languages.

1.1 Programming Languages and Software Engineering

Programming languages are used in several phases in the software development process: in the implementation phase obviously, but also in the design phase to describe the decomposition of the system into modules that later will be coded and tested.

There are various design methods in use, for example: top-down design, functional design, object-oriented design. Some languages provide better support for design methods than others:

– Older languages such as Fortran (the first version was reported in 1954 [4]) do not support any specific design method.
– More modern languages were designed to support a specific design method: for example, Pascal [5] was designed to support top-down development and structured programming, Haskell [6] supports functional design, Java [7] supports object-oriented design and programming.

If the design method is not compatible with the programming language in which the application will be coded, the programming effort increases. For large applications in particular, it is advisable to choose a design method and a programming language that are compatible. The style of the programming language should be reflected in the design of the software application. In this way, the design abstractions can easily be mapped into program components. For instance, we should think in terms of functions if we are going to use a functional language, or in terms of objects if we are going to use an object-oriented language.

1.2 Programming Paradigms

A programming language induces a particular style of programming and a particular set of methods and techniques to reason about programs, called a *programming paradigm*. Programming languages are usually classified according to the paradigm they support. The main classes of programming languages are:

- **Imperative Languages**: Programs are decomposed into *computation steps* (also called commands, statements, or instructions), reflecting the step-wise execution of programs in usual hardware. Subprograms (also called routines, procedures, etc.) are used to build programs in a modular way. Programs written in imperative languages give accurate descriptions of *how* to solve a given problem. For example: Fortran, Algol [8], Pascal, C [9], Python [10] and Java are imperative languages.
- **Functional Languages**: Programs are functions, which can be composed to build new functions as in the mathematical theory of functions (the basis of these languages). This class of languages is also called declarative, since the focus is on *what* should be computed, not *how* it should be computed. Functional languages emphasise the use of expressions, which are evaluated by simplification. For example: Haskell, SML [11], Caml [12] and Clean [13] are functional languages. LISP [14], introduced by John McCarthy in the 1950s, is considered to be the ancestor of all functional programming languages.
- **Object-oriented Languages**: Programs are collections of objects which can only be accessed through the operations (or methods) provided for them, and are usually hierarchically organised. For example: Java and Python are object-oriented languages. An object can be thought of as an entity combining data (fields) and operations (methods). In the object-oriented design methodology, the designer produces a hierarchical description of the structure of the system, which is the basis for the implementation in an object-oriented language. Object-orientation is sometimes considered as a feature of imperative languages, however, it can also be found in functional languages and it can be combined with logic languages too. Therefore we see it as a paradigm of programming in its own right. However, this class of languages is out of the scope of this book.
- **Logic Languages**: Programs describe a problem rather than defining an algorithmic implementation. Again this class of languages is declarative, since the focus is on the specification of the problem that needs to be solved and not on how it is solved. A logic program is a description (usually using the language of first-order logic) of facts and properties about a problem. The most well-known logic programming language is Prolog [15], which was designed by Colmerauer, Roussel and Kowalski in the 1970s. More modern logic programming languages combine logic programming and constraint-solving.

This list is not exhaustive. There are other classes of languages, for example, real-time programming languages, interaction-based languages, and scripting languages, such as JavaScript [16] and PHP [17] used in web programming. In this book we will focus on imperative, functional and logic languages.

1.3 Components of a Programming Language

A programming language has three main components:

1. *Syntax*: defines the form of programs. It describes the way expressions, commands and declarations are built and put together to form a program.

2. *Semantics*: gives the *meaning* of programs. It describes the way programs behave when they are executed.
3. *Implementation*: a software system that can read a program and execute it in a computer. It usually consists of a compiler or interpreter, plus a set of tools, such as editors and debuggers, which help programmers write and test programs. Programming languages usually include a runtime support, which provides functionalities such as memory management primitives (e.g., a garbage collector), mechanisms to implement calls to subprograms including parameter passing, etc.

We will describe each of these components in this section, starting from implementation. But first, to help understanding how programming languages are implemented, we give a brief overview of computer architecture.

1.3.1 Computer Architecture

The main components of a *Von Neumann machine* (the most popular kind of computer) are:

- Memory, which contains data and machine instructions represented as sequences of bits;
- Processor (also called Central Processing Unit, CPU), which consists of an arithmetic logic unit with a set of processor registers, and a control unit with an instruction register and program counter;
- Peripherals, which may include a keyboard, display, mouse, printer, etc;
- File systems, which permit to store data externally.

The set of machine instructions for arithmetic and logic operations used by the processor is usually called *machine language*. The *operating system* supplies higher-level primitives than those of the machine language (e.g. input/output operations, file management system, editors). For example, Linux, Unix, MS DOS and Mac OS are operating systems. Language implementations are built on top of these, and user programs or applications form the top layer, as shown in the following diagram.

user programs

---

language implementation

---

operating system

---

hardware

The three layers hardware, operating system and language implementation are sometimes called a *virtual machine*. This is because if we have an implementation of say, the language C, then by abstracting the intermediate levels we can think of the system as a machine that executes C instructions. In other words, we can see it as a computer whose machine language is C.

1.3.2 Language Implementation

Programming languages can be classified as low level or high level, depending on how close they are to machine language. Low-level languages are machine dependent. For example, machine instructions, and even assembly languages in which names are given to machine instructions and data, are low-level languages. In this book we are concerned with high-level programming languages, which are (more or less) independent from the machine.

Machine independence is good in terms of portability (the ease with which code can be moved from one machine to another), but bad in that the hardware of the computer is not able to execute the language commands directly. Therefore, if we use high-level languages we need special programs (which are themselves executable) to translate our high-level programs into executable code, or simply to read and execute our high-level programs. In order words, we need an implementation of the language.

High-level programming languages can be implemented by:

- *Compiling* programs into machine language: a compiler is a program that can read a high-level program and produce executable code for it;
- *Interpreting* programs: an interpreter is a program that can read a high-level program and execute its instructions;
- using a *Hybrid Method*, which combines compilation and interpretation, that is, the program is compiled into intermediate code, which it is later interpreted.

Although compilation, interpretation and the hybrid method are fundamentally different, they share some features. For instance, the three methods require first reading the program and identifying its components. We will describe the compilation method below, and then highlight the distinguishing features of the other two methods in relation to compilation.

1.3.2.1 Compilation

A compiler is a program that translates a *source language* (usually a high-level language) into *object language* (usually machine language). The output of the compiler is a program that can be executed directly on the computer, although often other programs are needed (for example, a *linker*) in order to include code from libraries into an executable binary program.

Once our original program has been compiled, we can run it by executing the binary program produced by the compiler (and possibly the linker). We can of course run the program many times without having to repeat the compilation process.

Usually compilers include optimisation phases, where the machine code generated is optimised to improve its efficiency, both in terms of memory use and execution time (although there is often a trade-off between the two). As a result, this method of implementation of programming languages provides fast program execution.

The main phases of the compilation process are:

1. *Lexical Analysis.*

   The building blocks of a programming language are lexical units called *tokens*. For example, identifiers (such as names of variables), keywords (such as begin, if, then, else, etc), separators (such as comma, colon, semicolon) are tokens. The lexical analyser, which is sometimes called the *lexer*, reads a file containing a program (that is, reads the sequence of characters that forms a program) and identifies a sequence of tokens, which are then passed to the syntax analyser. The lexical analyser may also produce an error message, if the characters in the input do not correspond to any of the tokens of the language.

2. *Syntax Analysis (Parsing).*

   The syntax analyser, which is often called the *parser*, reads a sequence of tokens and produces a parse tree (also called syntax tree) for the program, or an error message if the sequence of tokens does not obey the rules of the language. In order to check that the sequence of tokens corresponds to a syntactically correct program, the parser uses a formal definition of the syntax of the language, usually given by a *grammar*.

3. *Type and Semantics Analysis.*

   Some programming languages are *typed* and at compile time programs are checked to detect type errors. Programs that do not respect the typing rules of the language are rejected by the compiler.[1] Usually the syntax tree generated by the parser is used for type checking, and also for (optional) code optimisations.

4. *Machine Code Generation.*

   The code generator produces machine code, more precisely, it generates a machine-language program equivalent to the optimised syntax tree (and to the original source program).

At this point, we are ready to execute the program. To actually run the program, we need to execute the object code produced by the compiler (and possibly by the linker). Machine code is executed in the CPU, but resides in memory. Therefore, to be executed, each instruction needs to be brought to the CPU, decoded and executed. This process is called the *fetch-execute cycle*. During the fetch-execute cycle,

---

[1] In some typed languages the compiler does not check types but introduces code so that types can be checked at run time.

instructions are moved one by one from the memory, where the program is stored, to the processor. The fetch-execute cycle consists of the following steps:

– Initialise the Program Counter (also called Instruction Pointer), in a register of the machine;
– Repeat:

  – fetch the instruction to which the Program Counter points;
  – increment the Program Counter;
  – decode and execute the instruction.

When the execution of the program finishes, control returns to the operating system (of course, in a system where more than one program is running the process is more complex).

1.3.2.2 Interpretation

In this case there is no translation to machine code: an interpreter is a program that reads, analyses and directly executes the instructions of a high-level language (or produces an error message when a lexical, syntactic or semantic error is detected).

The interpreter simulates a machine whose fetch-execute cycle deals with high-level program instructions; in other words, the interpreter provides us with a *virtual machine* whose machine code is a high-level language.

Interpretation has some advantages over compilation: interpreters are easier to implement than compilers and provide better error messages, so interpreted programs are easier to debug. However, there are also some disadvantages: there is limited scope for optimisation if instructions have to be directly executed; for this reason in general the execution of programs in interpreted languages is slower.

Simpler languages, and prototyping languages, are usually interpreted (for example: LISP and Unix Shell Scripts are interpreted).

Some languages have both an interpreted and a compiled version. The interpreter can be used for didactic purposes, to write prototype software applications, or to develop and debug programs that are later compiled to increase execution speed. For example, for the study of functional programming languages later in this book we will use an interpreter for Haskell (called Hugs) but compilers are also available (for example, ghc).

1.3.2.3 Hybrid Implementation

Some languages are implemented by translation (compilation) to an intermediate simpler language, instead of machine language. This intermediate language is then interpreted.

The advantage of this solution is portability: in this way programs can be executed in any machine that has an interpreter for the intermediate language.

There are many examples of this technique. Pascal was one of the first languages implemented in this way. Many functional languages are translated to abstract machine code, which is interpreted. Java compilers also produce code in an intermediate language (bytecode) and programs can then be executed in any machine with a bytecode interpreter. Just-in-time implementations are hybrid, but instead of simply interpreting the intermediate code, a Just-in-time implementation compiles subprograms in the intermediate language the first time they are called; the code will then be reused in subsequent calls.

We will not study language implementation techniques in more detail in this book (the interested reader can find in the Further Reading section at the end of this chapter references to books where these topics are studied in detail). The rest of this chapter will introduce the tools used to describe the syntax and semantics of programming languages.

1.3.3 Syntax

The *syntax* of a programming language is concerned with the *form* of programs. It specifies the set of characters that can be used to write programs, and provides rules indicating how to form lexical units (such as keywords, identifiers, constants, etc.) and how to combine them to build expressions, commands, etc.

We have to distinguish between *concrete syntax* and *abstract syntax* of programming languages. The concrete syntax describes which sequences of characters are well-formed programs, whereas the abstract syntax describes the syntax trees that represent programs. In other words, the concrete syntax describes the actual programs, whereas the abstract syntax describes their representation (the output of the syntax analyser). For this reason, definitions of concrete syntax often include explanations about things like the use of indentation and how comments should be written. The abstract syntax does not deal with these details, since indentation and comments are not included in the representation of the program. Below we give more examples to illustrate the differences between concrete and abstract syntax, using arithmetic expressions. First we need to introduce some terminology.

Formally, a language is a set of *words* built out of characters from a given alphabet. In the case of programming languages, the words are programs. In order to describe the set of words that belong to the language, we use *grammars*.

The grammar of a programming language describes the set of programs that are syntactically correct; it specifies the concrete syntax of the language.

Grammars can be used as generators, that is, as a mechanism to generate the words of a language, or as checkers, that is, as a tool to check that a given word belongs to a given language.

A grammar is specified by:

– an alphabet: a set of symbols containing all the characters, or *terminals*, of the language, plus additional *non-terminal* symbols used to describe the generation of words;

- a set of rules of the form $A \rightarrow s$, also called *productions*, where A is a non-terminal and s a sequence of terminals and non-terminals, which indicate how words are built; and
- a distinguished non-terminal (called *initial symbol*), which is used as a starting point for the generation of words.

Sometimes the alphabet is not explicitly given, since it can be deduced from the rules of the grammar. Also, the initial symbol is usually omitted: it is assumed to be the left-hand side of the first rule. Rules with the same left-hand side are often grouped: we write $A \rightarrow s_1 \mid s_2$ as an abbreviation for the two rules $A \rightarrow s_1$ and $A \rightarrow s_2$.

Example 1.1(Arithmetic Expressions)
The following grammar defines the concrete syntax of a simple language of arithmetic expressions, where the alphabet contains the terminals 0, 1, 2, 3, 4, 5, 6, 7, 8, 9, $+$, $-$, $*$, div, and the non-terminals Exp, Num, Op, $Digit$. Exp is the initial symbol. The rules to form expressions are:

$$
\begin{aligned}
Exp &\rightarrow Num \mid Exp\ Op\ Exp \\
Op &\rightarrow + \mid - \mid * \mid div \\
Num &\rightarrow Digit \mid Digit\ Num \\
Digit &\rightarrow 0 \mid 1 \mid 2 \mid 3 \mid 4 \mid 5 \mid 6 \mid 7 \mid 8 \mid 9
\end{aligned}
$$

To generate the words in the language, we use the grammar rules from left to right. In this example we have grouped the rules with the same left-hand side. The symbol $\mid$ in the right hand side of a rule is understood as an "or". For instance, the first rule says that an expression is generated by the non-terminal Num, or has the form $Exp\ Op\ Exp$. So, this grammar indicates that there are only two kinds of expressions in the language: an expression is a number, or is formed by an expression followed by an operator, followed by another expression.

More precisely, to build an expression, we start with the initial symbol, in this case the non-terminal Exp, and use the rules from left to right until we obtain a word containing only terminals.

For instance, we can generate the expression $2 * 3 + 4$ as follows:

$$
\begin{aligned}
Exp &\rightarrow Exp\ Op\ Exp & &\rightarrow Num\ Op\ Exp \\
&\rightarrow Digit\ Op\ Exp & &\rightarrow 2\ Op\ Exp \\
&\rightarrow 2 * Exp & &\rightarrow 2 * Exp\ Op\ Exp \\
&\rightarrow 2 * Num\ Op\ Exp & &\rightarrow 2 * Digit\ Op\ Exp \\
&\rightarrow 2 * 3\ Op\ Exp & &\rightarrow 2 * 3 + Exp \\
&\rightarrow 2 * 3 + Num & &\rightarrow 2 * 3 + Digit \\
&\rightarrow 2 * 3 + 4
\end{aligned}
$$

A sequence of applications of rules that starts with the initial symbol and ends with a sequence of terminals (that is, a word in the language) is called a *derivation* of the word. For example, the sequence of steps from Exp to $2 * 3 + 4$ shown above is a derivation.

The problem with the definition of arithmetic expressions given in Example 1.1 is that there are several ways of deriving an expression: the grammar is *ambiguous*. Ambiguity is problematic, because the parser for the language, which translates the concrete syntax into abstract syntax, produces different outputs depending on the derivation used to generate the expression. For example, the expression $2 * 3 + 4$ can also be derived as:

$$
\begin{aligned}
Exp \to\ &Exp\ Op\ Exp && \to Exp\ Op\ Num \\
\to\ &Exp\ Op\ Digit && \to Exp\ Op\ 4 \\
\to\ &Exp\ +\ 4 && \to Exp\ Op\ Exp\ +\ 4 \\
\to\ &Exp\ Op\ Num\ +\ 4 && \to Exp\ Op\ Digit\ +\ 4 \\
\to\ &Exp\ Op\ 3\ +\ 4 && \to Exp\ *\ 3\ +\ 4 \\
\to\ &Num\ *\ 3\ +\ 4 && \to Digit\ *\ 3\ +\ 4 \\
\to\ &2\ *\ 3\ +\ 4
\end{aligned}
$$

The first derivation, shown in Example 1.1, identifies the operator $*$ as the main operator in the expression, with arguments 2 and $3 + 4$. It produces a syntax tree corresponding to $2 * (3 + 4)$, that is, the root of the generated syntax tree represents the operator $*$. The second derivation selects $+$ as the main operator, with arguments $(2 * 3)$ and 4, so it produces a syntax tree corresponding to $(2 * 3) + 4$, where the root of the syntax tree represents the operator $+$.

Since compilers generate code for an expression based on its syntax tree, this means that depending on the derivation chosen by the compiler we could get different code and possibly different results for the same expression (as in this example). This is of course something that must be avoided; for this reason, various techniques have been devised to ensure that the grammars defining the syntax of programming languages are non-ambiguous (unfortunately, there is no algorithm to transform an arbitrary grammar into an equivalent non-ambiguous one; the problem is undecidable in general).

The grammar given in Example 1.1 could be transformed into a non-ambiguous one by taking into account the priority of the operators and introducing brackets in the concrete syntax of the language. For example, a standard non-ambiguous grammar for arithmetic expressions defines separate syntactical categories for terms and factors:

$$
\begin{aligned}
Exp &\to Term \mid Term\ LowOp\ Exp \\
LowOp &\to +\mid - \\
Term &\to Factor \mid Factor\ HighOp\ Term \\
HighOp &\to *\mid div \\
Factor &\to (\ Exp\ )\mid Num \\
Num &\to Digit \mid Digit\ Num \\
Digit &\to 0\mid 1\mid 2\mid 3\mid 4\mid 5\mid 6\mid 7\mid 8\mid 9
\end{aligned}
$$

The translation from concrete syntax to abstract syntax is performed by the lexer and parser during the first phase of the compilation or interpretation process.

To specify the form of the abstract syntax trees generated by the parser, we can also use a grammar. However, the alphabet of this grammar will be different from the alphabet of the grammar specifying the concrete syntax: now the terminals are the tokens recognised by the lexer (the input for the parser). Moreover, since this grammar specifies trees (representing programs) rather than strings, we need a notation for trees. We will introduce it with an example.

Example 1.2

The abstract syntax of the language of arithmetic expressions defined in Example 1.1 is defined by the following grammar. The terminal n represents numerical tokens; E and Op are non-terminals. The terminals $+$, $-$, $*$, div are tokens corresponding to the arithmetic operators (we have chosen to use the same names for the operators in the concrete and in the abstract syntax).

$$E \ \rightarrow n \mid Op(E, E)$$
$$Op \rightarrow + \mid - \mid * \mid div$$

The first rule specifies that arithmetic expressions are either a number token or a tree where the root is labelled by a binary operator and the two subtrees are arithmetic expressions (the second rule, defining Op, specifies the kind of operators that can be used). Graphically, we can visualise the form of the tree as:

$$Op$$

$$/ \ \backslash$$

$$E \quad E$$

This grammar generates all the *abstract syntax trees* representing arithmetic expressions in the language. In this case, according to the grammar, in the syntax trees the leaves are numbers and the internal nodes are labelled with operators. Importantly, there is no ambiguity since the grammar specifies trees rather than strings.

For example, the abstract syntax tree $*(2, +(3, 4))$, where we denote the number tokens directly by their values (2, 3, 4 in this case), represents the expression with concrete syntax $2 * (3 + 4)$. Graphically, this tree is represented as follows:

$$*$$

$$/ \ \backslash$$

$$2 \quad +$$

$$/ \ \backslash$$

$$3 \quad 4$$

We see that the operator ∗ at the root is applied to the arguments 2 and +(3, 4), respectively. The latter is the tree representation of the string 3 + 4. The expression (2 ∗ 3) + 4 will instead be represented by the abstract syntax tree +(∗(2, 3), 4), shown below.

```
            +

          / \

        *   4

      / \

     2   3
```

In the rest of the book we will only work with the abstract syntax of programming languages. This is because we are interested in the *semantics* of the various constructs of programming languages. The concrete syntax is not relevant from a semantics point of view, although of course when writing a program it is important to know the concrete syntax of the language, as programs that do not respect the constraints will be rejected by the compiler or the interpreter.

1.3.4 Semantics

The *semantics* of a language defines the meaning of programs, that is, how they behave when they are executed on a computer.

Since similar constructs are often used in different languages with different syntax and different semantics, it is important to have a precise description of their behaviour. Variations in concrete syntax are in general superficial, but differences in meaning are important since constructs that are apparently similar may produce very different results.

The semantics of a programming language can be defined at two levels: *static semantics* (also called *typing*), and *dynamic semantics*, or just semantics. We will briefly describe both.

1.3.4.1 Static Semantics

Types can be seen as specifications of programs, and therefore they are part of the semantics of the language, but they are a form of static semantics. The goal is to detect (before the actual execution of the program) programs that are syntactically correct but will give errors during execution.

Example 1.3

Consider a language with arithmetic and Boolean expressions where the abstract syntax is given by:

$$E \rightarrow n \mid b \mid Op(E, E)$$
$$Op \rightarrow + \mid - \mid * \mid div \mid nand \mid nor$$

Here n represents numbers and b Booleans. The expression $+(1, True)$ is syntactically correct (it can be generated by this grammar), but it is not typeable: attempting to add a number and a Boolean should produce a type error.

Most typed languages require type declarations associating types with program constructs. In some functional languages, types can be *inferred*, which frees the programmer from the need of writing type declarations. We will study type checking and type inference systems in Chaps. 5 and 6.

1.3.4.2 Dynamic Semantics

The dynamic semantics of the language describes the behaviour of programs at execution time. It is often given by informal definitions and explanations in natural language (e.g., English) in language manuals. However, natural language explanations are in general imprecise and incomplete. An alternative is to provide a formal semantics. This is in general more difficult but can be very useful, and even essential in some contexts, for several reasons:

1. Language Implementation: A formal definition of the semantics of the language facilitates its implementation. This is because the semantics specifies the behaviour of each construct in abstract terms, providing a full description of the execution process that is independent of the actual machine. Compilers and interpreters are ultimately software applications, and as for any software application, it is easier to write it if we have a clear and complete specification of what it should do.
2. Programming: Programmers obviously benefit from a clear description of the constructs in the language. Moreover, the techniques used to give a formal semantics of a programming language are usually accompanied by techniques and tools to reason about programs and to prove properties of programs. Formal verification of programs, which aims at providing proofs of correctness (i.e., proving that a program satisfies its specification), is only possible if a formal description of the behaviour of the program is available.
3. Language Design: A formal semantics prevents ambiguities in the constructs and helps detect omissions (a notorious example where an omission remained undetected for some time was C: the evaluation order for function parameters was not specified in the first version of the language). A formal semantics guides the design of the language and suggests improvements and new constructs. For example, the use of the λ-calculus as a tool to give a formal semantics to programming languages has influenced the design of functional and object-oriented languages.

However, formal semantic descriptions of general programming languages can be hard to produce and difficult to read, so they are usually available for parts of the language only, or for special purpose languages (for instance, they are a standard feature in hardware description languages).

There are different approaches to the formal definition of the semantics of programming languages. The main semantic styles are:

– *Denotational*: The meaning of expressions, and in general, the meaning of the constructs in the language, is given in an abstract way using a mathematical model for the language. The semantics describes the *effect* of each construct.

   This approach has some similarities with the approach used in natural sciences to explain natural processes, where a mathematical model of the system under study is built, then natural processes are explained in terms of the model. In the case of programming languages, the model deals with computation, and it should be sufficiently powerful to allow us to explain the meaning of all the constructs in the language.

– *Axiomatic*: The meaning of programs is given by describing the properties that hold before and after the execution of the program, using axioms and deduction rules in a specific logic. For each kind of construct, predicates or assertions are given, describing the constraints on program variables before and after the execution of the statement. These are called *preconditions* and *postconditions*. This approach is particularly useful to programmers, since it shows clearly the effect of each program construct. It has been used as a basis for the development of program verification tools.

– *Operational*: The meaning of each construct is given in terms of computation steps. *Transition systems* are used as a tool to give the operational semantics of programs: the execution of the program is described as a sequence of transitions. Transition systems can be presented as abstract machines, where the transitions represent changes of state in the machine, or using axioms and rules to define a transition relation (this is called structural operational semantics). The operational approach was one of the first used to give a formal definition of the semantics of programming languages.

Each style of semantics has its advantages, they are complementary. Operational semantics is very useful for the implementation of the language and for proving correctness of compiler optimisations, since it describes the computation steps that are required to execute each command. On the other hand, denotational semantics and axiomatic semantics are useful to reason about programs and to prove properties of programs.

In this book we will only study operational semantics of programming languages, using transition systems. In the next chapter we give the necessary mathematical background.

1.4 Further Reading

Readers interested in the history of programming languages can find more information in Sebesta's book [18]. The notion of abstract syntax was first used by McCarthy [19] in connection with the language LISP. For more information on compiler techniques, Aho et al.'s [20] book is an excellent reference. Further information on programming language semantics can be found in [21]; for advanced readers, we recommend Winskel's book [22]. Additional references are provided in the following chapters.

1.5 Exercises

1. Using the grammar that specifies the concrete syntax for arithmetic expressions in Example 1.1:

   (a) Show that $1 - 2 - 3$ and $1 + 2 * 3$ are valid expressions in this language, and list their possible results, assuming that the arithmetic operators have the usual semantics.
   (b) Are $1 + (2 - 3)$ and -1 valid expressions in this language?
   (c) Using Haskell evaluate the expressions[2] $1 - 2 - 3$ and $1 + 2 * 3$.
       From the results obtained, can you explain how Haskell has parsed these expressions? Identify the main operator (i.e., the root of the syntax tree generated by Haskell) and its arguments, in each of the expressions.

2. Modify the grammar for the concrete syntax of arithmetic expressions in Example 1.1 so that it precludes leading zeros in numbers.
3. Using the grammar given in Example 1.2 to specify the abstract syntax of arithmetic expressions:

   (a) Show that both $-(-(1, 2), 3)$ and $-(1, -(2, 3))$ are valid. What are their values (assuming that the arithmetic operators have the usual semantics)?
   (b) Explain why $-(1, 2, 3)$ is not a valid abstract syntax tree according to this grammar.

4. Modify the grammars given in Examples 1.1 and 1.2 to specify the concrete and abstract syntax for arithmetic expressions, in order to include a unary subtraction operator. The idea is to allow users to write expressions such as -1 in the concrete syntax.
   Now modify the grammars again to take into account the fact that the language should also allow users to write expressions of the form x^y where x and y are two arithmetic expressions.

---

[2] Simply use the interactive evaluator in your browser, see http://www.tryhaskell.org. To evaluate an expression, type the expression after the prompt and press the return key.

5. Assume we want to design a language L in which variable identifiers are sequences of letters or numbers, starting with a capital letter. Give a grammar for the concrete syntax of identifiers in L.
6. The following grammar defines the concrete syntax of identifiers in Haskell. Non-terminals are written in italics. In the first rule, we use a special notation to represent set difference: (*small rest*)–*keywords* denotes the strings generated by *small rest* minus the ones generated by *keywords*. In the third rule, the symbol ϵ denotes an empty string.

varid → (*small rest*) − *keywords*

small → a | b | c | ... | z

rest → ϵ | *sldq rest*

sldq → *small* | *large* | *digit* | '

large → A | B | C | ... | Z

digit → 0 | 1 | 2 | ... | 9

keywords → case | class | data | default | deriving | do | else | if | import | in | infix | infixl | infixr | instance | let | module | newtype | of | then | type | where | _

(a) Explain in English how identifiers are formed.
(b) We extend the grammar with a rule to specify the form of function declarations in Haskell:

decl → let *varid args* = *expr1* in *expr2*

where *varid* is the name of the function, *args* its arguments, *expr1* its definition and *expr2* the expression where it is used (we omit the grammar rules defining *args, expr1, expr2*).

For example, the following is a valid function declaration for a function called double, with an argument x, defined by the expression 2 * x and used to compute the double of 3.

let double x = 2 * x in double 3

The following Haskell programs have syntax errors. Try to run the programs and explain why they produce error messages.[3] Using the grammar given, can you identify the errors and suggest ways to correct them?

---

[3] Type each of the lines using the interactive evaluator for Haskell in your browser, see http://www.tryhaskell.org, and explain the errors found.

let Double x = 2 * x in Double 3

let dou?ble x = 2 * x in dou?ble 3

let data = 1 in data + 1.

References

1. G. Gordon, The development of the general purpose simulation system (GPSS). Newsletter, in ACM SIGPLAN Notices. Special issue: History of programming languages conference, vol. **13**, pp. 183–198 (1978)
2. World Wide Web Consortium. XSL Transformations (XSLT), version 1.0 (1999), www.w3.org/TR/xslt
3. E. Jendrock, J. Ball, D. Carson, I. Evans, S. Fordin, K. Haase, The Java EE 5 Tutorial. Oracle (first published 2007) (2010)
4. IBM, *Preliminary Report, Specifications for the IBM Mathematical FORmula TRANslating System* (IBM Corporation, New York, 1954)
5. N. Wirth, The programming language Pascal. Acta Informatica **1**(1), 35–63 (1971)
6. S.L. Peyton Jones, *Haskell 98 Language and Libraries* (Cambridge University Press, Cambridge, 2003)
7. J. Gosling, B. Joy, G. Steele, *The Java Language Specification* (Addison-Wesley, Boston, 1996)
8. P. Naur, Report on the algorithmic language ALGOL 60. Commun. ACM **3**(5) (1960)
9. B.W. Kernighan, D.M. Ritchie, *The C Programming Language*, 2nd edn. Software Series (Prentice Hall, Upper Saddle River, 1988)
10. G. van Rossum, A tour of the Python language, in TOOLS 1997: 23rd International Conference on Technology of Object-Oriented Languages and Systems, 28 July–1 August 1997 (IEEE Computer Society, Santa Barbara, USA, 1998), p. 370
11. R. Milner, M. Tofte, R. Harper, *The Definition of Standard ML* (MIT Press, Cambridge, 1990)
12. P. Weiss, X. Leroy, *Le Langage CAML* (Dunod, Paris, 1999)
13. Clean Development Team. Concurrent Clean Language Report (version 2.2). clean.cs.ru.nl/Documentation.
14. J. McCarthy, P. Abrahams, D. Edwards, T. Hart, M. Levin, *LISP 1.5 Programmer's Manual*, 2nd edn. (MIT Press, Cambridge, 1965)
15. P. Roussel, PROLOG: Manuel de référence et d'utilisation, *Research Report* (Artificial Intelligence Team, University of Aix-Marseille, France, 1975)
16. D. Flanagan, *JavaScript: The Definitive Guide*, 6th edn. (O'Reilly Media, California, 2011)
17. T. Converse, J. Park, *PHP Bible*, 2nd edn. (Wiley, 2002)
18. R. Sebesta, *Concepts of Programming Languages*, 10th edn. (Addison Wesley, Boston, 2012)
19. J. McCarthy, Towards a mathematical science of computation, in IFIP Congress (1962), pp. 21–28
20. A.V. Aho, M.S. Lam, R. Sethi, J.D. Ullman, *Compilers: Principles, Techniques, and Tools* (Prentice Hall, Upper Saddle River, 2006)
21. H.R. Nielson, F. Nielson, *Semantics with Applications: An Appetizer (Undergraduate Topics in Computer Science)* (Springer, Berlin, 2007)
22. G. Winskel, *The Formal Semantics of Programming Languages. Foundations of Computing* (MIT Press, Cambridge, 1993)

Chapter 2
Mathematical Background

We start this chapter with a summary of basic concepts and notations for sets and first-order logic formulas, which will be used in the rest of the book. Our aim is to try to make the book self contained; readers who are familiar with set theory and first-order logic can skip the first two sections of this chapter and go directly to Sect. 2.3, where we define transition systems. Section 2.4 introduces induction as a technique to define sets and to prove their properties.

2.1 Sets and Relations

We will denote the *empty set*, that is, a set with no elements, by $\emptyset$ or $\{\}$. Non-empty sets will be given extensionally when possible, by enumerating their elements between curly brackets. For instance, the set of Boolean values can be given extensionally as follows.

$$Booleans = \{True, False\}$$

To indicate that an element is in a set we use the symbol $\in$, as in $True \in Booleans$. The symbol $\in$ denotes membership; its negation is written $\notin$, as in $0 \notin Booleans$.

When sets are infinite, it is not possible to enumerate all the elements so we will define them intensionally, by characterising their elements. We do this by giving a property that all the elements in the set satisfy. For example, even natural numbers are characterised by the fact that the remainder of the division by 2 is 0, that is, a natural number n is even if $n\ mod\ 2 = 0$. Thus, if $\mathcal{N}$ is the set of natural numbers we can define the set of even natural numbers intensionally as follows.

$$Even = \{n \in \mathcal{N} \mid n\ mod\ 2 = 0\}$$

This kind of definition is called definition by comprehension.

Another way of defining sets intensionally is by using induction; we will discuss induction in Sect. 2.4.

Two essential notions in set theory are inclusion and equality of sets.

M. Fernández, *Programming Languages and Operational Semantics*,
Undergraduate Topics in Computer Science, DOI: 10.1007/978-1-4471-6368-8_2,
© Springer-Verlag London 2014

Definition 2.1 (Set inclusion, equality)

A set A is *included* in the set B, written $A \subseteq B$, if all the elements in A are also in B. In this case, we say that A is a *subset* of B.

Using inclusion, we can define equality of sets: Two sets are *equal* if they have exactly the same elements, that is, $A = B$ if and only if $A \subseteq B$ and $B \subseteq A$.

Therefore, to check that two sets are equal we need to check that they contain the same elements. For example, the sets $\{True, False\}$ and $\{False, True, True\}$ are equal. This is an instance of a more general property: the order in which we write the elements of a set is irrelevant, and repeating elements is not very elegant but does not change the set either.

The standard operations on sets are:

– *Union*, written $\cup$, which, given two sets A and B builds a new set containing all the elements in A and all the elements in B:

$$A \cup B = \{e \mid e \in A \ or \ e \in B\}$$

Thus, the set $A \cup B$ is empty only if A and B are both empty.
Union is an associative and commutative operator, that is:

$$(A \cup B) \cup C = A \cup (B \cup C)$$
$$A \cup B = B \cup A$$

Since union is associative, we can write $A \cup B \cup C$ without brackets (there is no confusion since any choice of brackets produces the same result).

– *Intersection*, written $\cap$, which, given two sets A and B builds a new set containing the elements that are in both sets:

$$A \cap B = \{e \mid e \in A \ and \ e \in B\}$$

Intersection is also an associative and commutative operator:

$$(A \cap B) \cap C = A \cap (B \cap C)$$
$$A \cap B = B \cap A$$

The intersection of two sets is empty when they have no elements in common; in particular, it is empty if either of the sets is empty. Since intersection is associative, we can write $A \cap B \cap C$ without brackets.

– *Set difference* (or just difference), written $-$, which, given two sets A and B builds a new set as follows:

$$A - B = \{e \in A \mid e \notin B\}$$

Thus, the difference set $A - B$ contains all the elements that are in A but not in B. Another way of defining this set is as a *relative complement*: it is the complement of B with respect to A. This is sometimes written as $\overline{B}$ (read complement of the set B), when the set A is obvious from the context.

Set difference is neither commutative nor associative.

– *Cartesian product* (or just product), written $\times$, which, given two sets A and B builds the set containing all the pairs where the first component is in A and the second in B:

$$A \times B = \{(a, b) \mid a \in A \text{ and } b \in B\}$$

Since we are dealing with ordered pairs here, product is neither commutative nor associative on sets.

This operation can be generalised to products of a finite number of sets. Thus, $A_1 \times \cdots \times A_n$ is a set of tuples $(a_1, \ldots, a_n)$ where each of the elements a_i $(1 \leq i \leq n)$ is in the set A_i.

Note that we have defined the sets resulting from an operation of union, intersection, difference or product by comprehension: we have specified the properties that characterise the elements of the resulting sets. We have relied on an intuitive understanding of the connectives "or", "and" and "not"; we will define them precisely in the next section.

Now, we will use products of sets to define relations.

Definition 2.2 (Relation)

A binary *relation* R between sets A and B is a subset of the Cartesian product $A \times B$:

$$R \subseteq A \times B$$

In other words, a binary relation R is a subset of the pairs where the first element is in A and the second in B. We will use the notation $R(a, b)$ to indicate that the pair (a, b) is in the relation R.

If the sets A and B coincide, we will simply say that R is a relation on A.

Binary relations will be used in the next section to define transition systems associated to programs, where a transition will relate two states in the system. In this context, we will consider two properties of relations:

Definition 2.3 A binary relation $R \subseteq A \times A$ is *reflexive* if it includes all the pairs (a, a) such that $a \in A$. It is *transitive* if each time we have $R(a, b)$ and $R(b, c)$ we also have $R(a, c)$.

If a relation on A is not reflexive, we can make it reflexive by adding the missing pairs (a, a), and similarly, if it is not transitive, we can make it transitive by adding the pair (a, c) whenever there exists b in A such that $R(a, b)$ and $R(b, c)$.

Definition 2.4 The *reflexive-transitive* closure of the relation $R \subseteq A \times A$ is the least reflexive and transitive relation on A that contains R. It is denoted by R^*.

The reflexive-transitive closure of the relation R is obtained simply by extending R with all the pairs needed to satisfy reflexivity and transitivity.

If we represent R as a graph (i.e., as a set of nodes and edges, where the nodes are the elements of A and there is an edge from a to b if and only if (a, b) is in R), then the reflexive-transitive closure of R is the relation representing reachability: if (a, b) is in R^* then there is a path from a to b in the graph. This idea will be useful later: we will use transition relations to specify the behaviour of programs, and the reflexive-transitive closure will represent sequences of computations.

Another useful notion is the closure of a set under an operator. In general, a set is said to be closed under an operation if the result of the operation on elements of the set is also a member of the set. The notion of closure can be stated using relations.

Definition 2.5 Let R be a binary relation on A. We will say that a subset A' of A is closed under the relation R if R relates elements of A' with elements of A'.

Again, this notion will be useful later, in particular to provide an inductive definition of the transition relation associated to a set of programs.

Some relations are *functions*. We can characterise functions from A to B as relations that associate at most one element in B with each element in A: for each $a \in A$, there is at most one $b \in B$ such that a and b are related.

Definition 2.6 A relation $R \subseteq A \times B$ is a function if $R(a, b)$ and $R(a, c)$ implies $b = c$, for every $a \in A$.

To emphasise the fact that a relation R is a function from A to B, we will write $R: A \to B$, and denote by $R(a)$ the unique element in B related with $a \in A$.

For example, the relation that associates each natural number n with the number $n + 1$ is a function, usually called the *successor* function S:

$$S: \mathcal{N} \to \mathcal{N} = \{(n, n + 1) \mid n \in \mathcal{N}\}$$

Another way of defining S is by writing $S(n) = n + 1$.

The notions of domain and image of a function can be formally defined:

If R is a function from A to B, its *domain* is the subset of A consisting of all the elements for which there exists an element b in B such that $(a, b) \in R$. In other words, the domain of the function R consists of all the elements a in A such that $R(a)$ is defined.

If R is a function from A to B, its *image* is the subset of B consisting of all the elements for which there exists an element a in A such that $(a, b) \in R$. In other words, the image of the function R consists of all the elements b in B for which there is some a in A such that $b = R(a)$. The element $R(a)$ is the *image of a* under R.

So far, we have considered only binary relations, however, the ideas can be extended to n-ary relations. An n-ary relation R on the sets $A_1, ..., A_n$ is a set of tuples $(a_1, \ldots, a_n)$ where each of the elements a_i is in the set A_i. Thus, $R \subseteq A_1 \times \cdots \times A_n$. We will use the notation $R(a_1, \ldots, a_n)$ to indicate that the tuple $(a_1, \ldots, a_n)$ is in the relation R. Thus, we can use a relation to characterise a set of tuples with a relevant property. In other words, we can see a relation as a predicate (indeed, relations are used to give a meaning to predicates in first-order logic).

2.2 Logic Formulas

In this section, we define the syntax of formulas in first-order logic and recall briefly their semantics. First we need to define *terms*.

Definition 2.7 (Terms)

Given an infinite but denumerable set $\mathcal{X}$ of symbols x, y, z, x_1, x_2, etc., which we call *variables*, and an infinite but denumerable set $\mathcal{F}$ of symbols f, g, h, f_1, f_2, etc., which we call *function symbols*, each with an associated arity (a natural number), the set of terms built out of $\mathcal{X}$ and $\mathcal{F}$ is generated by the grammar:

$$T \rightarrow x \mid f(T, \ldots, T)$$

where x is an element of $\mathcal{X}$, f is in $\mathcal{F}$ and if the arity of f is n then any occurrence of f in a term must be applied to exactly n terms $t_1, \ldots, t_n$.

The grammar given above describes the abstract syntax of terms. In other words, terms are either variables or are built using a function symbol and a number of previously built terms corresponding to the arity of the function symbol. We say that $t_1, \ldots, t_n$ are the arguments of f in the term $f(t_1, \ldots, t_n)$. Thus, an n-ary function symbol must always have exactly n arguments. Note that n could be zero, in this case the function symbol is called a *constant*.

For example, we can define a language of terms representing natural numbers using just two function symbols: $zero$, of arity 0, and suc of arity 1. In this case, we do not need variables. The number 0 will be represented by the term $zero()$. To improve readability, when function symbols have arity 0 we will omit the brackets. Thus, to represent the number 0 we write simply $zero$; similarly, the term $suc(suc(zero))$ represents the number 2. We will sometimes write $suc(n)$ as $n + 1$.

Formulas in first-order logic are built using a set of terms, a set of *predicate symbols*, each with a given arity, and additionally a set of *connectives* and *quantifiers* (see below). Terms and predicate symbols are used to build *atomic formulas*, also called *atoms*, of the form $P(t_1, \ldots, t_n)$, where P is a predicate of arity n and $t_1, \ldots, t_n$ are terms. We will distinguish two 0-ary predicates, T and F, which will denote true and false values, respectively.

For example, using the binary predicate $>$, we can write the atomic formula $>(suc(zero), zero)$. We will usually write this predicate using an infix notation, that is, we write $suc(zero) > zero$.

Atomic formulas may also have variables, for example, we could write $suc(x) > zero$. In this case, we will say that the variable x is *free* in the formula.

To build more complex formulas, in this book we will use the binary connectives $\wedge$ (read "and"), $\vee$ (read "or"), $\Rightarrow$ (read "implies"), and the unary connective $\neg$ (read "not"). So, if ϕ and ψ are logic formulas, then $\phi \wedge \psi$, $\phi \vee \psi$, $\phi \Rightarrow \psi$ and $\neg\phi$, are also formulas. In addition, first-order logic formulas may have *quantifiers* $\forall$ and $\exists$ (read "for all" and "there exists"), denoting universal and existential quantification, respectively: If ϕ is a formula and x is a variable, then $\forall x.\phi$ and $\exists x.\phi$ are formulas.

In a formula of the form $\forall x.\phi$ or $\exists x.\phi$, the variable x is said to be *quantified* or *bound*.

Formally, the language of first-order formulas can be defined using a grammar; see the Exercises at the end of this chapter. A precise definition of the sets of free and bound variables in a formula is also left as an exercise. A formula without free variables is said to be *closed*.

Once we have defined the syntax of the formulas, we can try to associate a meaning (a truth value) to each formula. However, if the formula has free variables, its truth value depends on the values of the variables, so the meaning of the formula can only be given in relation to a *valuation* that assigns values to the variables. In addition, to establish the truth value of the formula we need to know how to interpret the function symbols and predicates.

We describe now how to map formulas to truth values.

We start by fixing a domain U of interpretation for the variables; this is sometimes called a *universe*. Now, assume each function symbol of arity n is interpreted by an n-ary function on U (in the particular case of $n = 0$, constants are interpreted by elements of U) and each predicate of arity n is interpreted by an n-ary relation on U. We will denote by $[f]$ the function associated to the function symbol f, and by $[P]$ the relation associated to the predicate symbol P. If the formula is closed, we do not need a valuation: the truth value of the formula depends only on the chosen universe, the meaning of the function symbols and the meaning of predicate symbols. Otherwise, assume we are also given a valuation σ mapping variables to elements of U.

Using the valuation σ and the interpretations of function symbols we can give a meaning to terms. Then, using the interpretations of terms and predicate symbols, we can give denotations for formulas.

Definition 2.8 (Denotation of terms)

The interpretation, or *denotation*, of a term t in U with respect to a valuation σ and interpretations for function symbols, written $[t]$, is defined as follows.

- The denotation of a variable x is $\sigma(x)$:
  $[x] = \sigma(x)$
- The denotation of $f(t_1, \ldots, t_n)$ is the image of $([t_1], \ldots, [t_n])$ under $[f]$:
  $[f(t_1, \ldots, t_n)] = [f]([t_1], \ldots, [t_n])$

Once we know the meaning of terms, we can specify the truth values of formulas.

Definition 2.9 (Denotation of formulas)

A formula $P(t_1, \ldots, t_n)$ is true if $([t_1], \ldots, [t_n]) \in [P]$, that is, if $[P]([t_1], \ldots, [t_n])$; otherwise it is false. For the distinguished symbols T and F, we define $[T]$ to be true and $[F]$ to be false. Finally, the connectives have the following meanings:

- $\wedge$ denotes conjuction, that is, $\phi \wedge \psi$ is true if both ϕ and ψ are true;
- $\vee$ denotes disjunction, that is, $\phi \vee \psi$ is true if at least one of ϕ or ψ are true;

 – ⇒ denotes implication, $\phi \Rightarrow \psi$ is true if each time ϕ is true, ψ is also true;
 – ¬ denotes negation: $\neg\phi$ is true if ϕ is false, and it is false if ϕ is true.

In addition, quantified formulas are interpreted as follows: the formula $\forall x.\phi$ is true if ϕ is true for every possible value of x, and the formula $\exists x.\phi$ is true if there is at least one value of x that satisfies ϕ (that is, it makes it true).

According to the previous definitions, under an interpretation each term has a value in U, and each formula is either true or false.

Example 2.10

Let us assume we interpret the variable x on the natural numbers, so our universe is $\mathcal{N}$.

To assign a meaning to the formula $suc(x) > zero$ we need a valuation, which will give us a value for x, let us say 0, and we need interpretations for the function symbols $zero$ and suc and predicate symbol $>$. Let us assume we interpret $zero$ as the number 0, suc as the successor function and $>$ as the relation containing all the pairs of natural numbers where the first element is greater than the second. Then the formula $suc(x) > zero$ with the valuation that assigns 0 to x is true under this interpretation. Actually, this formula is true for any valuation, if we interpret the variable x on the natural numbers.

Therefore, the formula $\forall x.suc(x) > zero$ is true if we interpret the variable x on the natural numbers, assuming $[suc]$ is the successor function, $[zero]$ is the number 0, and $[>]$ is the relation containing all the pairs of natural numbers where the first element is greater than the second.

The formula $zero > suc(x)$ is false for all valuations in $\mathcal{N}$, but some formulas are true for certain valuations and false for others. For example $suc(zero) > x$ is only true for the valuation that assigns to x the value 0.

We will denote the equality predicate by $=$ as usual, and write it in infix notation. Then, we can write a formula $\exists x.suc(x) = zero$, but this formula is not true if we interpret x on the natural numbers and interpret suc as the successor function, $zero$ as the number 0, and $=$ as the relation containing all the pairs of natural numbers where the first element is equal to the second.

According to our definitions, the formulas $\phi \vee \psi$ and $\psi \vee \phi$ have the same meaning: they are both true if at least one of the formulas ϕ, ψ are true, and false if both are false. We conclude that $\vee$ is commutative. Similarly, $\wedge$ is commutative, and both $\vee$ and $\wedge$ are associative.

Note that in the case of quantified formulas, the name of the bound variable is not important, since the formula's truth value (which we are taking as its meaning) does not change if we rename the variable. We will not define the renaming operation formally here, but the intuition is that we can consistently change the name of the variable everywhere in the formula.

The meaning of a quantified formula may of course change if we change the domain of interpretation of the bound variables, that is, if we change the set of values that the quantified variables may take.

To make clear which is the domain of interpretation we have in mind, when we write first-order logic formulas with quantifiers we will write explicitly the domain next to the quantified variable. For instance, we may write $\forall n \in \mathcal{N}.(P(n) \Rightarrow P(suc(n)))$.

2.3 Transition Systems

A transition system is a mathematical device that can be used to model computation.

Definition 2.11 (Transition System)

A *transition system* is specified by

- a set Config of *configurations* or *states*;
- a binary relation $\rightarrow \subseteq Config \times Config$, called the *transition relation*.

We use the notation $c \rightarrow c'$ (infix) to indicate that c and c' are related by $\rightarrow$.

The expression $c \rightarrow c'$ denotes a *transition* from c to c'. A transition can be understood simply as a change of state. It will represent a step of computation.

To describe the computation performed by a program, we need to specify sequences of transitions. For this, we can use the reflexive-transitive closure of the relation $\rightarrow$, denoted by $\rightarrow^*$. By definition, $\rightarrow^*$ is a binary relation that contains $\rightarrow$, contains all the pairs $c \rightarrow^* c$ (reflexivity), and all the pairs $c \rightarrow^* c'$ such that $c \rightarrow^* c''$ and $c'' \rightarrow^* c'$ for some c'' (transitivity). Therefore, $c \rightarrow^* c'$ holds if and only if there is a sequence of transitions:

$$c \rightarrow c_1 \rightarrow \cdots \rightarrow c_n = c' \quad \text{where } n \geq 0.$$

We will distinguish *initial* and *final* (also called *terminal*) subsets of configurations, written I, T respectively. A final configuration c is characterised by the fact that there is no transition out of c, more precisely: for all c in T, there is no configuration c' such that $c \rightarrow c'$. This can be written in a more compact way as follows.

$$\forall c \in T, c \nrightarrow .$$

The intuitive idea is that a sequence of transitions from an initial state $i \in I$ to a final state $t \in T$ represents a run of the system.

Definition 2.12 A transition system is *deterministic* if for every configuration c, whenever $c \rightarrow c_1$ and $c \rightarrow c_2$ we have $c_1 = c_2$.

According to the definition, in a deterministic system, at each point of the computation there is at most one possible transition. In other words, the transition relation is a function. In the context of programming languages, this means that if a program is associated to a deterministic transition system, then at each point in the execution the next step of computation is uniquely defined.

In this book, we will be concerned mostly with deterministic programming languages. We will consider non-deterministic systems when giving examples in concurrent languages. Indeed, non-determinism is one of the defining features of concurrent languages.

Historically, transition systems were the first tool used to give the formal semantics of a programming language. In fact, the first formal description of the behaviour of a program was in terms of an abstract machine, which is a particular kind of transition system.

Definition 2.13 (Abstract Machine)

An *abstract machine* for a programming language is a transition system that simulates the execution of programs. An abstract machine specifies how each construct in the language is executed and for this reason can be seen as an interpreter for a programming language.

In Chap. 4 we will give an abstract machine for a simple imperative language.

Abstract machines are very useful for implementing a programming language since they describe the execution of each command, step by step. However, for users of the language they are not always easy to understand: abstract machines deal with implementation details that are not always useful to programmers. For the same reason, abstract machines are not an ideal tool for analysing programs, reasoning about programs or proving properties of programs.

It is possible to specify the operational semantics of the language in a more structured way, abstracting some of the implementation details. The structural approach to operational semantics based on transition systems gives an *inductive* definition of the execution of a program, where the transition relation is defined by induction and each command is described in terms of its components. We will give examples of structural operational semantics for imperative and functional languages, in Chaps. 4 and 6. We end this chapter with an overview of induction principles.

2.4 Induction

Induction is a powerful technique to define sets and prove their properties. An inductive set is usually defined as the closure of a given set under some operations, that is, the inductive set is the least subset of the given set that is closed under the operations.[1]

The most well known instances of this technique are the inductive definition of the set of natural numbers, with its associated Principle of Mathematical Induction, and inductive definitions of data structures, with the associated Principle of Structural Induction. We will use structural induction to prove properties of abstract syntax.

---

[1] More formally, an inductive set is defined as the least fixed point of an operator, which, under certain conditions, is guaranteed to exist.

Another useful version of induction is Rule Induction, which we will use to define transition systems. Its associated Principle of Rule Induction will be used to prove properties of the transition relation.

Mathematical Induction. The set $\mathcal{N}$ of natural numbers is defined inductively, as the *smallest* set that contains the number 0 and is closed under the successor operation. The latter means that if n is a natural number then its successor $n + 1$ is also in the set of natural numbers. Also, since it is the smallest set satisfying this condition, the only elements in $\mathcal{N}$ are 0 and its successors. Instead of writing $0, 0 + 1, 0 + 1 + 1$, etc., it is traditional to write the elements of the set $\mathcal{N}$ as $0, 1, 2, \ldots$.

The *Principle of Mathematical Induction* says that to prove that a certain property P holds for all the natural numbers, which we write as

$$\forall n \in \mathcal{N} \cdot P(n)$$

to mean "$P(n)$ is true for every natural number n", it is sufficient to prove the property P for 0 and to prove that if P holds for an arbitrary number n, then it holds for $n + 1$. Thus, each proof by mathematical induction has two parts:

- In the first part, called *Basis*, we need to prove $P(0)$, that is, prove that the property holds for the number 0.
- In the second part, called *Induction Step*, we need to prove the property for the number $n + 1$ under the assumption that it is true of the number n. This is written:

$$\forall n \in \mathcal{N} \cdot (P(n) \Rightarrow P(n + 1)).$$

The assumption $P(n)$ in the induction step is called *Induction Hypothesis*.

The reason this is sufficient to deduce that P holds for all natural numbers is that, according to its inductive definition, $\mathcal{N}$ is the *least* set containing 0 and closed under successor. All the natural numbers are generated from 0 using the successor operation, thus, if we can prove the property for 0 and we can prove it is closed under successor, then we have proved that all natural numbers have the property.

The Principle of Mathematical Induction is used frequently in arithmetic, and is a useful technique to reason about programs that manipulate numbers, as the following example shows.

Example 2.14

Suppose that we need to compute the value of an expression that depends on an index i (a natural number). We write exp_i to highlight the fact that the expression exp depends on i. Moreover, suppose that we need to find the total value of expressions with indices in a given range, for example, we need the sum of all the expressions with indices between j and k. We use the notation

$$\sum_{i=j}^{k} exp_i$$

to represent the sum of exp_j, $exp_{j+1}, \ldots$, exp_k, where we assume that j is less than or equal to k. If j is greater than k then we have an empty sum, which is 0 by definition.

For instance, if the expression is just i and the range is 0 to n, then

$$\sum_{i=0}^{n} i = 0 + 1 + \cdots + n$$

Writing a program to compute such a sum is not a difficult task, but if we need to compute a lengthy sum, instead of writing a program that adds the expressions one by one, we can simply compute $n(n + 1)/2$. If n is a large number, this is a much better way to obtain the required result. But how can we be sure that this program and the one that computes the lengthy addition produce the same result, for any natural number n? Program equivalence is in fact a difficult problem (it is undecidable in general). In this particular case, we can easily prove, by induction, that replacing the lengthy addition $0 + 1 + \cdots + n$ by $n(n + 1)/2$ is indeed a correct optimisation.

The property that we want to prove states that the sum $0 + 1 + \ldots + n$ produces the same result as $n(n + 1)/2$, for any natural number n. In other words, we want to prove

$$\forall n \cdot (\sum_{i=0}^{n} i = n(n + 1)/2)$$

Similarly, if the expression is $2i - 1$ and we need to compute

$$\sum_{i=1}^{n} (2i - 1) = 1 + 3 + \cdots + (2n - 1)$$

we can avoid the lengthy sum and simply output n^2. To show that this is indeed a valid optimisation, we can simply by prove by induction that for any natural number n this sum is equal to n^2.

According to the Principle of Mathematical Induction, we need to prove the required property first for the base case and then the induction step. We leave the proof of the first property as an exercise (see the list of exercises at the end of the chapter), and show below the proof of the second property, which we can write as

$$\forall n \cdot (\sum_{i=1}^{n} (2i - 1) = n^2)$$

Basis: Here we need to prove the property for $n = 0$, in other words, we need to show

$$\sum_{i=1}^{0} (2i - 1) = 0^2$$

The left-hand side is an empty sum, which is 0 by definition, and the right-hand side is also 0, so the basis is trivial in this case.

Induction Step: Assume $\sum_{i=1}^{n}(2i-1) = n^2$ (induction hypothesis). We need to prove that $\sum_{i=1}^{n+1}(2i-1) = (n+1)^2$. First, notice that

$$\sum_{i=1}^{n+1}(2i-1) = \sum_{i=1}^{n}(2i-1) + (2(n+1)-1)$$

Using the induction hypothesis we obtain

$$\sum_{i=1}^{n}(2i-1) + (2(n+1)-1) = n^2 + 2n + 1$$

and the latter is equal to $(n+1)^2$ as required.

Structural Induction. Programs usually deal with various kinds of data structures, such as strings, lists and trees, in addition to numbers. To prove universal properties of data structures we can use induction on the size of the structure. For example, to show that a certain property P is true for all lists, we can prove that for every natural number n, P holds for all lists of length n. In this way, we translate a property of lists to a property of numbers. However, instead of translating our property, we can adapt the induction principle to work directly on the data structures of interest (specifically, recursively-defined structures such as strings, lists or trees). Let us consider first the case of lists.

Assume we denote an empty list by *nil*, and a non-empty list by *cons*(*h, l*) where *h* is the head element and *l* is the tail of the list. For simplicity, let us assume that we are building lists of natural numbers, so *h* is a natural number. For example, the list containing just the element 0 is written *cons*(0, *nil*). The operator *cons* is a *constructor* for lists, hence its name.

There are only two alternatives: either the list is empty (*nil*), or it is not empty and in this case it must have a head *h* and a tail *l*. Since these are the only possible ways of building lists, we can define the set of lists of numbers as an inductive set, as follows.

Definition 2.15 (Lists of natural numbers)

The set L of lists of natural numbers is the smallest set that contains the empty list *nil* and is closed under the operator that takes a list *l* of natural numbers and a natural number *h* and produces the list *cons*(*h, l*). The latter means that if the set L contains a list *l*, then it also contains *cons*(*h, l*) for any natural number *h*.

For example, the list containing the numbers 1, 3, 5 can be obtained starting with the empty list (nil) and building first $cons(5, nil)$, then $cons(3, cons(5, nil))$, and finally $cons(1, cons(3, cons(5, nil)))$.

According to Definition 2.15:

– nil is a list, and
– if we know that l is a list and h is a natural number, then $cons(h, l)$ is a list.

Moreover, we can state that there are no other cases, since we defined the set L as the *smallest* set that contains nil and is closed under the $cons$ operator.

As a consequence of this observation, we can derive a mechanism to define functions on lists (recursion) and a principle of induction to prove properties on lists (induction on the structure of lists).

To define a function f on lists, and ensure that every element in the inductive set of lists has an image, it is sufficient to define the image of the empty list (i.e., define $f(nil)$) and define the image $f(cons(h, l))$ of a non-empty list $con(h, l)$, assuming we already know how to compute $f(l)$.

For example, we can define the length of a list by cases as follows.

– $length(nil) = 0$,
– $length(cons(h, l)) = length(l) + 1$.

The principle of induction for lists mimics the definition of the set L.

Definition 2.16 (Principle of induction for lists)

To prove that a property P holds for every list of natural numbers, that is, for every element of the set L we have defined, it is sufficient to prove:

– *Basis*: $P(nil)$. This means that we need to prove that the property holds for the empty list.
– *Induction Step*: $P(l)$ implies $P(cons(h, l))$ for each element h and list l; this is written:
$$\forall h \in \mathcal{N}, \forall l \in L.(P(l) \Rightarrow P(cons(h, l))).$$

It means that we need to prove the property for the list $cons(h, l)$ under the assumption that it is true of the list l. Here the assumption $P(l)$ is the Induction Hypothesis.

Consider the following definition of the mirror image of a list, which we call its *reverse*.

– $reverse(nil) = nil$,
– $reverse(cons(h, l)) = append(reverse(l), h)$, where the append operation simply adds the element h at the end of the list $reverse(l)$.

Equipped with the principle of induction for lists, we can now prove properties of lists by induction directly, without needing to reword the property as a property of numbers. For instance, we can prove by induction that the reverse of a list is a list of the same length, for any list.

- *Basis*: The reverse of *nil* is also *nil*, so the property holds trivially in this case.
- *Induction Step*: Given a non-empty list $cons(h, l)$, we remark that, by the induction hypothesis, l and its reverse have the same length n. Since both the original list $cons(h, l)$ and its reverse have one additional element, we conclude that they both have length $n + 1$.

The induction principle for lists is a particular case of the Structural Induction Principle, which applies to any set built out of a finite set of basic elements $e_1, \ldots, e_n$ using a finite set of constructors $c_1, \ldots, c_k$ to generate new elements from previously built elements. The set of terms defined in Sect. 2.2 is such a set. The basic elements correspond to variables and 0-ary function symbols, and each function symbol f of arity n greater than 0 can be seen as a term constructor that allows us to generate a new term $f(t_1, \ldots, t_n)$ using previously built terms $t_1, \ldots, t_n$.

In general, we can use structural induction to define sets of finite labelled trees. The Structural Induction Principle that we used for lists can be easily adapted to deal with trees, as we will show below. This provides a useful tool to reason on the abstract syntax of programming languages.

First, we define the set of finite labelled trees.

Definition 2.17 (Finite Labelled Trees)

Assume the basic elements are trees $l_1, \ldots, l_m$ consisting of just one node (a leaf). To build more trees, we use constructors $c_1, \ldots, c_k$, each with an associated arity. Given trees $t_1, \ldots, t_{n_i}$, the constructor c_i of arity n_i builds the tree $c_i(t_1, \ldots, t_{n_i})$, which has a root labelled c_i and subtrees $t_1, \ldots, t_{n_i}$.

The set of finite labelled trees is the smallest set that contains all the basic trees $l_1, \ldots, l_m$ and is closed under the constructor operators.

The constructors could also have other parameters, for instance, we could also include numbers or strings to be stored at each node of the tree (see the exercises at the end of this chapter).

Before stating the induction principle for trees, let us give an example.

Example 2.18

If we have just one kind of leaf l, and only one constructor, of arity 2, let us call it *btree*, we can build the following binary trees:

- l: a leaf is a tree;
- $btree(l, l)$: this tree has just a root node and two leaves;
- $btree(btree(l, l), l)$ and $btree(l, btree(l, l))$: these are the only trees with three leaves;
- $btree(btree(l, l), btree(l, l))$: this tree has a root, two internal nodes, and four leaves.

The induction principle follows the inductive definition of tree (Definition 2.17).

Definition 2.19 (Principle of Induction for Trees)

To prove a property P for all finite labelled trees, it is sufficient to show:

– *Basis*: $P(l_1), ..., P(l_m)$.
   This means that we need to prove that the property holds for every basic tree.
– *Induction Step*:
   For each tree constructor c_i (with $n_i \geq 1$ arguments), if the property holds for any
   trees $t_1, \ldots, t_{n_i}$ then it holds for $c_i(t_1, \ldots, t_{n_i})$. More precisely:

$$\forall c, t_1, \ldots, t_n.(P(t_1) \wedge \cdots \wedge P(t_n) \Rightarrow P(c(t_1, \ldots, t_n)))$$

   It means that, for each tree constructor c of arity n, we need to prove the property
   for the tree $c(t_1, \ldots, t_n)$ under the assumption that the property holds for the trees
   $t_1, \ldots, t_n$.

In the induction step, $P(t_1), \ldots, P(t_n)$ are the induction hypotheses.

Similarly, to define a function on all the elements of a set defined by structural
induction, it is sufficient to define it for the basic elements, and to give a recursive
definition for the elements defined by constructors. More precisely, to define function
f on a set defined by structural induction from the basic elements $l_1, \ldots, l_m$, using
constructors $c_1, \ldots, c_k$, where c_i has arity n_i, we need to define:

– $f(l_i)$ for each i such that $1 \leq i \leq m$, and
– $f(c_i(t_1, \ldots, t_{n_i}))$, for each constructor c_i $(1 \leq i \leq k)$ and arbitrary elements
   $t_1, \ldots, t_{n_i}$; in the definition of $f(c_i(t_1, \ldots, t_{n_i}))$ we may use $f(t_j)$ for any $1 \leq j \leq n_i$.

For example, the function that computes the number of leaves in a binary tree (see
Example 2.18), can be defined as follows.

– $leaves(l) = 1$
– $leaves(btree(t_1, t_2)) = leaves(t_1) + leaves(t_2)$.

Since programs are represented as abstract syntax trees, the principle of induction
we have just given for finite labelled trees can be applied when we need to prove
that all the programs written in a given programming language satisfy a certain
property. For this, it is sufficient to specialise the induction principle to take into
account the specific sets of basic elements and constructors in the abstract syntax
under consideration.

Example 2.20

Let us consider the particular case of arithmetic expressions (which are part of all
general purpose programming languages). We have already given the abstract syntax
of arithmetic expressions in Example 1.2: the grammar provided defines the set
of trees representing arithmetic expressions. There are two cases, corresponding,
respectively, to tokens representing numbers and expressions defined by applying
a binary operator to two subtrees. Thus, the set of labelled trees corresponding to

arithmetic expressions can be built inductively: the basic trees are built using number tokens, and the inductive trees are built using four constructors, one for each of the four binary operators $+, *, -, div$ in our language.

To prove that a property P holds for all the abstract syntax trees corresponding to arithmetic expressions in the language, we proceed as follows:

1. Basis: Prove $P(n)$ for all number tokens n.
2. Induction Step: For each operator $Op \in \{+, *, -, div\}$, and each pair E, E' of abstract syntax trees of arithmetic expressions, prove that $P(E)$ and $P(E')$ implies $P(Op(E, E'))$.

Rule Induction. All the induction principles we discussed so far are in fact particular cases of a more general mechanism. We will now give a definition of an inductive set as a subset of a universal set characterised by its generators, that is, a subset defined by

– a finite set of basic elements and
– a finite set of rules that specify how to generate elements of the subset.

Any set of objects can be used as a universal set. Once we have fixed our universal set T, we can define the basic elements of the inductive subset by enumerating them, and define the generators by showing how new elements are constructed in terms of previously defined objects. Formally, we will write inductive definitions using *axioms* to represent the basic elements (the *basis* of the inductive definition) and *rules* to define the way constructors work.

We will then give an induction principle associated with the definition of the inductive subset. The axioms will provide the basis for the induction, and the rules will represent the induction step. We will give examples below, but first let us define more precisely the notions of axiom and rule.

Definition 2.21 (Axioms and Rules)

Let T be a set of objects (i.e. our universal set).

An axiom is simply an element of T. The standard notation for axioms is:

$$\frac{}{t}$$

A rule is a pair (H, c) where

– H is a non-empty subset $\{h_1, \ldots, h_n\}$ of T, called the *hypotheses* or *premises* of the rule;
– c is an element of T, called the *conclusion* of the rule.

The standard notation for rules is:

$$\frac{h_1 \quad \ldots \quad h_n}{c}$$

Rules may have conditions, which we write on the side (we give examples below).

We now define precisely the inductive set specified by a collection of axioms and rules.

Definition 2.22 (Inductive Set Specified by Axioms and Rules)

The subset I of T inductively defined by a collection A of axioms and R of rules is the smallest subset of T that includes the set A of axioms and is closed under all the rules in R.

According to this definition, the inductive set I consists of those elements t in T such that

- $t \in A$ (that is, t is an axiom), or
- there are $t_1, \ldots, t_n \in I$ and a rule $(H, c) \in R$ such that $H = \{t_1, \ldots, t_n\}$ and $t = c$.

We can apply this technique to define the inductive sets we have already studied.

Example 2.23

We can define the set of natural numbers using one axiom:

$$\frac{\quad}{0}$$

and one rule:

$$\frac{n}{n+1}$$

The set of lists of natural numbers can be defined by the axiom:

$$\frac{\quad}{nil}$$

and the rule:

$$\frac{l}{cons(h, l)} \quad \text{if } h \in \mathcal{N}$$

Note the condition on the rule, which specifies that h is a natural number.

Another example is the definition of the set of strings that have an even number of characters from an alphabet Σ. In this case the universal set is the set of all the sequences of characters in Σ. Let us denote the empty string by ϵ. We can define the subset of strings whose length is an even number using just the axiom

$$\frac{\quad}{\epsilon}$$

and a set of rules of the form

$$\frac{s}{a\,s\,b} \quad \text{if } a, \ b \in \Sigma$$

According to this rule, we can build a string with an even number of characters using a previously built string s, which has an even number of characters, and two arbitrary characters a and b in Σ; $a\,s\,b$ denotes the string obtained by adding a at the beginning of s and b at the end. We will often omit ϵ when there is no confusion, so we will write $a\,b$ instead of $a\,\epsilon\,b$.

We can think of this as a rule scheme: there is one rule for each pair of characters.

To show that an element t of T is in the inductive set I it is sufficient to show that t is an axiom, or that there is a way of generating t starting from the axioms and using the rules. The latter can be shown by building a *proof tree* for t.

Definition 2.24 (Proof tree)

Given an inductive definition of I using axioms A and rules R, a proof tree for t has root, also called *conclusion*, t. Its leaves correspond to axioms in A, and for each non-leaf node t_i there is a rule $(\{t_{i1}, \dots, t_{im_i}\}, t_i)$ in R relating t_i and its children $t_{i1}, \dots, t_{im_i}$ in the proof tree.

This kind of proof tree is usually written:

$$
\cfrac{
\cfrac{\vdots}{t_{11}} \quad \cdots \quad \cfrac{\vdots}{t_{1m_1}} \qquad\qquad
\cfrac{\vdots}{t_{n1}} \quad \cdots \quad \cfrac{\vdots}{t_{nm_n}}
}{\strut}
$$

$$
\cfrac{t_1 \qquad\qquad \cdots \qquad\qquad t_n}{t}
$$

For example, the proof tree for the number 2, using the inductive definition of the set of natural numbers given in Example 2.23, is:

$$
\cfrac{\cfrac{\dfrac{\overline{}}{0}}{1}}{2}
$$

Similarly, we can build a proof tree for the string $abab$:

$$
\cfrac{\cfrac{\dfrac{\overline{}}{\epsilon}}{b\,a}}{a\,b\,a\,b}
$$

In the following example, we use axioms and rules to give an inductive definition of an evaluation relation for arithmetic expressions. Here, the universal set is the set of pairs where the first element is an abstract syntax tree representing an arithmetic expression, and the second a value (an integer number in this case).

Example 2.25 (Inductive Definition of Evaluation)

Consider the abstract syntax of arithmetic expressions given in Example 1.2. We define now, using axioms and rules, a binary relation that associates the (abstract syntax tree of an) arithmetic expression E with a number n. We will write $E \Downarrow n$ to indicate that the expression E evaluates to the number n.

Axioms.

A number is already a value. Therefore for each number we need an axiom: $0 \Downarrow 0$, $1 \Downarrow 1$, $2 \Downarrow 2$, etc. Instead of writing these explicitly, we will use an *axiom scheme*:

$$n \Downarrow n$$

which represents the infinite set of axioms obtained by replacing n with a number.

From now on, we will not distinguish between axioms and axiom schemes. We will simply write $n \Downarrow n$, with the assumption that n is any number.

Rules.

Similarly, we will need rules for each operator $Op \in \{+, *, -, div\}$, which we represent as *rule schemes*:

$$\frac{E_1 \Downarrow n_1 \quad E_2 \Downarrow n_2}{Op(E_1, E_2) \Downarrow n} \text{ if } n = (n_1 \ Op \ n_2)$$

The condition " if $n = (n_1 \ Op \ n_2)$" on the rule simply states that the number n in the conclusion of the rule is the result of the operation denoted by Op on the values n_1 and n_2.

From now on, rule schemes will simply be called rules.

Associated to inductive definitions using axioms and rules, there is a principle of induction, called the *Principle of Rule Induction*.

Let I be a set defined by induction with axioms and rules (A, R). To show that a property P holds for each element of the set I, that is, to prove

$$\forall i \in I . P(i)$$

it is sufficient to prove:

– *Basis*: $\forall a \in A . P(a)$
– *Induction Step*:
  $\forall(\{h_1, \dots h_n\}, c) \in R. \ P(h_1) \wedge \cdots \wedge P(h_n) \Rightarrow P(c)$.

Thus, every proof by rule induction has two parts. In the first part, the property is proved for the axioms. In the second part, for each rule, assuming that the property is true for the premises of the rule (this is the induction hypothesis), the property is proved for the conclusion of the rule.

Example 2.26

We can prove using rule induction that each arithmetic expression has a unique value under the evaluation relation given in Example 2.25. In other words, the relation $\Downarrow$ is a function, and it is defined for every expression (we assume the arithmetic operators are total).

Basis: The basis of the induction holds trivially, since numbers have unique values (according to the axioms, the value of an expression n is the number n itself).

Induction Step: For non-atomic expressions, we remark that the value of an arithmetic expression of the form $Op(E_1, E_2)$ is uniquely determined by the values of its arguments E_1 and E_2, which are unique by the induction hypotheses.

2.5 Further Reading

Makinson's book [1] provides a gentle introduction to logic, set theory and induction. Harper's book [2] and Winskel's book [3] include chapters on induction with a variety of examples, and Dowek's book [4] provides a formal definition of an inductive set as a least fixed point, including concise explanations of the notions underlying the definition.

2.6 Exercises

1. Show the following properties of the intersection and union operators on sets:

$$A \cup B = B \cup A$$
$$(A \cup B) \cup C = A \cup (B \cup C)$$
$$A \cup A = A$$
$$A \cap B = B \cap A$$
$$(A \cap B) \cap C = A \cap (B \cap C)$$
$$A \cap A = A$$

2. Show that for every formula ϕ in first-order logic, and every choice of universe U, valuation σ and interpretations for function and predicate symbols, the interpretations of ϕ and $\neg(\neg\phi)$ coincide, that is, double negation does not change the truth value of a formula.
3. Prove, by mathematical induction, that for any natural number n:
   - $\sum_{i=1}^{n} i = n(n+1)/2$
   - $\sum_{i=1}^{n} 2^{i-1} = 2^n - 1$
4. Describe the set of trees generated by the following inductive definition:
   Nil is a tree;
   If n is a number and t_1 and t_2 are trees, then $Tree(n, t_1, t_2)$ is a tree.
5. Prove that the principle of structural induction corresponds to a particular application of the principle of mathematical induction.
6. Define the abstract syntax of first-order logic formulas using a grammar.
   Using structural induction, define for each formula its set of free variables and bound variables.

7. Define by rule induction the set E of even natural numbers, using $n+2$ to generate the even number after n. Prove by rule induction that $2n$ is in the set E, for every natural number n.

8. Let $R \subseteq A \times A$ be a binary relation on A. Define by rule induction the relation R^*, that is, the reflexive-transitive closure of R.

9. (†) Let I be a set defined by rule induction using axioms A and rules R. An alternative way of defining I is by taking the intersection of all the subsets of T that include A and are closed under R:

$$ I = \bigcap \{J \subseteq T \mid A \subseteq J \text{ and } J \text{ } R\text{-closed}\} $$

Prove that both definitions are equivalent.

References

1. D. Makinson, *Sets, Logic and Maths for Computing*, 2nd edn., Undergraduate topics in computer science (Springer, Berlin, 2012)
2. R. Harper, *Practical Foundations for Programming Languages* (Cambridge University Press, Cambridge, 2013)
3. G. Winskel, *The Formal Semantics of Programming Languages*, Foundations of computing (MIT Press, Cambridge, 1993)
4. G. Dowek, *Proofs and Algorithms—An Introduction to Logic and Computability*, Undergraduate topics in computer science (Springer, Berlin, 2011)

Part II
Imperative Languages

Chapter 3
General Features of Imperative Languages

The first programming languages were designed to follow closely the physical design of a computer. The languages that evolved from them, usually called *imperative* programming languages, are still influenced by the architecture of the computer: they mirror the features of the Von Neumann machine, abstracting from superfluous details and retaining the essential aspects of this architecture.

All imperative languages provide memory and processor abstractions. Low-level imperative languages provide a very limited level of abstraction, whereas high-level languages provide powerful memory manipulation and input/output primitives that are hardware independent.

The memory is one of the main components of the Von Neumann architecture; it stores data as well as the program to be executed. In an imperative language, the part of the memory used to store data is abstracted by variables, which represent memory cells. Imperative languages provide assignment statements to modify their contents.

The other important component of the Von Neumann machine is the processor. In imperative languages, it is abstracted by control structures, also known as commands. Imperative programs contain commands that specify the order of execution of instructions in the processor.

Although the level of abstraction provided by imperative languages varies greatly from low-level assembly languages to sophisticated high-level languages such as C++, Python or Java, there are common features in the design of all the imperative languages. In order to understand the behaviour of imperative programs, we need to know the *properties of variables* and the *flow of control among instructions*.

3.1 Variables

A variable is characterised by its properties or attributes:

– *Name*: usually a string of characters chosen by the programmer. In most programming languages, there is a set of reserved words that cannot be used to name

M. Fernández, *Programming Languages and Operational Semantics*,
Undergraduate Topics in Computer Science, DOI: 10.1007/978-1-4471-6368-8_3,
© Springer-Verlag London 2014

variables (e.g., *class* is a reserved word in C++), and there are restrictions on the maximum length of a name and what character sequences are valid (e.g., variable names are usually required to start with an upper or lower case letter).

Variable names are also called *identifiers*. The concrete syntax of the language specifies the kind of strings that can be used as identifiers. For example, in Python an identifier may contain letters, digits and underscores (without spaces between them), and must start with a letter or an underscore; see also Exercise 6 in Chap. 1 for an example of concrete syntax for identifiers.[1] Imperative programs usually contain *variable declarations*, which specify the name of the variables, as well as other attributes such as type and initial value, as described below.

– *Type*: indicates the range of values that can be assigned to the variable, as well as the operations that can be performed on it. Some languages (for example, assembly languages) are untyped, so no types are associated with variables. Many high-level imperative languages have *static typing*, which means that each variable is associated with a type at compile time when a variable declaration is processed (either by using the type explicitly declared for the variable, or by using a type inference algorithm if there are no type declarations, as in the languages from the ML family). In languages with *dynamic typing*, such as Python, PHP and JavaScript, variables are given types at run time, when values are assigned to them. This provides some flexibility, but makes it impossible to type check programs at compile time and for this reason less errors can be detected before the programs are executed. Moreover, code added to perform the type checking at run time in dynamically typed languages introduces overheads.

– *Address*: the memory location associated with the variable, which is sometimes called its *left-value* or *l-value*, since it is required when the variable occurs on the left-hand side of an assignment statement (the behaviour of assignment statements is described in Sect. 3.2 below).

The association between memory addresses and names of variables is not simple: the same name may be associated with different addresses in different parts of the program, and in some imperative languages it is possible to associate more than one name with the same address (e.g., using the EQUIVALENCE statement in Fortran, variant records in Pascal, or union types in C and C++).

– *Value*: the contents of the memory location associated with the variable. Assignment statements are used in imperative languages to change the values of variables at run time. The value of a variable is also called its *right-value* or *r-value*, since it is required when the variable occurs on the right-hand side of an assignment statement.

Some languages include variables whose values are specified once and for all (either statically, when the variable declaration is processed, by giving the variable a value which cannot be changed during the execution of the program, or dynamically, by using a unique assignment instruction for the variable). This kind

---

[1] The language Haskell mentioned in Exercise 6 in Chap. 1 is functional, not imperative. Although the semantics of identifiers in functional languages is very different from the semantics of variables in imperative languages, the concrete syntax is similar.

of variable is usually called a *constant*. For example, in Java, programmers can declare constants using the keyword "final"; Java constants can be bound to values statically (by giving a value when the variable is declared) or dynamically (by using an assignment instruction).

- *Lifetime*: the time during which the variable is allocated to a specific memory location (between *allocation* and *deallocation*). Allocation is the process of assigning free memory space to variables. Deallocation occurs when the space used for the variable is placed back in the pool of available memory. In some languages, there are specific commands to allocate and deallocate variables. In other languages, the run time support performs one or both of these tasks in a transparent way.

The memory is usually divided into different areas and the way variables are allocated and deallocated depends on the area of memory used. In most imperative languages, there are three areas: *static memory*, *run time stack* (or simply stack), and *heap*. The static memory is used for variables whose storage requirements are known at compile time and will not change at run time. The run time stack is used to manage calls to subprograms that require storage space for local variables and parameters. The heap is an unstructured area of memory (usually organised as linked lists), used for variables that are dynamically allocated during the program execution. We can distinguish four classes of variables depending on the area of memory where they reside and the kind of mechanism used to allocate and deallocate their memory space.

1. *Static Variables* are bound to memory locations in the static area before the execution of the program begins, and remain bound until the end of the execution.

   The advantage of this kind of allocation is efficiency, since all addressing can be resolved at compile time and there is no allocation/deallocation at run time.

   The disadvantage is that the storage occupied by static variables cannot be reused, and we need to know in advance the number of memory cells that are required. In some cases, this is not possible: for instance, local variables in recursive programs cannot be static because each recursive call requires its own local variables and the number of recursive calls is not known before the execution of the program. In C and C++, programmers can use the keyword "static" on variable definitions in functions to indicate that static allocation should be used.[2]

2. *Stack Dynamic Variables* are allocated to a memory location on the stack when the declaration of the variable is processed at run time. For example, the variables declared at the beginning of a Java method are allocated when the method is called, and deallocated when the method finishes. More generally, local variables of recursive procedures are typically stack dynamic variables: each recursive call will create a new frame in the stack, allocating space for the local variables. At

---

[2] This should not be confused with the use of the keyword "static" as a modifier in the declaration of a variable in a C++ or Java class, where it indicates that the variable is a *class variable* rather than an instance variable. As their name suggests, instance variables belong to the objects that are instances of the class, so there is a copy of the variable for each object, whereas there is only one copy of a class variable.

the end of the recursive call, when the control returns to the caller, the frame is destroyed and the local variables are deallocated, so the memory space becomes again available (Sect. 3.5 describes memory management for subprograms in more detail).

3. *Explicit Heap Dynamic Variables* are nameless variables that are allocated and deallocated in the heap at run time, by program instructions, using pointers. For example, in C++

```
int *intvar;
...
intvar = new int; /* allocates memory for an int variable*/
...
delete intvar; /* deallocates the space to which intvar

                                                points*/
```

The amount of storage needed for the variable in the heap depends on its type, which can be statically defined or dynamically computed. It is possible for a language to be statically typed and include dynamically allocated variables.

When an allocation instruction (such as the new in the C++ example above) is executed, the variable is bound to a specific storage space in the heap, and remains bound to this address until a deallocation command for the same variable is executed. If the deallocation is performed by means of program instructions (as in the example above with the delete instruction), the programmer must remember to include the commands to deallocate space, otherwise the program may run out of space and a run time error will occur. To avoid this kind of error, which arises quite often in practice, in some programming languages only the allocation is done explicitly by program instructions—the deallocation is implicit. For example, objects in Java are explicit heap dynamic, and are accessed through reference variables, but there is no way to destroy them explicitly: implicit garbage collection is used.

The *garbage collector* is the part of the run time support that performs deallocation of unused segments of the heap, returning them to the pool of available space. In a language with implicit deallocation of heap variables, the run time support must include mechanisms to detect if a variable in the heap is no longer needed. This is usually done by keeping count of the number of pointers to each variable in the heap, with the associated run time overheads. Implicit garbage collection is not suitable for applications where full control of the processor is needed. In that case, a programming language that offers instructions to perform heap allocation and deallocation is preferable. Otherwise, transparent memory management is usually preferred.

4. *Implicit Heap Dynamic Variables* are allocated memory space only when they are assigned values at run time, and their attributes may change when their values change. Examples of this kind of variable are strings and arrays in Perl and JavaScript.

The advantage of implicit heap dynamic variables over explicit ones is that they provide flexibility in the use of the memory space. The disadvantage is cost (in execution time) since all the attributes of the variable may vary during the execution (including type, array ranges, etc). This also makes error detection more difficult.

— *Scope*: the part of the program in which the variable is visible and therefore can be used. Programs in imperative languages are usually divided into *blocks* and *subprograms*, which may contain their own variable declarations. So the scope of a variable refers to the block(s) or subprogram(s) where it can be used. We discuss blocks and subprograms in Sect. 3.5; for the moment it is sufficient to think of a block of code as a sequence of instructions (each language has its own rules to identify the beginning and the end of a block) and of a subprogram as a block of code with a name that identifies it (and often also some parameters). The concrete syntax of blocks and subprograms varies depending on the language. Subprograms are some times called procedures or functions; in object-oriented languages, classes, objects, and methods could be seen as blocks or subprograms. Variables can be classified as *local* or *global* depending on their scope. Local variables are those declared in the block of program or subprogram. Variables that are visible but not local are global.
Some languages have static scoping rules whereas others have dynamic scoping rules:
— A *statically scoped language* is one where the scope of each variable can be determined before the execution of the program, that is, at compile time. When a variable is referenced, the compiler looks for its declaration in the same block or subprogram, and if there is no declaration then it looks in the parent block/subprogram, and continues in this way until it reaches the main program. If no declaration is found then an error is reported.
For example, the following Pascal program contains several references to the variable x.

```
program main;
   var x : real;
   procedure P1;
      var x : integer;              { local variable }
      begin
      ... x ...
      end;
   procedure P2;
      begin
      ... x ...                     { global variable }
      end;
begin
... x ...
end.
```

Since Pascal has static scoping, the reference to x in P1 corresponds to the local integer variable, whereas the references to x in P2 and in the main program correspond to the global real variable.

- A *dynamically scoped language* is one where the scope of each variable depends on the calling sequence of subprograms. In other words, it depends on the order in which the instructions are executed. In the previous example, if we assume dynamic scoping, the reference to x in P2 may refer to the variable in P1 or in the main program, depending on who called P2.

This implies that languages with dynamic scoping rules cannot have static type checking (with the disadvantages that were already mentioned), and programs may be more difficult to understand. Some languages that were originally defined with dynamic scoping were later changed to implement static scoping (e.g., LISP used dynamic scoping rules, but its descendant Scheme is statically scoped). Most modern languages adopt static scoping rules, however, dynamic scoping also has some advantages: it provides an efficient mechanism to pass information to the called subprogram, and often programs in dynamically scoped languages are more concise, with less lines of code. Examples of modern languages with dynamic scoping rules are JavaScript and Python.

3.2 Assignment

The assignment statement is generally of the form:

variable-name = expression

but the = sign should not be confused with equivalence in the mathematical sense. To emphasise the difference, in some languages : = is used instead of =.

An assignment statement associates the variable named on the left-hand side with the value of the expression indicated on the right-hand side, until a new value is stored with another assignment to the variable or by a side-effect of another instruction.

In typed languages, typing controls are performed (at compile time if the language has static typing) in order to ensure that the expression and the variable in an assignment statement have compatible types.

The language C introduced a notation for combining assignment and increment: i++ and ++i change the value of i to the current value plus 1 and return the value of i and i+1 respectively. There are also statements combining assignment and decrement (written i- - and - -i, a-). These instructions can be used on their own, or as expressions within other instructions. For example, in C we can write

```
result = sum++;
```

which has the effect of storing in the variable result the current value of the variable sum, then incrementing the value in the variable sum.

3.3 Control Statements

Programs in imperative languages are sequences of instructions. The sequencing is indicated by textual juxtaposition. The next instruction that will be executed is therefore the one that follows in the text of the program, unless a control statement is used to alter the flow of control.

The main control statements in imperative languages are:

- *selection constructs*, also called *conditionals*, which are used to choose between alternative flows of control,
- *iterative constructs*, also called *loops*, which are used to repeat the execution of the same code several times, and
- *branching instructions*, also called *jumps*, which are used to force a change in the flow of control.

Moreover, imperative languages provide ways to build *compound control statements* by grouping together several instructions in *blocks*, for example using braces in C or Java.

It has been proved that any sequential algorithm can be coded with just two control statements (in addition to assignment statements and sequence): a selection construct (such as if-then-else) and a logically controlled iteration (such as while). Branching instructions (such as the controversial goto, which gave rise to heated discussions amongst programming language designers in the 1960s and 1970s) are therefore superfluous and have been excluded from some modern languages (for example, Java and Python do not include a goto statement). Instead, modern languages include specific mechanisms to deal with errors.

Although a conditional and a loop would be sufficient to define a universal language, all languages provide several constructs of each class, in order to facilitate the writing and reading of programs. For instance, most imperative languages include several kinds of iterative constructs (e.g., while loops and for loops). We discuss below the most common features of the constructs within each class.

3.3.1 Selection Statements

Selection constructs are used to choose between two or more execution paths in a program. We distinguish *two-way selectors* and *multiple selectors*.

- *Two-way selectors*, also known as "if-then-else" constructs, are standard in modern imperative languages. The concrete syntax varies depending on the language, the usual forms are:

> if *condition* then *then-branch* else *else-branch*
>
> or
>
> if (*condition*) *then-branch* else *else-branch*

These constructs cause the evaluation of the condition, and the selection of the *then-branch* if the condition is true, or the *else-branch* otherwise. Sometimes the `else` *else-branch* part is omitted and when the condition is false the next instruction in the program is executed. Usually the condition is a Boolean expression, although some languages, such as C, allow programmers to use arithmetic expressions in two-way selectors; an expression that evaluates to 0 is considered False. Although the semantics of a single selector is quite clear, the semantics of nested selectors varies depending on the language. For example, given the following program:

```
if (a == 0)
    if (b == 0)
    (result = 0)
else
    (result = 1)
```

the question "is the `else` paired with the outer or inner `if`?" may have different answers depending on the language.

In some languages, like Python for example, indentation is important. The concrete syntax of a two-way selector in Python is

`if` *condition* :
   then-branch
`else` :
   else-branch
statements after the conditional

Note that the `else` keyword lines-up with the `if`. This is a requirement in Python for the else branch to be paired with the `if`. The rule is that the `else` will be paired with the closest `if` in the *same* column, and the statements in the then-branch and the else-branch must be indented exactly the same amount. Python is very precise about indentation, because indentation is used to determine the flow of control in the program. But most languages, including Java, specify that the `else` is matched with the most recent unpaired `then` clause (the inner one in the example above), ignoring the indentation of the statements.

Since the use of implicit association rules may be confusing, some languages require the use of specific syntax for nesting selectors. For example, in Algol 60, the keywords `begin` and `end` are used to enforce the association of an `else` branch with an `if`, as in the following example where the `else` is paired with the inner `if`.

```
if a = 0 then
begin
   if b = 0 then
   result := 0
   else
   result := 1
end
```

To associate the `else` with the outer `if`, we write:

```
if a = 0 then
begin
   if b = 0 then
      result := 0
end
else
   result := 1
```

Note that to obtain the latter semantics in Java we also need to use extra syntax (braces).

— *Multiple selectors* are a generalisation of two-way selectors. The idea is that more than two alternative paths can be specified. Multiple selectors are usually associated with keywords such as `case` or `switch`.

For example, in Java, C, or C++ we can write:

```
switch (expression) {
case expr-1 : statement-1;
...
case expr-n : statement-n;
[default : statement-n+1]
}
```

In some languages (e.g., Pascal), at the end of a branch, the control goes to the instruction that follows the multiple selector, while in others (e.g., Java) we need an explicit `break` at the end of the branch in order to go to the end of the switch (or a `return` to exit the method).

Multiple selectors can be simulated with nested chains of two-way selectors, but the use of a multiple selector, if available in the language, improves the readability of programs.

3.3.2 Iterative Statements (Loops)

Iterative constructs cause a statement or sequence of statements (the *body* of the loop) to be repeated, until a certain condition becomes true.

If the test for loop completion is done before the execution of the body we say that it is a *pre-test* loop, and if it occurs after the body is executed, we say that it is a *post-test* loop.

In addition, we can distinguish between two kinds of loops, depending on the way the iteration is controlled:

- *Counter-controlled loops*: The number of repetitions of the body of the loop depends on the value of a counter. For example, the `for` statement in C and Java, which has the form:

```
for (expr-1; expr-2; expr3)
    loop-body
```

is executed as follows: `expr-1` initialises the counter, `expr-2` is the loop control and is evaluated before each execution of the loop-body (it is used to stop the loop), and `expr-3` is evaluated after each execution of the loop-body. For example, the `for` instruction in the following program

```
int sum;
int index;
sum = 0;
for (index = 0; index < 5; index++)
    sum = sum + list[index];
```

initialises the counter `index` to 0. The condition `index < 5` is evaluated before each repetition of the assignment instruction, and `index` is incremented after each repetition, until it becomes equal to 5 and fails the test `index < 5`.

In Java the control expression must be Boolean, but C also accepts arithmetic expressions, in which case 0 is understood as False.

In other languages, the `for` statement only indicates the name of the counter and the range. For example, in Pascal we can write:

```
for index = 0 to 4 do
    sum := sum + list[index];
```

In this case the increment is implicitly assumed to be 1 (this is sometimes called the *step* of the `for` loop).

A variant of counter-controlled loop is the loop over a sequence of elements. This version of the `for` loop, also known as an iterator or "foreach" statement, was added in Java 5.0 to simplify the writing of programs that require iterating through the elements in an array or in a collection. In Python, for example, it is possible to iterate over a string using a for-loop. This means that the body of the loop is executed once for each character in the string. The for-loop in Python has the following form:

```
for variable in sequence :
    loop-body
statements after the loop
```

Again, indentation is crucial here: it is used to determine the sequence of instructions in the loop body, which should be repeated. The variable specified in this `for` statement is an arbitrary variable chosen by the programmer; it will initially be assigned to the first element of the sequence, then the loop body will be executed and afterwards the variable will be updated to the next element of the sequence. The number of repetitions of the loop body corresponds to the length of the sequence: if the sequence is empty, it will not be executed, otherwise it will be executed once for each element in the sequence, so in this sense this is also a counter-controlled loop. To simulate a for-loop based on a counter name and range, as the one in Pascal, we can simply create a sequence of values (list) and then iterate over the list.

– *Logically-controlled loops*: Most imperative languages include both pre-test and post-test logically-controlled loop constructs. For example, in C++ and Java there is a `while` loop which has the form:

```
while (expression)
    loop-body
```

and a `do` loop, which has the form:

```
do
    loop-body
while (expression)
```

The `while` is pre-test, that is, the expression is evaluated first, and the loop-body is executed as long as the expression evaluates to True. The `do` loop is post-test, therefore the loop-body is executed first and then the expression is evaluated, but in this case the loop-body is repeated until the expression evaluates to False. There are other variants of logically-controlled loops. For example, in Pascal there is a post-test `repeat` loop which has the form:

```
repeat
    loop-body
until (expression)
```

This iterative construct executes the loop-body until the expression evaluates to True.

Finally, we remark that some languages, such as C, C++ and Java, allow the programmer to include in the loop-body statements that break the repetition (by exiting the loop body), but this makes programs more difficult to understand and reason about.

3.4 Branching Statements

A branching instruction, also known as a "jump" or "goto" instruction, allows programmers to specify in a direct way the next instruction to be executed, thus transferring execution control to a specific part of the program.

If used in an unrestricted way, this kind of instruction can make programs very difficult to understand, increasing the maintenance cost. For this reason, some languages do not include a goto (for example, Java and Python, amongst others). However, most modern languages include branching statements of some kind, whether they be unrestricted goto statements or a limited form of jumping construct within particular contexts (for instance, within iterative statements to exit the body of a loop, or in a multi-way selector to exit a branch and jump to the instruction that follows the selector).

3.5 Structuring the Program: Blocks and Subprograms

A *block* is simply a group of statements, delimited by keywords such as begin and end, or by separators, like { and }. A block of statements is syntactically equivalent to one instruction, in other words, we can use a block in constructs where just one statement is expected. A block may contain not only commands but also declarations (of constants, variables or types). If the language has static scope, these will only be visible inside the block (they are local).

Subprogram is a generic name for a block that has a name and can be invoked explicitly. In this case the block of statements is executed upon invocation (the caller is suspended while the invoked subprogram is executed), and control returns to the calling point after the execution of the subprogram. Typical examples are *procedures* in Pascal, *functions* in C, or *methods* in Java. Usually, the word function is used to refer to subprograms that return values to the caller.

All high-level programming languages include some mechanism to define and invoke subprograms. Subprograms are essential to the development of well-structured programs, and improve their readability. Moreover, by using subprograms, programmers can avoid repetition of code, which simplifies the task of finding and correcting bugs, making programs easier to maintain.

Although the concrete syntax and implementation mechanisms for subprograms vary depending on the language, most notions of subprogram share the following features: When a subprogram is declared, together with the name we can associate *parameters* or *arguments*, usually given between brackets after the name of the subprogram. These are called *formal parameters*, whereas the ones provided when the subprogram is called are the *actual parameters*.

The values of the actual parameters are substituted for the formal parameters when the subprogram is invoked. This can be done in different ways, and imperative programming languages often offer several *parameter passing mechanisms*. The most common are *call-by-value*, where a copy of the value of the actual parameter is passed to the invoked subprogram, *call-by-name*, where a textual copy of the actual parameter is used in place of the formal parameter in the called subprogram, and *call-by-reference*, where a pointer to the actual parameter is passed to the called subprogram. For example, in Java all parameters are passed by value, including objects, but since objects can only be accessed through reference variables, for object parameters a reference to the object is passed. However, this reference is still passed by value.[3] Parameter passing is discussed in more detail for functional languages, in Chaps. 5 and 6.

In addition to the parameters, subprograms can contain their own local variables and can access the global variables in their scope. Although in general procedures do not return a value to the caller, they can communicate values back to the caller by updating global variables, or parameters passed by reference. In some languages, such as Fortran 95 and Ada [1], parameters can be declared to be "in", "out", or "inout", depending on whether they are intended to be passed from the caller to the callee, from the callee to the caller, or both.

The implementation of subprogram calls in modern languages requires sophisticated memory management mechanisms, due to the fact that subprogram declarations can be nested. When a subprogram is called, it is necessary to allocate the stack-dynamic local variables and parameters, and implement a reference chain that will allow the subprogram to access non-local variables that are in its scope. Usually this is done as follows.

Each time a subprogram is called, an *activation record* is placed in the run time stack. The activation record contains the local variables, parameters, a pointer to the caller, a return address (so the control can go back to the caller when the subprogram invoked completes its execution), and additional information to retrieve the global variables that are in the scope of the subprogram.

The way global variables are accessed depends on the scoping rules of the language. In languages with dynamic scope, the scoping rules state that the invoked subprogram can access all the variables in the caller. Since the caller subprogram is still active, its variables are available in the corresponding activation record in the run time stack and can be easily found using the pointer to the caller stored in the activation record of the subprogram. For languages with static scope, it is necessary to implement a static chain: each activation record should include a pointer to the activation record of the static parent. When a reference to a global variable is

---

[3] As a consequence, although it is possible to modify the state of the object passed as parameter using the reference variable, it is not possible to replace it with another object: the latter would require a change in the reference passed as parameter, which is not possible since it was passed by value.

processed, the variable can be found by following the pointers in the static chain, until an activation record containing the variable is found.

3.6 Further Reading

There is a vast literature on imperative programming languages, ranging from theoretical work (on models of computation underlying imperative programming, the expressive power and formal semantics of programming constructs, and techniques used to analyse imperative programs, amongst others) to practical work on programming language design and implementation, programming techniques, readability and reliability of programs, etc. The books by Sipser [2] and by Hopcroft et al. [3] contain detailed descriptions of automata and Turing machines, which are early models of computation relating to imperative programming languages. Amongst the early theoretical results on expressivity of imperative constructs, we can cite Böhm and Jacopini's paper [4], which shows that for an imperative language to be able to simulate a universal Turing machine, it is sufficient to include, in addition to an assignment construct and sequence, a two-way selector and a logically controlled loop. This answered negatively the open question of whether a branching instruction (goto) was needed or not to obtain a Turing-complete imperative programming language, and suggested minimal requirements for imperative programming language designers. However, from a practical point of view, minimality is not the most important property of a programming language, since programmers are often more interested in properties such as readability, writability and efficiency of programs. Readability is the ease with which programs can be read and understood. Writability refers to the ease with which programs can be created for a chosen domain of application. Efficiency is measured in terms of memory space and time needed to execute programs. Reliability is a property related to correctness, in the sense that a program is said to be reliable if it performs to its specification in all circumstances. For more information on these properties, as well as details on the history of programming language constructs and evolution of languages, we refer the reader to Sebesta's book [5].

3.7 Exercises

1. Some programming languages are untyped. What are the disadvantages of using a language without types? Is there any advantage?
2. What are the advantages of static variables in a programming language?
3. (a) Define static scope and dynamic scope.
   (b) What are the advantages and disadvantages of dynamic scoping?

4. Consider the following Pascal program:

```
program main;
    var a : integer;
    procedure P1;
    begin
      writeln('a =', a)
    end;
    procedure P2;
    var a : integer;
    begin
      a := 10;
      P1
    end;
  begin a := 4;
      P2
    end.
```

   Pascal uses static scoping rules. What is the value of a printed by P1?
   Under dynamic scoping rules, what would be the value printed?
5. Which kind of scoping rules (static or dynamic) does your favourite programming language use?

   (a) Try to find the answer to this question in the documentation available for the language.
   (b) Write a test program and use its results to justify your answer to the previous question.

6. The while-do and do-while statements available in Java are equally expressive: show how to obtain the effect of a while-do using a do-while and vice versa.
7. Some programming languages have a post-test logically controlled loop of the form:

```
repeat C until B
```

   where the loop-body C will be repeated until the Boolean expression B evaluates to True.
   Show that it is possible to simulate this kind of loop in a language that provides a pre-test loop such as:

```
while B do C
```

8. Consider a programming language with a branching statement (goto), and a program containing an instruction goto p.

   (a) Suppose that p is the address of an instruction inside the body of a loop statement. Should this be considered a mistake? If not, when and how should the counter (if it is a counter-controlled loop) or the Boolean condition (if it is a logically-controlled loop) be evaluated?

(b) Suppose that p is the address of an instruction inside the body of a subprogram. Should this be considered a mistake? If not, how should the local variables and parameters be treated?

References

1. Ada Resource Association, *Ada 2005 Reference Manual: Language and Standard Libraries, International Standard ISO/IEC 8652:1995(E) with Technical Corrigendum 1 and Amendment 1* (Springer, Berlin, 2005)
2. M. Sipser, *Introduction to the Theory of Computation* (Course Technology—Cengage Learning, Stamford, 2006)
3. J.E. Hopcroft, R. Motwani, J.D. Ullman, *Introduction to Automata Theory, Languages and Computability* (Addison-Wesley, Boston, 2000)
4. C. Böhm, G. Jacopini, Flow diagrams, Turing machines and languages with only two formation rules. Commun. ACM **9**(5), 366–371 (1966)
5. R. Sebesta, *Concepts of Programming Languages*, 10th edn (Adison Wesley, Boston, 2012)

Chapter 4
Operational Semantics of Imperative Languages

The discussion of programming language features in the previous chapter was informal. However, informal semantic descriptions may be imprecise, as the following example shows.

Consider the expression $f(i++, --i)$ in C, where f is the name of a function. This is a function call, and the parameters $i++$ and $--i$ will be passed by value (recall that $i++$ returns the value stored in the variable i and increments it, and $--i$ decrements the value stored in i and returns the result). According to the description given in the previous chapter (see Sect. 3.5):

> The values of the actual parameters are substituted for the formal parameters when the subprogram is invoked. This can be done in different ways, and imperative programming languages often offer several *parameter passing mechanisms*. The most common are *call-by-value*, where a copy of the value of the actual parameter is passed to the invoked subprogram, *call-by-name*, where a textual copy of the actual parameter is used in place of the formal parameter in the called subprogram, and *call-by-reference*, where a pointer to the actual parameter is passed to the called subprogram.

Therefore, in this case f will receive the *values* of the expressions $i++$ and $--i$ and use those values to replace the formal parameters in the code defined for the function. So, what are the values of the parameters passed to f in this function call, if the variable i contains the number 0?

Depending on the order of evaluation of the parameters (e.g., left to right, or right to left) the answers to this question will be different.

Actually, the order of evaluation of parameters of functions was not specified in Sect. 3.5; it was not specified in the original definition of the language C either. Different C compilers could evaluate the parameters in a different order, and produce very different code for the same program. In practice, this means that programs have to be tested again if a different version of the compiler is used.

When programs are used in safety-critical domains (e.g., medical applications, transport systems), or when the financial cost of programming errors is considerable, it is not possible to rely on informal semantic descriptions.

M. Fernández, *Programming Languages and Operational Semantics*,   61
Undergraduate Topics in Computer Science, DOI: 10.1007/978-1-4471-6368-8_4,
© Springer-Verlag London 2014

In this chapter, we give a precise meaning to the language constructs in use in imperative languages, using a mathematical tool: transition systems. We present a small imperative language, which we call SIMP, and describe its semantics formally, following the operational approach introduced in Chap. 1.

4.1 Abstract Syntax of SIMP

SIMP is a simple imperative programming language that supports only a limited set of features: assignment, sequencing, conditionals, loops and integer variables.

Since our goal is to provide a formal specification of the operational semantics of SIMP programs, from now on we will only consider SIMP programs that are syntactically correct.

We will not define a concrete syntax for SIMP, instead, we assume that a parser is available to transform syntactically correct programs into abstract syntax trees and simply give below the definition of the abstract syntax trees that are used to represent SIMP programs (see Chap. 1 for definitions and properties of concrete and abstract syntax).

In the rest of this chapter, when we talk about "a SIMP program", we will always mean "an abstract syntax tree representing a SIMP program".

Programs in SIMP are of three kinds: commands (C), integer expressions (E), or Boolean expressions (B). Their abstract syntax trees are generated by the following grammar.

$$P ::= C \mid E \mid B$$

where C, E and B, defined below, are the initial symbols of the grammars generating commands, arithmetic expressions and Boolean expressions, respectively.

Commands. As in every imperative language, in SIMP we have sequencing and assignment statements. Sequences are represented using the binary operator ;. The abstract syntax tree representing the command sequence C_1; C_2 is given by

```
      ;
     / \
   C₁   C₂
```

where the root is labelled by the symbol ;, which identifies a sequence, and the two subtrees are the representations of the commands to be sequentially executed.

Assignment instructions are represented by abstract syntax trees of the form:

where l is a label denoting a memory location (the address of the variable that will be updated) and E is an abstract syntax tree representing an arithmetic expression.

In SIMP there is also a two-way selector, a loop construct, and a skip instruction, which simply passes control to the following statement. The corresponding abstract syntax trees have the form:

$$
\begin{array}{ccc}
if & while & skip \\
/\,|\,\backslash & /\ \ \backslash & \\
B\ C_1\ C_2 & B\ \ \ C &
\end{array}
$$

Formally, the abstract syntax of commands is specified by the grammar below, where trees are represented using a textual notation. We use infix notation for the sequencing operator, and mixfix notation for the conditional and loop (the tokens *then* and *else* separate the branches of the tree representing an if-then-else, and *do* is used to separate the branches of a *while* tree).

$$C ::= l := E \mid C; C \mid if\ B\ then\ C\ else\ C \mid while\ B\ do\ C \mid skip$$

The *skip* instruction is useful to simulate an *if-then* using an *if-then-else*: if the concrete syntax of SIMP includes an if-then construct of the form *if B then C*, in the abstract syntax this can be represented as *if B then C else skip*.

Integer Expressions. In SIMP, we only consider simple expressions built out of integers, variables and the arithmetic operators addition, subtraction, multiplication and integer division. In the abstract syntax of integer expressions, the basic elements (i.e., leaves of the abstract syntax trees) are number tokens, denoted by n,[1] and variable labels (written $l, x, y, z, \ldots$). The internal nodes of the trees correspond to the arithmetic operators $(+, -, *, /)$. In fact, when a variable is used in an arithmetic expression, it is the content of the memory location associated with the variable (its r-value) that is needed, so instead of l we write $!l$ in the abstract syntax tree. The expression $!l$ denotes the value stored at address l. The symbol ! should be understood as a de-referencing operator.

The abstract syntax trees of integer expressions are generated by the following grammar (again we use a textual notation for the trees, see Chap. 1 for a graphical representation of arithmetic expressions).

$$E ::= !l \mid n \mid E\ op\ E$$

$$op ::= + \mid - \mid * \mid /$$

In the grammar rules above, n represents an integer value (that is, $n \in Z = \{\ldots, -2, -1, 0, 1, 2, \ldots\}$, where Z is the set of integer numbers) and l a label ($l \in L = \{l_0, l_1, \ldots\}$, where L is a set of *memory locations*, which we will simply call *variables*).

---

[1] Recall that abstract syntax trees are built using the tokens produced by the lexer; see Chap. 1 for more details.

Boolean Expressions. We build abstract syntax trees to represent Boolean expressions in a similar way: the tokens corresponding to the Boolean constants *True* and *False* (which we denote sometimes in a generic way by *b*) are the basic elements (leaves of the tree), and internal nodes are labelled by Boolean operators such as conjunction (*and*, which we represent with the symbol $\land$) and negation (represented by $\neg$), and relational operators $>$, $<$, $=$ representing comparisons (thus, each of the nodes labelled by a comparison operator should have two subtrees, corresponding to the integer expressions to be compared).

The abstract syntax trees of Boolean expressions are generated by the following grammar, where again we use a textual notation to represent the trees.

$$B ::= \; True \mid False \mid E \; bop \; E \mid \neg B \mid B \land B$$

$$bop ::= \; > \; \mid \; < \; \mid \; =$$

More logical connectives and comparison operators could easily be added (see the exercises at the end of the chapter).

We emphasise the fact that the grammar presented in this chapter for SIMP specifies the *abstract* syntax of the language, therefore the expressions should not be understood as strings, but rather as labelled trees. The leaf nodes of the trees are labelled by elements of $Z \cup \{True, False\} \cup L \cup \{skip\}$, while the non-leaf nodes are labelled by operators and commands. In the rest of the chapter we will often abuse the notation by writing these two-dimensional tree structures in a convenient one-dimensional form. Some examples will help to clarify the notation.

Example 4.1
The following program swaps the contents of the variables x and y.[2]

$$z := \; !x \; ; \; (x := \; !y \; ; \; y := \; !z)$$

The abstract syntax tree is depicted below.

```
                    ;
                  /   \
                :=      ;
               / \     / \
              z  !x   :=   :=
                      / \  / \
                     x  !y y  !z
```

----

[2] The brackets are not part of the syntax; they are not needed if we draw the two-dimensional tree, but are used to disambiguate the textual syntax: in this example the root of the tree corresponds to the first sequencing operator.

Although the abstract syntax trees represented by

$$z := !x \; ; \; (x := !y \; ; \; y := !z)$$

and

$$(z := !x \; ; \; x := !y) \; ; \; y := !z$$

are different, we will see later that both have exactly the same semantics (i.e. produce the same results), which suggests that there is no need to include brackets in sequences in the concrete syntax.

Example 4.2

Assuming a natural number n is stored in the variable l, the program depicted below computes its factorial $n!$ using the *while* command (the only iterative construct available in SIMP). It starts by storing 1 in the variable *factorial*, using an assignment statement. Then, it iterates the sequence of assignments

$$factorial := \, ! factorial * !l \; ; \; l := \, !l - 1$$

until $!l$ becomes 0.

The abstract syntax tree of the iteration is shown below.

```
                    while
                    /    \
                   >      ;
                  / \    / \
                !l  0  :=   :=
                       / \  / \
                 factorial *  l  -
                           / \  / \
                     !factorial !l !l 1
```

In the textual notation this loop is written as follows:

$$while \; !l > 0 \; do \; (\, factorial := !factorial * !l; \; l := !l - 1)$$

Note the use of brackets, to avoid ambiguity.

4.2 An Abstract Machine for SIMP

To give a precise description of the behaviour of SIMP programs, in this section we define an abstract machine. It consists of four main elements:

1. a *control stack* c, where instructions are stored;
2. an *auxiliary stack* r, also called the *results stack*, where intermediate results are stored;
3. a *processor*, which performs simple arithmetic operations, comparisons, and Boolean operations (and, not); and
4. a *memory*, or *store*, modelled by a partial function m mapping locations to integers.

For simplicity, we assume the processor performs only integer-valued binary operations: addition, subtraction, multiplication and division. Moreover, we assume the processor always returns a result for an arithmetic operation; division by zero produces a number rather than an error.

We represent the memory as a *function* because each location can hold at most one value; it is partial because some locations might not hold any value. We use the notation $dom(m)$ for the set of locations where m is defined, and use the notation $m(l)$ to denote the value stored at location l in m. We write $m[l \mapsto n]$ to denote the function that maps each $l' \neq l$ to the value $m(l')$, and l to the value n (so the function $m[l \mapsto n]$ coincides with m everywhere except in l, where they may differ).

Formally, an abstract machine is a transition system, and is therefore defined by a set of *configurations* and a *transition relation* (see Sect. 2.3 in Chap. 2). The transition relation will be defined by transition rules.

Configurations. The configurations of the abstract machine for SIMP are triples $\langle c, r, m \rangle$ of control stack, results stack and memory. Stacks are inductively defined: an empty stack is denoted by *nil*, and a non-empty stack $i \cdot c$ is obtained by pushing an instruction i on top of a stack c. The formal definition of the stacks c and r is given by the grammar:

$$c ::= nil \mid i \cdot c$$

$$i ::= P \mid op \mid \neg \mid \wedge \mid bop \mid := \mid if \mid while$$

$$r ::= nil \mid P \cdot r \mid l \cdot r$$

where P, op and bop are the non-terminals used in the rules defining the abstract syntax of SIMP in Sect. 4.1.

In other words, the control stack may be empty, or contain programs, operators such as $+, -, *, /, \neg, \wedge, >, <, =, :=$, and keywords such as *if* or *while*. In the same way, the results stack may be empty or contain programs or locations. In a non-empty stack $i \cdot c$, i is the element at the top of the stack and c is the rest of the stack.

To model the execution of SIMP programs we will use sequences of transitions from initial to final configurations.

Definition 4.3 (Initial and Final Configurations)
To execute the command C in a given memory state m, the abstract machine starts from a configuration $\langle C \cdot nil, nil, m \rangle$. Configurations of this form are called *initial*.

Final configurations have the form $\langle nil, nil, m \rangle$, since the machine stops when the stacks are empty.

Transition Rules. The transition relation, denoted by $\rightarrow$, specifies how to execute the commands available in the language SIMP, and how to evaluate arithmetic and Boolean expressions. It is a binary relation between configurations: a transition

$$\langle c, r, m \rangle \rightarrow \langle c', r', m' \rangle$$

corresponds to a step of computation of the abstract machine, which will transform the configuration $\langle c, r, m \rangle$ into a new configuration $\langle c', r', m' \rangle$.

The transition performed by the machine depends on the command that needs to be executed or the expression that needs to be evaluated. These will be placed at the top of the control stack. Therefore, to define the transition relation we use generic rules that show how configurations evolve depending on the instruction at the top of the control stack.

Evaluating Expressions. The following rules describe the transitions that take place when the element at the top of the control stack is an integer expression. There are three cases, which correspond to the three different kinds of abstract syntax trees representing integer expressions in SIMP. We describe them below.

1. If the expression is simply a number n, we use the following rule.

$$\langle n \cdot c, r, m \rangle \rightarrow \langle c, n \cdot r, m \rangle$$

In this case, since the expression at the top of the control stack in the configuration shown on the left-hand side of the rule is already a value, there is no need to evaluate it, and therefore the machine simply pops this value off the control stack and pushes it onto the results stack. Note how the control stack $n \cdot c$ in the configuration on the left-hand side of the rule becomes just c on the right-hand side, and the results stack r on the left-hand side becomes $n \cdot r$ on the right-hand side. The memory is not affected.

2. If the expression is a reference to a variable, $!l$, then the value of the expression is the number stored at the location l in the memory. The following rule defines the transition performed by the machine.

$$\langle !l \cdot c, r, m \rangle \rightarrow \langle c, n \cdot r, m \rangle \text{if } m(l) = n$$

According to this rule, if the content of location l in m, denoted by $m(l)$, is n, and the expression to be evaluated is $!l$, then the machine pops $!l$ from the control stack, and pushes n onto the results stack. Note how the control stack $!l \cdot c$ in the configuration on the left-hand side of the rule becomes just c on the right-hand side, and the results stack r on the left-hand side becomes $n \cdot r$ on the right-hand side. The evaluation of this kind of expression does not change the memory m.

3. If the expression has an arithmetic operator at its root, we use the following rules.

$$\langle (E_1 \text{ op } E_2) \cdot c, r, m \rangle \rightarrow \langle E_1 \cdot E_2 \cdot op \cdot c, r, m \rangle$$
$$\langle op \cdot c, n_2 \cdot n_1 \cdot r, m \rangle \rightarrow \langle c, n \cdot r, m \rangle \qquad \text{if } n_1 \text{ op } n_2 = n$$

The first rule specifies a transition from a configuration that contains an element of the form $E_1 \ op \ E_2$ at the top of the stack, to a configuration that contains $E_1 \cdot E_2 \cdot op \cdot c$. This is achieved by popping the expression from the top of the control stack, then disassembling it into its constituent parts, i.e., E_1, op and E_2, and then pushing the root operator and each of the subexpressions back onto the control stack. Note that the configuration on the right-hand side of the first rule has E_1 at the top of the control stack. Then depending on whether E_1 is a number, a variable or another compound expression with an operator at its root, one of the three rules we have defined will apply. The process continues until the expression on top of the control stack is a number or a variable, in which case the rules for numbers and variables, as given above, are applied. At that point, the expression E_1 will have been evaluated and E_2 will be at the top of the control stack, and the process continues. After E_2 is evaluated, its value will be pushed onto the results stack, leaving finally the operator op at the top of the control stack. Then, the rule

$$\langle op \cdot c, n_2 \cdot n_1 \cdot r, m \rangle \rightarrow \langle c, n \cdot r, m \rangle$$

is applied, and the machine makes a transition to $\langle c, n \cdot r, m \rangle$, where n is the number obtained by performing the arithmetic operation op (in the processor) with the arguments n_1 and n_2, which have been stored in the results stack. Since we assume that the processor always returns a result for the arithmetic operations if the arguments are integers, n is well defined.

The transition rules for the evaluation of Boolean expressions work in a similar way.

With these transition rules, we can prove that the abstract machine is able to evaluate any integer or Boolean expression in SIMP, provided the expression is placed at the top of the control stack, and all the variables used in the expression are valid memory locations. The machine might need to perform several transition steps in order to evaluate the expression, but it will eventually stop leaving the value of the expression at the top of the results stack. The value computed by the machine is the semantics of the expression.

Definition 4.4 (Semantics of SIMP Expressions)
If there is a sequence of transitions[3]

$$\langle E \cdot c, r, m \rangle \rightarrow^* \langle c, v \cdot r, m' \rangle$$

or

$$\langle B \cdot c, r, m \rangle \rightarrow^* \langle c, v \cdot r, m' \rangle$$

then we say that the *value of the expression E* (respectively B) in state m is v. In this case, the semantics of the expression E (respectively B) in m is v.

---

[3] Recall that $\rightarrow^*$ denotes the reflexive-transitive closure of $\rightarrow$, that is, $\langle E \cdot c, r, m \rangle \rightarrow^* \langle c, v \cdot r, m' \rangle$ if there are zero or more reduction steps from $\langle E \cdot c, r, m \rangle$ to $\langle c, v \cdot r, m' \rangle$.

In addition to giving the precise semantics of each integer and Boolean expression in SIMP, the abstract machine also provides a description of the evaluation process step by step, which is very useful if we have to implement the language. Basically, Definition 4.4 tells us that, to find the value of an expression, it is sufficient to place the expression on top of the control stack (ahead of any other unspecified commands c that happen to be there) and apply the transition rules, until we reach a configuration containing a value v on top of the results stack (ahead of any other unspecified results r that happen to be there), leaving the control stack with just c, and the memory possibly updated.

Since the semantics is precisely defined, it is possible to prove properties of programs. For example, to prove that a property P holds for all integer expressions in SIMP, we can use the Structural Induction Principle:

1. *Basis:*

    – For all numbers n, prove $P(n)$.
    – For all locations l, prove $P(!l)$.

2. *Induction Step:*
   For all integer expressions E, E' and operators op:
   Prove that $P(E)$ and $P(E')$ implies $P(E \; op \; E')$.

Example 4.5
We can prove that the semantics of integer expressions given above, guarantees that for any integer expression E occurring in a SIMP program working on a memory m, if E uses valid addresses (i.e., addresses that are defined on m) then the value of E is defined. In other words, for any such expression there is a sequence of transitions that leads to a configuration containing the value of that expression at the top of the results stack. This means that the machine cannot block or loop forever. More precisely:

For any configuration $\langle E \cdot c, r, m \rangle$, where c and r are arbitrary control and results stack, there is a configuration $\langle c, n \cdot r, m \rangle$ such that $\langle E \cdot c, r, m \rangle \rightarrow^* \langle c, n \cdot r, m \rangle$.

Let us denote by $locations(E)$ the set of locations referenced by E. Formally, we have to prove $\forall E . P(E)$ where P is the property:

$$\forall m . (locations(E) \subseteq dom(m) \Rightarrow \exists n . \forall c . \forall r . \langle E \cdot c, r, m \rangle \rightarrow^* \langle c, n \cdot r, m \rangle)$$

This is proved by induction on the structure of E:

– *Basis:* If E is a number n or $!l$ then the transition rules specified for constants and locations prove $P(E)$.
– *Induction Step:* Assume $P(E_1)$ and $P(E_2)$ hold, we prove $P(E_1 \; op \; E_2)$ using the transition rules as follows.

$$
\begin{aligned}
\langle (E_1 \; op \; E_2) \cdot c, r, m \rangle \;\rightarrow\;& \langle E_1 \cdot E_2 \cdot op \cdot c, r, m \rangle \\
\rightarrow^*\;& \langle E_2 \cdot op \cdot c, n_1 \cdot r, m \rangle \quad \text{by } P(E_1) \\
\rightarrow^*\;& \langle op \cdot c, n_2 \cdot n_1 \cdot r, m \rangle \quad \text{by } P(E_2) \\
\rightarrow^*\;& \langle c, n \cdot r, m \rangle \quad \text{where } n = n_1 \; op \; n_2.
\end{aligned}
\tag{4.1}
$$

In a similar way, we can prove that if a Boolean expression (that mentions only valid memory locations) is placed at the top of the control stack, the machine will reach a configuration where the value of the expression will be available at the top of the results stack (see Exercise 4 at the end of the chapter).

Executing Commands. For commands, the idea is similar: the transition relation specifies the changes that take place in the configuration of the machine during the execution of the command that is currently at the top of the control stack. There are rules for each kind of command.

For example, the command *skip* does not produce any change in the state of the machine. This is specified by the transition rule:

$$
\langle skip \cdot c, r, m \rangle \;\rightarrow\; \langle c, r, m \rangle
$$

An assignment instruction changes the contents of a variable in memory. This is precisely specified by the following transition rules.

$$
\begin{aligned}
\langle (l := E) \cdot c, r, m \rangle \;&\rightarrow\; \langle E \cdot := \cdot c, l \cdot r, m \rangle \\
\langle := \cdot c, n \cdot l \cdot r, m \rangle \;&\rightarrow\; \langle c, r, m[l \mapsto n] \rangle
\end{aligned}
$$

The first transition rule specifies that when an assignment instruction $l := E$ is at the top of the control stack, it should be popped, disassembled into its constituent parts, $:=$ and E pushed onto the control stack (in that order), and l pushed onto the results stack (because it will be needed later). Since in the resulting configuration the expression E is at the top of the control stack, the transition rules for the evaluation of integer expressions will be applied, until a value n for the expression is pushed onto the top of the results stack and the operator $:=$ reaches the top of the control stack. The second rule specifies the transition that will be performed when the operator $:=$ is at the top of the control stack: in the configuration on the right, we see that the location l in memory now holds the value of the expression, the operator $:=$ has been popped from the control stack and both n and l have been popped from the results stack.

A sequence $C_1; C_2$ of commands is executed from left to right, first C_1 and then C_2. This is specified by the following transition rule.

$$
\langle (C_1; C_2) \cdot c, r, m \rangle \;\rightarrow\; \langle C_1 \cdot C_2 \cdot c, r, m \rangle
$$

By popping $C_1; C_2$ and pushing first C_2 and then C_1, we obtain a new configuration where the command C_1 is at the top of the control stack. Therefore, C_1 will be executed first.

If the command at the top of the control stack is a two-way selector, then the machine should first evaluate the condition (a Boolean expression) and then execute either the *then* branch (if the value obtained is True) or the *else* branch (if the value obtained is False). This behaviour is specified by the following transition rules, where in the first rule we see that the Boolean expression is at the top of the control stack, with the instruction *if* below, and the commands C_1 and C_2 (corresponding to the *then* branch and the *else* branch, respectively) are placed in the results stack. Here the results stack is used to store the commands until the value of the Boolean expression is computed. By placing the Boolean expression at the top of the control stack, we ensure that the abstract machine will evaluate the condition of the two-way selector first.

$$\langle (if \ B \ then \ C_1 \ else \ C_2) \cdot c, r, m \rangle \rightarrow \langle B \cdot if \cdot c, C_1 \cdot C_2 \cdot r, m \rangle$$
$$\langle if \cdot c, True \cdot C_1 \cdot C_2 \cdot r, m \rangle \rightarrow \langle C_1 \cdot c, r, m \rangle$$
$$\langle if \cdot c, False \cdot C_1 \cdot C_2 \cdot r, m \rangle \rightarrow \langle C_2 \cdot c, r, m \rangle$$

Note that the second and third rules above will be triggered after the expression is evaluated (and its value pushed on to the results stack): the transition rules for the evaluation of expressions ensure that after evaluating the expression the machine reaches a configuration where the top of the stack contains the instruction *if* (see Exercise 4). The next transition depends on whether there is True or False at the top of the results stack.

Finally, a while loop is executed as follows.

$$\langle (while \ B \ do \ C) \cdot c, r, m \rangle \rightarrow \langle B \cdot while \cdot c, B \cdot C \cdot r, m \rangle$$
$$\langle while \cdot c, True \cdot B \cdot C \cdot r, m \rangle \rightarrow \langle C \cdot (while \ B \ do \ C) \cdot c, r, m \rangle$$
$$\langle while \cdot c, False \cdot B \cdot C \cdot r, m \rangle \rightarrow \langle c, r, m \rangle$$

The first rule specifies that to execute a while statement, the machine should pop the while statement from the control stack, and push first the keyword *while*, then the Boolean condition B. In this way, the Boolean condition will be at the top of the control stack and will be evaluated first, as expected since this is a pre-test loop (the body of the loop will be executed only if the condition is True). Note that in the first transition rule, the configuration in the right-hand side has B and C in the results stack. They need to be stored until the result of B is obtained. At that point, the machine reaches a configuration where the top element in the control stack is *while*, and the top element of the results stack is the value of B. The transition rule to be applied depends on the value of B. If it is True, the machine moves to a configuration where C is at the top of the control stack, with the while statement (in its entirety, in the same form as it was when it was first pushed onto the control stack) immediately behind. Thus, the body of the loop will be executed, and then the while statement will be executed again. However, if the value of B is False, the last transition rule applies, and all the components of the while statement are popped from the stacks.

We can now give a precise definition of the meaning of the commands in the language SIMP.

Definition 4.6 (Semantics of SIMP Commands)
If there is a sequence of transitions

$$\langle C \cdot nil, nil, m \rangle \rightarrow^* \langle nil, nil, m' \rangle$$

then we say that the program C executed in state m terminates successfully producing the state m'.

The *semantics of a command C in state m* is described by giving the sequence of *transitions* that transform the configuration $\langle C \cdot nil, nil, m \rangle$ into $\langle nil, nil, m' \rangle$.

Note that, unlike expressions, commands may generate infinite sequences of transitions. We give examples below, and summarise in Fig. 4.1 the full set of transition rules that generate the transition relation on the configurations of the abstract machine.

Example 4.7
Let C be the program
$$while\ B\ do\ C'$$

where B is the Boolean expression $!l > 0$ and C' is the command

$$factorial := !factorial * !l;\ l := !l - 1$$

(see Example 4.2). Let m be the function that maps l to 4 and $factorial$ to 1, which we denote by $\{l \mapsto 4, factorial \mapsto 1\}$.

Starting from the initial configuration $\langle C \cdot nil, nil, m \rangle$, the abstract machine will perform the following transition steps:

$$
\begin{aligned}
\langle C \cdot nil, nil, m \rangle &\rightarrow \langle B \cdot while \cdot nil, B \cdot C' \cdot nil, m \rangle \\
&\rightarrow \langle !l \cdot 0 \cdot > \cdot while \cdot nil, B \cdot C' \cdot nil, m \rangle \\
&\rightarrow \langle 0 \cdot > \cdot while \cdot nil, 4 \cdot B \cdot C' \cdot nil, m \rangle \\
&\rightarrow \langle > \cdot while \cdot nil, 0 \cdot 4 \cdot B \cdot C' \cdot nil, m \rangle \\
&\rightarrow \langle while \cdot nil, True \cdot B \cdot C' \cdot nil, m \rangle \\
&\rightarrow \langle C' \cdot C \cdot nil, nil, m \rangle \\
&\rightarrow \ldots \\
&\rightarrow \langle nil, nil, m[l \mapsto 0, factorial \mapsto 24] \rangle
\end{aligned}
$$

The last configuration is final, therefore the sequence of transitions above gives the semantics of the program

while $!l > 0$ *do*
     $(factorial := !factorial * !l;$
     $l := !l - 1)$

working in a memory where l contains the value 4 and *factorial* the value 1. The final configuration shows that the program stops leaving the value 0 in l and 24 in *factorial*, as expected.

1. Evaluation of Expressions:

$$\langle n \cdot c, r, m \rangle \quad \rightarrow \quad \langle c, n \cdot r, m \rangle$$
$$\langle b \cdot c, r, m \rangle \quad \rightarrow \quad \langle c, b \cdot r, m \rangle$$

$$\langle \neg B \cdot c, r, m \rangle \quad \rightarrow \quad \langle B \cdot \neg \cdot c, r, m \rangle$$
$$\langle (B_1 \wedge B_2) \cdot c, r, m \rangle \quad \rightarrow \quad \langle B_1 \cdot B_2 \cdot \wedge \cdot c, r, m \rangle$$
$$\langle \neg \cdot c, b \cdot r, m \rangle \quad \rightarrow \quad \langle c, b' \cdot r, m \rangle \qquad \text{if } b' = not\ b$$
$$\langle \wedge \cdot c, b_2 \cdot b_1 \cdot r, m \rangle \quad \rightarrow \quad \langle c, b \cdot r, m \rangle \qquad \text{if } b_1\ and\ b_2 = b$$

$$\langle (E_1\ op\ E_2) \cdot c, r, m \rangle \quad \rightarrow \quad \langle E_1 \cdot E_2 \cdot op \cdot c, r, m \rangle$$
$$\langle (E_1\ bop\ E_2) \cdot c, r, m \rangle \quad \rightarrow \quad \langle E_1 \cdot E_2 \cdot bop \cdot c, r, m \rangle$$
$$\langle op \cdot c, n_2 \cdot n_1 \cdot r, m \rangle \quad \rightarrow \quad \langle c, n \cdot r, m \rangle \qquad \text{if } n_1\ op\ n_2 = n$$
$$\langle bop \cdot c, n_2 \cdot n_1 \cdot r, m \rangle \quad \rightarrow \quad \langle c, b \cdot r, m \rangle \qquad \text{if } n_1\ bop\ n_2 = b$$

$$\langle !l \cdot c, r, m \rangle \quad \rightarrow \quad \langle c, n \cdot r, m \rangle \qquad \text{if } m(l) = n$$

2. Evaluation of Commands:

$$\langle skip \cdot c, r, m \rangle \quad \rightarrow \quad \langle c, r, m \rangle$$

$$\langle (l := E) \cdot c, r, m \rangle \quad \rightarrow \quad \langle E \cdot := \cdot c, l \cdot r, m \rangle$$
$$\langle := \cdot c, n \cdot l \cdot r, m \rangle \quad \rightarrow \quad \langle c, r, m[l \mapsto n] \rangle$$

$$\langle (C_1; C_2) \cdot c, r, m \rangle \quad \rightarrow \quad \langle C_1 \cdot C_2 \cdot c, r, m \rangle$$

$$\langle (if\ B\ then\ C_1\ else\ C_2) \cdot c, r, m \rangle \quad \rightarrow \quad \langle B \cdot if \cdot c, C_1 \cdot C_2 \cdot r, m \rangle$$
$$\langle if \cdot c, True \cdot C_1 \cdot C_2 \cdot r, m \rangle \quad \rightarrow \quad \langle C_1 \cdot c, r, m \rangle$$
$$\langle if \cdot c, False \cdot C_1 \cdot C_2 \cdot r, m \rangle \quad \rightarrow \quad \langle C_2 \cdot c, r, m \rangle$$

$$\langle (while\ B\ do\ C) \cdot c, r, m \rangle \quad \rightarrow \quad \langle B \cdot while \cdot c, B \cdot C \cdot r, m \rangle$$
$$\langle while \cdot c, True \cdot B \cdot C \cdot r, m \rangle \quad \rightarrow \quad \langle C \cdot (while\ B\ do\ C) \cdot c, r, m \rangle$$
$$\langle while \cdot c, False \cdot B \cdot C \cdot r, m \rangle \quad \rightarrow \quad \langle c, r, m \rangle$$

Fig. 4.1 Transition rules of the abstract machine for SIMP

For some initial configurations, the machine may produce an infinite computation. If there is an infinite sequence of transitions out of $\langle C \cdot nil, r, m \rangle$, we say that the program C is *non-terminating* in state m.

For example, replacing the last command in the loop body of the program in the example above by $l := \ !l + 1$ would give a non-terminating program:

$$while\ !l > 0\ do\ (factorial := \ !factorial * !l;\ l := \ !l + 1)$$

The abstract machine describes the exact behaviour of a while loop, in contrast with the informal definition given in Chap. 3:

The while is pre-test, that is, the expression is evaluated first, and the loop-body is executed as long as the expression evaluates to True.

However, although the abstract machine semantics is very useful for the implementation of the language, for users of the language (programmers) it is too detailed, and not always intuitive. Many transitions are doing just phrase analysis, only a few really perform computations. To overcome this problem, another approach to operational semantics, also based on transition systems, was developed: the *structural approach* due to Plotkin [1].

The idea is that transition systems should be structured in a way that reflects the structure of the language. The transitions for a compound statement should be defined in terms of the transitions for its substatements. In other words: the definition should be *inductive*.

For example, to describe the semantics of integer expressions in SIMP we can give an inductive definition of the evaluation process using axioms and rules,[4] instead of sequences of transitions in the abstract machine. We write $(E, m) \Downarrow n$ to indicate that the expression E evaluates to n in state m. The evaluation relation is defined by the axioms:

- $(n, m) \Downarrow n$ for all integer numbers n
- $(!l, m) \Downarrow n$ if $l \in dom(m)$ and $m(l) = n$

and rules of the form:

$$\frac{(E_1, m) \Downarrow n_1 \quad (E_2, m) \Downarrow n_2}{(E_1 \ op \ E_2, m) \Downarrow n} \quad \text{if } n = n_1 \ op \ n_2$$

In the next section we define the structural operational semantics of SIMP as an alternative to the abstract machine.

4.3 Structural Operational Semantics for SIMP

There are two styles of structural operational semantics:

- Small-step semantics, based on a *reduction* relation,
- Big-step semantics, based on an *evaluation* relation.

We will consider each style in turn.

---

[4] See Def. 2.22, Chap. 2.

4.3.1 Reduction Semantics: Small-Step Semantics

The transition system defining the reduction semantics of SIMP is defined by:

- Configurations of the form

$$\langle P, s \rangle$$

where P is a SIMP program (that is, a command C, an arithmetic expression E, or a Boolean expressions B, as specified by the grammar for P given in Sect. 4.1) and s is a store represented by a partial function from locations to integers, as in the previous section. Recall that $s[l \mapsto n]$ denotes the function s' that coincides with s except that it maps l to the value n, more precisely:

$$s[l \mapsto n](l) = n \text{ and } s[l \mapsto n](l') = s(l') \text{ if } l \neq l'.$$

- A transition relation between configurations, also called the *reduction* relation, which is inductively defined by axioms and rules. The axioms specify reduction steps, whereas the rules specify how to generate new reduction steps using the ones that have already been defined. Since the reduction relation is inductively defined, it is the least relation containing the pairs of configurations specified in the axioms and closed under the rules.

First we give the axioms and rules involving expressions.

For each configuration where the first component consists of a reference to a variable, we have a reduction step as follows.

$$\langle !l, s \rangle \rightarrow \langle n, s \rangle \text{ if } s(l) = n$$

This is an axiom scheme, since there is one such axiom for each variable l. According to this definition, a reference to location l in the memory s is replaced by the value stored at location l, without changing the memory (i.e., accessing a location in memory does not alter its content).

The following axiom schemes specify the reductions that take place to evaluate an expression consisting of an operator and two numbers:

$$\langle n_1 \text{ op } n_2, s \rangle \rightarrow \langle n, s \rangle \quad \text{if } n = (n_1 \text{ op } n_2)$$
$$\langle n_1 \text{ bop } n_2, s \rangle \rightarrow \langle b, s \rangle \quad \text{if } b = (n_1 \text{ bop } n_2)$$

Here, *op* and *bop* are arithmetic and relational operators, respectively, as defined by the grammars given in Sect. 4.1. These axioms specify that an expression that contains only numbers and an operator should be replaced by its value.

Similarly, we have axiom schemes for the evaluation of conjunctions and negation, when the arguments are Boolean values:

$$\langle b_1 \wedge b_2, s \rangle \rightarrow \langle b, s \rangle \quad \text{if } b = (b_1 \text{ and } b_2)$$
$$\langle \neg b, s \rangle \rightarrow \langle b', s \rangle \quad \text{if } b' = \text{not } b$$

For configurations containing expressions of the form $E_1 op E_2$ or $E_1 bop E_2$, first the value of E_1 and then the value of E_2 are computed, as the following rules state.

$$\frac{\langle E_1, s \rangle \rightarrow \langle E_1', s' \rangle}{\langle E_1 op E_2, s \rangle \rightarrow \langle E_1' op E_2, s' \rangle} \qquad \frac{\langle E_2, s \rangle \rightarrow \langle E_2', s' \rangle}{\langle n_1 op E_2, s \rangle \rightarrow \langle n_1 op E_2', s' \rangle}$$

$$\frac{\langle E_1, s \rangle \rightarrow \langle E_1', s' \rangle}{\langle E_1 bop E_2, s \rangle \rightarrow \langle E_1' bop E_2, s' \rangle} \qquad \frac{\langle E_2, s \rangle \rightarrow \langle E_2', s' \rangle}{\langle n_1 bop E_2, s \rangle \rightarrow \langle n_1 bop E_2', s' \rangle}$$

Similarly, we have rules to reduce configurations containing expressions of the form $B_1 \wedge B_2$ and $\neg B$.

$$\frac{\langle B_1, s \rangle \rightarrow \langle B_1', s' \rangle}{\langle \neg B_1, s \rangle \rightarrow \langle \neg B_1', s' \rangle}$$

$$\frac{\langle B_1, s \rangle \rightarrow \langle B_1', s' \rangle}{\langle B_1 \wedge B_2, s \rangle \rightarrow \langle B_1' \wedge B_2, s' \rangle} \qquad \frac{\langle B_2, s \rangle \rightarrow \langle B_2', s' \rangle}{\langle b_1 \wedge B_2, s \rangle \rightarrow \langle b_1 \wedge B_2', s' \rangle}$$

Now we give the axioms and rules for commands.

For assignment statements where the expression is a number, we have the following axiom:

$$\langle l := n, s \rangle \rightarrow \langle skip, s[l \mapsto n] \rangle$$

where we can see that the assignment produces a change in memory (the value in location l is now n).

For conditionals, we have two axioms:

$$\langle if \ True \ then \ C_1 \ else \ C_2, s \rangle \rightarrow \langle C_1, s \rangle$$
$$\langle if \ False \ then \ C_1 \ else \ C_2, s \rangle \rightarrow \langle C_2, s \rangle$$

which reduce configurations where the condition in the *if* statement is *True* or *False*, respectively.

In addition, we include in the definition of the reduction relation the following axioms to simplify while statements and sequences:

$$\langle while \ B \ do \ C, s \rangle \rightarrow \langle if \ B \ then \ (C; while \ B \ do \ C) \ else \ skip, s \rangle$$
$$\langle skip; C, s \rangle \rightarrow \langle C, s \rangle$$

According to these axioms, the execution of a program *while B do C* triggers the execution of *if B then (C; while B do C) else skip*, as expected since the while-loop is pre-test (the condition is evaluated first, and the body of the loop is executed if and only if the condition is True, in which case, after executing the body the condition will be tested again, and the whole process will be repeated). For a sequence of the form $skip; C$, the axiom specifies that it reduces to just C.

A sequence $C_1; C_2$ will trigger the execution of C_1 first, as the following rule specifies.

$$\frac{\langle C_1, s \rangle \rightarrow \langle C_1', s' \rangle}{\langle C_1; C_2, s \rangle \rightarrow \langle C_1'; C_2, s' \rangle}$$

There is also a rule for configurations containing an *if* statement where the condition is not a Boolean value (in this case, the condition has to be evaluated first):

$$\frac{\langle B, s \rangle \rightarrow \langle B', s' \rangle}{\langle if\ B\ then\ C_1\ else\ C_2, s \rangle \rightarrow \langle if\ B'\ then\ C_1\ else\ C_2, s' \rangle}$$

The full definition of the reduction relation is shown in Fig. 4.2.

We now give some examples of transitions.

Example 4.8
Let P be the program $z: =!x; (x: =!y; y: =!z)$ as discussed in Example 4.1, and assume the memory s is such that $s(z) = 0, s(x) = 1, s(y) = 2$.

Using the axioms and rules given in Fig. 4.2, we can show that there is a sequence of transitions:

$$\begin{aligned}
\langle z:=!x; (x:=!y; y:=!z), s \rangle &\rightarrow \langle z := 1; (x :=!y; y :=!z), s \rangle \\
&\rightarrow \langle skip; (x :=!y; y :=!z), s[z \mapsto 1] \rangle \\
&\rightarrow \langle x :=!y; y :=!z, s[z \mapsto 1] \rangle \\
&\rightarrow \langle x := 2; y :=!z, s[z \mapsto 1] \rangle \\
&\rightarrow \langle skip; y :=!z, s[z \mapsto 1, x \mapsto 2] \rangle \\
&\rightarrow \langle y :=!z, s[z \mapsto 1, x \mapsto 2] \rangle \\
&\rightarrow \langle y := 1, s[z \mapsto 1, x \mapsto 2] \rangle \\
&\rightarrow \langle skip, s[z \mapsto 1, x \mapsto 2, y \mapsto 1] \rangle
\end{aligned}$$

which shows that the program P is correctly swapping the contents of the variables x and y as specified.

In contrast with the abstract machine, each transition here is doing a part of the computation that leads to the result (this is not true of the abstract machine, where some transitions only manipulate syntax). However, to show that a transition is valid, i.e., is in the inductive set defined by the axioms and rules, a proof is required. A pair $c \rightarrow c'$ is in the inductive set if it is an instance of an axiom scheme, or it is obtained by using a rule (see Definition 2.22 in Chap. 2). For example, to prove the validity of the first transition in the sequence above:

$$\langle z :=!x; (x :=!y; y :=!z), s \rangle \rightarrow \langle z := 1; (x :=!y; y :=!z), s \rangle$$

when $s(z) = 0, s(x) = 1, s(y) = 2$, we use the axiom (**var**) and the rules (**seq**) and (**:=**$_R$) as follows:

Reduction Semantics of Expressions:

$$\frac{}{\langle !l, s \rangle \rightarrow \langle n, s \rangle \quad \text{if } s(l) = n} \text{ (var)}$$

$$\frac{}{\langle n_1 \ op \ n_2, s \rangle \rightarrow \langle n, s \rangle \quad \text{if } n = (n_1 \ op \ n_2)} \text{ (op)}$$

$$\frac{}{\langle n_1 \ bop \ n_2, s \rangle \rightarrow \langle b, s \rangle \quad \text{if } b = (n_1 \ bop \ n_2)} \text{ (bop)}$$

$$\frac{\langle E_1, s \rangle \rightarrow \langle E_1', s' \rangle}{\langle E_1 op E_2, s \rangle \rightarrow \langle E_1' op E_2, s' \rangle} \text{ (op}_\text{L}) \qquad \frac{\langle E_2, s \rangle \rightarrow \langle E_2', s' \rangle}{\langle n_1 op E_2, s \rangle \rightarrow \langle n_1 op E_2', s' \rangle} \text{ (op}_\text{R})$$

$$\frac{\langle E_1, s \rangle \rightarrow \langle E_1', s' \rangle}{\langle E_1 bop E_2, s \rangle \rightarrow \langle E_1' bop E_2, s' \rangle} \text{ (bop}_\text{L}) \qquad \frac{\langle E_2, s \rangle \rightarrow \langle E_2', s' \rangle}{\langle n_1 bop E_2, s \rangle \rightarrow \langle n_1 bop E_2', s' \rangle} \text{ (bop}_\text{R})$$

$$\frac{}{\langle b_1 \wedge b_2, s \rangle \rightarrow \langle b, s \rangle \quad \text{if } b = (b_1 \ and \ b_2)} \text{ (and)}$$

$$\frac{}{\langle \neg b, s \rangle \rightarrow \langle b', s \rangle \quad \text{if } b' = not \ b} \text{ (not)} \qquad \frac{\langle B_1, s \rangle \rightarrow \langle B_1', s' \rangle}{\langle \neg B_1, s \rangle \rightarrow \langle \neg B_1', s' \rangle} \text{ (notArg)}$$

$$\frac{\langle B_1, s \rangle \rightarrow \langle B_1', s' \rangle}{\langle B_1 \wedge B_2, s \rangle \rightarrow \langle B_1' \wedge B_2, s' \rangle} \text{ (and}_\text{L}) \qquad \frac{\langle B_2, s \rangle \rightarrow \langle B_2', s' \rangle}{\langle b_1 \wedge B_2, s \rangle \rightarrow \langle b_1 \wedge B_2', s' \rangle} \text{ (and}_\text{R})$$

Reduction Semantics of Commands:

$$\frac{\langle E, s \rangle \rightarrow \langle E', s' \rangle}{\langle l := E, s \rangle \rightarrow \langle l := E', s' \rangle} \text{ (:=}_\text{R}) \qquad \frac{}{\langle l := n, s \rangle \rightarrow \langle skip, s[l \mapsto n] \rangle} \text{ (:=)}$$

$$\frac{\langle C_1, s \rangle \rightarrow \langle C_1', s' \rangle}{\langle C_1; C_2, s \rangle \rightarrow \langle C_1'; C_2, s' \rangle} \text{ (seq)} \qquad \frac{}{\langle skip; C, s \rangle \rightarrow \langle C, s \rangle} \text{ (skip)}$$

$$\frac{\langle B, s \rangle \rightarrow \langle B', s' \rangle}{\langle if \ B \ then \ C_1 \ else \ C_2, s \rangle \rightarrow \langle if \ B' \ then \ C_1 \ else \ C_2, s' \rangle} \text{ (if)}$$

$$\frac{}{\langle if \ True \ then \ C_1 \ else \ C_2, s \rangle \rightarrow \langle C_1, s \rangle} \text{ (if}_\text{T})$$

$$\frac{}{\langle if \ False \ then \ C_1 \ else \ C_2, s \rangle \rightarrow \langle C_2, s \rangle} \text{ (if}_\text{F})$$

$$\frac{}{\langle while \ B \ do \ C, s \rangle \rightarrow \langle if \ B \ then \ (C; while \ B \ do \ C) \ else \ skip, s \rangle} \text{ (while)}$$

Fig. 4.2 Axioms and rules defining reduction for SIMP

$$\frac{}{\langle !x, s \rangle \rightarrow \langle 1, s \rangle} \text{ (var)}$$

$$\frac{}{\langle z := !x, s \rangle \rightarrow \langle z := 1, s \rangle} \text{ (:=}_\text{R})$$

$$\frac{}{\langle z := !x; (x := !y; y := !z), s \rangle \rightarrow \langle z := 1; (x := !y; y := !z), s \rangle} \text{ (seq)}$$

The definition of the reduction relation is *syntax directed*: that is to say, the selection of the rules used in a proof is guided by the syntax of the program in the configuration on the left-hand side of the transition. More precisely, to build a proof for the transition $\langle P_1, s_1 \rangle \rightarrow \langle P_2, s_2 \rangle$ we traverse the abstract syntax tree of the program P_1, and apply the rule or axiom that corresponds to the label of the root. In the program $z :=!x; (x :=!y; y :=!z)$ above, the root is the sequencing construct, therefore we first apply the rule (seq), with the hypothesis $\langle z :=!x, s \rangle \rightarrow \langle z := 1, s \rangle$. The latter can be proved using the rule $(:=_R)$, which in turn requires the hypothesis $\langle !x, s \rangle \rightarrow \langle 1, s \rangle$. The latter is a particular case of the axiom (var), since $s(x) = 1$.

Note that there are some configurations to which no axiom or rule applies (i.e., they are irreducible). An example of an irreducible configuration is $\langle n, s \rangle$, where the expression is already a value.

Definition 4.9 (Final Configurations)

All irreducible configurations are *final*. In particular, configurations of the form:

- $\langle n, s \rangle$ where n is an integer;
- $\langle b, s \rangle$ where b is a boolean;
- $\langle !l, s \rangle$ where $l \notin dom(s)$;
- $\langle skip, s \rangle$

are final.

Final configurations where the program is not *skip*, or an integer or Boolean value, are *blocked* (the computation stops even though the configuration may still contain commands or expressions to be evaluated).

For example, a configuration of the form $\langle !x, s \rangle$ where $x \notin dom(s)$ is *blocked*, and so is $\langle if \ !x > 0 \ then \ C \ else \ C', s \rangle$, for any commands C and C', because to reduce this configuration we need the value of $!x > 0$, which cannot be obtained if $x \notin dom(s)$.

The transition system defining the reduction relation is *deterministic*: at each point, there is at most one possible transition. This can be proved by induction (see Exercise 6 at the end of the chapter).

Therefore, given a configuration $\langle P, s \rangle$ there is a unique sequence of transitions that starts from $\langle P, s \rangle$ and has maximal length. This sequence, that is, the longest sequence starting from $\langle P, s \rangle$, is used to formally define the semantics of P when executed in memory state s. More precisely, we associate with P an *execution process* in s, also called an *evaluation sequence*, which corresponds to the longest sequence of reductions out of $\langle P, s \rangle$, as the following definition states. We give examples of evaluation sequences below.

Definition 4.10 (Evaluation)

The *evaluation sequence* for $\langle P, s \rangle$ is the uniquely defined sequence of transitions that starts with $\langle P, s \rangle$ and has maximal length.

If the evaluation sequence is infinite, we say that the program is *divergent*.

Finite sequences can be classified according to the form of their final configuration: A *finite* evaluation sequence is said to be *terminating* if it eventually reaches a final non-blocked configuration (that is, $\langle n, s \rangle$, $\langle b, s \rangle$ or $\langle skip, s \rangle$), otherwise it is said to be *blocked*.

Example 4.11

1. The program *while True do skip* is divergent: the configuration $\langle while\ True\ do\ skip, s \rangle$ has an infinite evaluation sequence for any store s:

$$\langle while\ True\ do\ skip, s \rangle \rightarrow$$
$$\langle if\ True\ then\ (skip;\ while\ True\ do\ skip)\ else\ skip, s \rangle \rightarrow$$
$$\langle skip;\ while\ True\ do\ skip, s \rangle \rightarrow$$
$$\langle while\ True\ do\ skip, s \rangle \rightarrow$$
$$\cdots$$

2. If $dom(s)$ does not contain x, the configuration $\langle while\ !x > 0\ do\ C, s \rangle$ is blocked, no matter what the command C does:

$$\langle while\ !x > 0\ do\ C, s \rangle \rightarrow$$
$$\langle if\ !x > 0\ then\ (C;\ while\ !x > 0\ do\ C)\ else\ skip, s \rangle \nrightarrow$$

There is no further transition since the rule (if) requires a transition for $!x > 0$, which in turn requires the evaluation of $!x$ which is undefined.

3. For any store s, the configuration $\langle if\ 4 = 0\ then\ skip\ else\ skip, s \rangle$ is terminating:

$$\langle if\ 4 = 0\ then\ skip\ else\ skip, s \rangle \rightarrow$$
$$\langle if\ False\ then\ skip\ else\ skip, s \rangle \rightarrow$$
$$\langle skip, s \rangle$$

We finish this section with the definition of the small-step semantics of SIMP programs, and an application to program equivalence.

Definition 4.12 (Semantics of SIMP Programs)
The *small-step semantics of a* SIMP*program P in state s* is the unique sequence of reductions from $\langle P, s \rangle$ to a final configuration.

If P is a command C and there is a sequence of transitions $\langle C, s \rangle \rightarrow^* \langle skip, s' \rangle$ then we say that the program C executed in state s terminates successfully producing s'.

If P is an integer expression E and there is a sequence of transitions $\langle E, s \rangle \rightarrow^*$ $\langle n, s' \rangle$, where n is an integer number, then we say that the expression E in state s has the value n.

If P is a Boolean expression B and there is a sequence of transitions $\langle B, s \rangle \rightarrow^*$ $\langle b, s' \rangle$, where b is either True or False, then we say that the expression B in state s has the value b.

We can use the semantics of SIMP programs to define a notion of program equivalence.

Definition 4.13 (Equivalence of programs)
Two programs P_1 and P_2 are *semantically equivalent* if, for all memory states s:

- $\langle P_1, s \rangle \rightarrow^* \langle c, s' \rangle$ if and only if $\langle P_2, s \rangle \rightarrow^* \langle c, s' \rangle$, whenever $\langle c, s' \rangle$ is a final configuration; and
- P_1 is divergent if and only if P_2 is divergent.

The notion of program equivalence can be used to show that the optimisations performed by a compiler are correct. For instance, we can show that for any commands C and C', the program

$$if\ 1 < 0\ then\ C\ else\ C'$$

is equivalent to C'. A compiler can optimise this program by generating just the code for C'. More generally, a program where the condition of a selector has a constant value can be optimised by replacing the selector with the code for the selected branch.

4.3.2 Evaluation Semantics: Big-Step Semantics

In the previous section, we defined for a each configuration a unique evaluation sequence, consisting of small-step transitions leading to a final configuration (see Definition 4.9). If the evaluation sequence associated with $\langle P, s \rangle$ is not blocked, the final configuration is the *result* of the evaluation of P in s.

The big-step semantics abstracts from the details of the execution process, and associates each configuration with its result, if it exists.

In this section, we define the big-step semantics of SIMP by means of a transition system on configurations $\langle P, s \rangle$. The transition relation, or *evaluation relation*, is denoted by $\Downarrow$.

Definition 4.14 (Evaluation Relation)
The *evaluation relation* associates $\langle P, s \rangle$ with the *last* configuration of its evaluation sequence, provided the latter is terminating. The usual notation for this is $\langle P, s \rangle \Downarrow \langle P', s' \rangle$.

The transition systems defining the small-step and the big-step semantics of SIMP have the same sets of configurations, but differ in the transition relation: transitions represent individual computation steps in the former and full evaluations in the latter.

The axioms and rules given in Fig. 4.3 define by induction the binary relation $\Downarrow$ on configurations. Compared with the definition of the small-step semantics (Fig. 4.2), the big-step semantics is more concise (there are less axioms and rules). For instance, we need only one rule for assignment (rule (:=)) whereas we needed two in the small-step semantics (rules (:=$_R$) and (:=)).

Example 4.15
Consider again a program P that swaps the contents of x and y. We represent it with the abstract syntax tree

$$(z := !x;\ x := !y)\ ;\ y := !z$$

$$\frac{}{\langle c, s\rangle \Downarrow \langle c, s\rangle \quad \text{if } c \in Z \cup \{True, False\}} \text{ (const)}$$

$$\frac{}{\langle !l, s\rangle \Downarrow \langle n, s\rangle \quad \text{if } s(l) = n} \text{ (var)}$$

$$\frac{\langle B_1, s\rangle \Downarrow \langle b_1, s'\rangle \quad \langle B_2, s'\rangle \Downarrow \langle b_2, s''\rangle}{\langle B_1 \wedge B_2, s\rangle \Downarrow \langle b, s''\rangle \quad \text{if } b = b_1 \text{ and } b_2} \text{ (and)}$$

$$\frac{\langle B_1, s\rangle \Downarrow \langle b_1, s'\rangle}{\langle \neg B_1, s\rangle \Downarrow \langle b, s'\rangle \quad \text{if } b = \text{not } b_1} \text{ (not)}$$

$$\frac{\langle E_1, s\rangle \Downarrow \langle n_1, s'\rangle \quad \langle E_2, s'\rangle \Downarrow \langle n_2, s''\rangle}{\langle E_1 \text{ op } E_2, s\rangle \Downarrow \langle n, s''\rangle \quad \text{if } n = n_1 \text{ op } n_2} \text{ (op)}$$

$$\frac{\langle E_1, s\rangle \Downarrow \langle n_1, s'\rangle \quad \langle E_2, s'\rangle \Downarrow \langle n_2, s''\rangle}{\langle E_1 \text{ bop } E_2, s\rangle \Downarrow \langle b, s''\rangle \quad \text{if } b = n_1 \text{ bop } n_2} \text{ (bop)}$$

$$\frac{}{\langle skip, s\rangle \Downarrow \langle skip, s\rangle} \text{ (skip)} \qquad \frac{\langle E, s\rangle \Downarrow \langle n, s'\rangle}{\langle l := E, s\rangle \Downarrow \langle skip, s'[l \mapsto n]\rangle} (:=)$$

$$\frac{\langle C_1, s\rangle \Downarrow \langle skip, s'\rangle \quad \langle C_2, s'\rangle \Downarrow \langle skip, s''\rangle}{\langle C_1; C_2, s\rangle \Downarrow \langle skip, s''\rangle} \text{ (seq)}$$

$$\frac{\langle B, s\rangle \Downarrow \langle True, s'\rangle \quad \langle C_1, s'\rangle \Downarrow \langle skip, s''\rangle}{\langle if B \text{ then } C_1 \text{ else } C_2, s\rangle \Downarrow \langle skip, s''\rangle} \text{ (if}_\mathsf{T})$$

$$\frac{\langle B, s\rangle \Downarrow \langle False, s'\rangle \quad \langle C_2, s'\rangle \Downarrow \langle skip, s''\rangle}{\langle if B \text{ then } C_1 \text{ else } C_2, s\rangle \Downarrow \langle skip, s''\rangle} \text{ (if}_\mathsf{F})$$

$$\frac{\langle B, s\rangle \Downarrow \langle True, s_1\rangle \quad \langle C, s_1\rangle \Downarrow \langle skip, s_2\rangle \quad \langle while B \text{ do } C, s_2\rangle \Downarrow \langle skip, s_3\rangle}{\langle while B \text{ do } C, s\rangle \Downarrow \langle skip, s_3\rangle} \text{ (while}_\mathsf{T})$$

$$\frac{\langle B, s\rangle \Downarrow \langle False, s'\rangle}{\langle while B \text{ do } C, s\rangle \Downarrow \langle skip, s'\rangle} \text{ (while}_\mathsf{F})$$

Fig. 4.3 Axioms and rules defining evaluation for SIMP

Suppose we start the execution of the program P in a state s such that $s(z) = 0$, $s(x) = 1, s(y) = 2$.

We can show, using the axioms and rules given in Fig. 4.3, that after the execution of P, the values of x and y have been swapped:

$$\langle P, s\rangle \Downarrow \langle skip, s'\rangle \quad where \ s'(z) = 1, \ s'(x) = 2, \ s'(y) = 1.$$

First notice that we can derive $\langle z :=!x, s \rangle \Downarrow \langle skip, s[z \mapsto 1] \rangle$:

$$\frac{\dfrac{}{\langle !x, s \rangle \Downarrow \langle 1, s \rangle} \text{ (var)}}{\langle z :=!x, s \rangle \Downarrow \langle skip, s[z \mapsto 1] \rangle} \text{ (:=)}$$

and also:

$$\frac{\dfrac{}{\langle !y, s[z \mapsto 1] \rangle \Downarrow \langle 2, s[z \mapsto 1] \rangle} \text{ (var)}}{\langle x :=!y, s[z \mapsto 1] \rangle \Downarrow \langle skip, s[z \mapsto 1, x \mapsto 2] \rangle} \text{ (:=)}$$

Therefore using the rule (seq) we obtain:

$$\langle z :=!x; x :=!y, s \rangle \Downarrow \langle skip, s[z \mapsto 1, x \mapsto 2] \rangle$$

We also have:

$$\frac{\dfrac{}{\langle !z, s[z \mapsto 1, x \mapsto 2] \rangle \Downarrow \langle 1, s[z \mapsto 1, x \mapsto 2] \rangle} \text{ (var)}}{\langle y :=!z, s[z \mapsto 1, x \mapsto 2] \rangle \Downarrow \langle skip, s[z \mapsto 1, x \mapsto 2, y \mapsto 1] \rangle} \text{ (:=)}$$

Finally, by using (seq) again, we can derive $\langle P, s \rangle \Downarrow \langle skip, s' \rangle$.

We remark that, as for the small step semantics, the big step semantics is syntax-oriented. In order to obtain the proof for $\langle P, s \rangle \Downarrow \langle skip, s' \rangle$ in the example above, we use the rule (seq) twice since there are two sequencing operators in the program, and for each of the three assignment instructions in the program we use (:=) and (var).

4.3.3 Equivalence between Small- and Big-Step Semantics

For the SIMP programs that are terminating, the results according to the small-step and big-step semantics coincide. This is formally stated as follows.

Property 4.16
For any SIMP program P and memory s, $\langle P, s \rangle \Downarrow \langle P', s' \rangle$ if, and only if, $\langle P, s \rangle \rightarrow^* \langle P', s' \rangle$ where $\langle P', s' \rangle$ is a final, non-blocked configuration.

Proof
We prove below that if $\langle P, s \rangle \Downarrow \langle P', s' \rangle$ then $\langle P, s \rangle \rightarrow^* \langle P', s' \rangle$ where $\langle P', s' \rangle$ is a final, non-blocked configuration. The proof is by induction on the definition of the evaluation relation. The reverse implication is left as an exercise (see Exercise 11 at the end of the chapter).

The base cases correspond to the axioms defining $\Downarrow$ (see Fig. 4.3).

– Assume $\langle c, s \rangle \Downarrow \langle c, s \rangle$ using the axioms (const) or (skip). We have to prove that $\langle c, s \rangle \rightarrow^* \langle c, s \rangle$ and $\langle c, s \rangle$ is a final, non-blocked configuration.

Since $\langle c, s \rangle \Downarrow \langle c, s \rangle$ using **(const)** or **(skip)**, c is an integer number, a Boolean constant, or *skip*. These are final, non-blocked configurations in the small step semantics, and $\langle c, s \rangle \rightarrow^* \langle c, s \rangle$ in zero steps.

- Assume $\langle !l, s \rangle \Downarrow \langle n, s \rangle$ using the axiom **(var)**. We have to prove that $\langle !l, s \rangle \rightarrow^*$ $\langle n, s \rangle$ and $\langle n, s \rangle$ is a final, non-blocked configuration.
  Since $\langle !l, s \rangle \Downarrow \langle n, s \rangle$ using **(var)**, n is a number and $s(l) = n$. In this case, $\langle !l, s \rangle \rightarrow \langle n, s \rangle$ using the axiom **(var)** in the small-step semantics (see Fig. 4.2), and $\langle n, s \rangle$ is a final, non-blocked configuration.

We consider now each of the rules in Fig. 4.3 in turn.

- If $\langle B_1 \wedge B_2, s \rangle \Downarrow \langle b, s'' \rangle$ using the rule **(and)**, where $b = b_1$ *and* b_2, then it must be the case that $\langle B_1, s \rangle \Downarrow \langle b_1, s' \rangle$ and $\langle B_2, s' \rangle \Downarrow \langle b_2, s'' \rangle$. Then, by the induction hypothesis, $\langle B_1, s \rangle \rightarrow^* \langle b_1, s' \rangle$ and $\langle B_2, s' \rangle \rightarrow^* \langle b_2, s'' \rangle$.
  Therefore, we can apply the rule **(and$_L$)** given in Fig. 4.2, repeatedly (for each step in the reduction sequence $\langle B_1, s \rangle \rightarrow^* \langle b_1, s' \rangle$), obtaining $\langle B_1 \wedge B_2, s \rangle \rightarrow^* \langle b_1 \wedge B_2, s' \rangle$. Applying now the rule **(and$_R$)** repeatedly (for each step in the reduction sequence $\langle B_2, s' \rangle \rightarrow^* \langle b_2, s'' \rangle$), we obtain $\langle b_1 \wedge B_2, s' \rangle \rightarrow^* \langle b_1 \wedge b_2, s'' \rangle$.

Finally, we use the axiom **(and)** in Fig. 4.2 to derive $\langle b_1 \wedge b_2, s'' \rangle \rightarrow \langle b, s'' \rangle$.

Hence, $\langle B_1 \wedge B_2, s \rangle \rightarrow^* \langle b, s'' \rangle$, and the latter is a final, non-blocked configuration.
- The cases for the rules **(not)**, **(op)**, and **(bop)** are similar.
- If $\langle l := E, s \rangle \Downarrow \langle skip, s'[l \mapsto n] \rangle$ using the rule **(:=)**, then $\langle E, s \rangle \Downarrow \langle n, s' \rangle$.
  By the induction hypothesis, we know that $\langle E, s \rangle \rightarrow^* \langle n, s' \rangle$.
  Therefore, by repeatedly applying the rule **(:=$_R$)** in Fig. 4.2, we obtain $\langle l := E, s \rangle \rightarrow^* \langle l := n, s' \rangle$, and applying now the rule **(:=)** in Fig. 4.2 we derive $\langle l := n, s' \rangle \rightarrow \langle skip, s'[l \mapsto n] \rangle$.

Hence, $\langle l := E, s \rangle \rightarrow^* \langle skip, s'[l \mapsto n] \rangle$.

- The cases for rules **(seq)**, **(if$_T$)** and **(if$_F$)** are proved in a similar way.
- Assume that $\langle while\ B\ do\ C, s \rangle \Downarrow \langle skip, s_3 \rangle$ using the rule **(while$_T$)**. Then, $\langle B, s \rangle \Downarrow \langle True, s_1 \rangle$, $\langle C, s_1 \rangle \Downarrow \langle skip, s_2 \rangle$ and $\langle while\ B\ do\ C, s_2 \rangle \Downarrow \langle skip, s_3 \rangle$. By the induction hypothesis, $\langle B, s \rangle \rightarrow^* \langle True, s_1 \rangle$, $\langle C, s_1 \rangle \rightarrow^* \langle skip, s_2 \rangle$ and $\langle while\ B\ do\ C, s_2 \rangle \rightarrow^* \langle skip, s_3 \rangle$.
  In the small-step semantics, using the axiom **(while)** we have the reduction:

$$\langle while\ B\ do\ C, s \rangle \rightarrow \langle if\ B\ then\ (C; while\ B\ do\ C)\ else\ skip, s \rangle$$

Since $\langle B, s \rangle \rightarrow^* \langle True, s_1 \rangle$, using repeatedly the rule **(if)** given in Fig. 4.2, we obtain the reduction $\langle if\ B\ then\ (C; while\ B\ do\ C)\ else\ skip, s \rangle \rightarrow^*$ $\langle if\ True\ then\ (C; while\ B\ do\ C)\ else\ skip, s_1 \rangle$.

Applying rule **(if$_T$)** from Fig. 4.2, we derive

$$\langle if\ True\ then\ (C; while\ B\ do\ C)\ else\ skip, s_1 \rangle \rightarrow \langle C; while\ B\ do\ C, s_1 \rangle.$$

By repeatedly applying rule (seq), the latter can be reduced to $\langle skip; while\ B\ do\ C, s_2 \rangle$, because $\langle C, s_1 \rangle \rightarrow^* \langle skip, s_2 \rangle$.

Now, axiom (skip) from Fig. 4.2 allows us to derive $\langle skip; while\ B\ do\ C, s_2 \rangle \rightarrow \langle while\ B\ do\ C, s_2 \rangle$.

Again by induction hypothesis, $\langle while\ B\ do\ C, s_2 \rangle \rightarrow^* \langle skip, s_3 \rangle$.

Therefore, we have a reduction sequence $\langle while\ B\ do\ C, s \rangle \rightarrow^* \langle skip, s_3 \rangle$ as required.

The case of rule (while$_F$) is similar. $\qquad\qquad\qquad\qquad\qquad\qquad$ □

4.4 Adding Blocks and Local Variables to SIMP

We can add the notion of *local state* to SIMP, by using blocks and local variable declarations. For this, we add to the syntax of SIMP a block constructor and local variable declarations and initialisations.

We will use static scoping rules, so that the scope of a newly created location corresponds precisely to the block where the location is created and initialised.

A local variable will either be stack dynamic, in which case it will be allocated a memory space when the declaration is elaborated at run time and deallocated at the end of the block, or explicit heap dynamic if it is declared as a reference, in which case its lifetime will not be limited to the execution of the block.

Let us first define the (abstract) syntax of the extended language.

Syntax. We extend the grammar that defines the abstract syntax of SIMP, adding a new rule for commands:

$$C ::= begin\ loc\ l := E;\ C\ end$$

and a new rule for arithmetic expressions:

$$E ::= ref\ E$$

All the expressions and programs that were valid in SIMP remain valid in the extended language, but the added rules allow us to generate also programs with blocks and references. We use the keywords *begin* and *end* to indicate the limits of the block (as in Algol and Pascal). The idea is that the variable l will only be visible inside the block in which it is declared (i.e., it is a local variable), and will be initialised with the value of the expression E, which in case we use references will be a pointer.

Semantics. To give a precise meaning to these constructs, we add two rules to the big-step semantics.

The rule (ref) defined below shows that the value of $ref\ E$ is a new location, which has as its contents the value of E.

$$\frac{\langle E, s \rangle \Downarrow \langle v, s' \rangle}{\langle ref\ E, s \rangle \Downarrow \langle l, s'[l \mapsto v] \rangle,\ if\ l \notin dom(s')} \text{(ref)}$$

In the rule (ref), the condition $l \notin dom(s')$ ensures that the location is new. Recall that the memory s is modelled as a partial function; the function $s'[l \mapsto v]$, where $l \notin dom(s')$, extends s' by mapping l to v.

The rule (loc) defined below gives the meaning of a block declaration. The location l used in this rule must be fresh, as specified by the condition in the rule. The notation $C\{z \mapsto l\}$ denotes the program C where the occurrences of z have all been replaced by l.

$$\frac{\langle E, s \rangle \Downarrow \langle v, s' \rangle \quad \langle C\{z \mapsto l\}, s'[l \mapsto v] \rangle \Downarrow \langle skip, s''[l \mapsto v'] \rangle}{\langle begin\ loc\ z := E;\ C\ end, s \rangle \Downarrow \langle skip, s'' \rangle} \text{(loc)}$$

where $l \notin dom(s') \cup dom(s'') \cup locations(C)$, that is, l is a fresh name.

The condition $l \notin dom(s') \cup dom(s'') \cup locations(C)$ ensures that, when C is executed, the variable z (which is renamed to l) is not confused with other variables with the same name in other parts of the program. We evaluate $C\{z \mapsto l\}$, that is, C where z has been replaced by the new variable l, in a memory in which l has the value v (obtained by evaluating E). After the execution of the block, the memory state is represented by s'', where l is no longer in the domain (it has "disappeared"). The renaming of the local variable z by l guarantees that if there is another z in the program, its value is not affected by the execution of the block.

Example 4.17
To see how the rule (loc) works, consider a program P that swaps the contents of x and y using a local variable z:

```
begin
  loc z := !x;
  x := !y;
  y := !z
end
```

According to the semantics of blocks, z is only visible inside the block.

We can show that the program P is correct by proving $\langle P, s \rangle \Downarrow \langle P, s' \rangle$, where s' coincides with s except that the contents of the variables x and y have been swapped: First we prove

$$\langle x := !y;\ y := !l, s[l \mapsto s(x)] \rangle \Downarrow \langle skip, s[l \mapsto s(x), x \mapsto s(y), y \mapsto s(x)] \rangle$$

as in Example 4.15. Let us call s_1 the store $s[l \mapsto s(x), x \mapsto s(y), y \mapsto s(x)]$ and s_2 the store $s[x \mapsto s(y), y \mapsto s(x)]$, then:

$$\frac{}{\langle !x, s\rangle \Downarrow \langle s(x), s\rangle}\text{(var)}$$

$$\frac{\langle x := !y \, ; \ y := !l, s[l \mapsto s(x)]\rangle \Downarrow \langle skip, s_1\rangle}{\langle P, s\rangle \Downarrow \langle skip, s_2\rangle}\text{(loc)}$$

The operational semantics we have just given does not specify how the memory is physically organised (this can also be formally specified, but it is out of the scope of this book). Our semantics assumes that there is always space for new variables in the memory (i.e., given a partial function s representing the memory state, we can always generate a location l that is not in the domain of the function s).

We can model procedure declarations and procedure calls in a similar way. SIMP could also be extended to include other looping constructs, or more powerful selectors such as a Java-style switch construct. However, this will not add more computational power to the language, and the semantic rules given in this chapter to describe the behaviour of while loops and conditionals can be easily adapted to model post-test loops and multiple selectors. We will not develop the operational semantics of imperative constructs further. Instead in the following chapters we will study two classes of languages that are strikingly different in their use of variables and control structures: functional languages and logic programming languages.

4.5 Further Reading

Several textbooks discuss the operational semantics of imperative programming languages using minimalistic languages similar to SIMP, see for example [2, 3]. For more advanced readers, we recommend [4, 5].

The use of abstract machines to study computation systems has its roots in the work done by Turing on abstract computation models, which had a deep influence on the design of computers and later on the design of programming languages for those computers. The influence of Turing's work on imperative programming languages is not limited to computer architecture. Abstract machines based on the notion of a state transition are used nowadays by programming language designers to analyse the behaviour of program constructs, and in compiler implementations to improve portability of code, amongst other properties. Interested readers can find more information in [6, 7].

4.6 Exercises

1. Draw the abstract syntax tree of the following SIMP programs:

    (a) $y := 0$;
        $if \, !x = !y \, then \, (x := !x + 1; \ y := !y - 1)$
        $else \, (x := !x - 1; \ y := !y + 1)$

(b) $C_1; (C_2; C_3)$ where C_1, C_2, C_3 are arbitrary programs.

(c) $(C_1; C_2); C_3$ where C_1, C_2, C_3 are arbitrary programs.

2. Assume y has the value n for some natural number n. Write a SIMP program to compute x^y (x to the power y).

3. Let C_1, C_2 and C_3 be arbitrary SIMP commands. Using the abstract machine semantics of SIMP, show that the programs $C_1; (C_2; C_3)$ and $(C_1; C_2); C_3$ are equivalent, that is, they produce the same results when executed in the same state. Therefore the brackets are not needed.

4. (a) Give the structural induction principle for Boolean expressions in SIMP.

   (b) Consider a configuration $\langle B \cdot c, r, m \rangle$ for the abstract machine, where c, r, m are arbitrary stacks and memory states, and B is a Boolean expression in SIMP, such that any integer expression E occurring in B mentions only valid memory locations.

   Prove by structural induction that for any such B, there is a sequence of transitions for the abstract machine:

   $$\langle B \cdot c, r, m \rangle \to^* \langle c, b \cdot r, m \rangle$$

   where b is a Boolean value (True or False),

5. Explain why in the rules defining the small-step semantics of SIMP (Fig. 4.2) there is no rule of the form:

   $$\frac{\langle C_2, s \rangle \to \langle C_2', s' \rangle}{\langle C_1; C_2, s \rangle \to \langle C_1; C_2', s' \rangle}$$

   Hint: show that using this rule we can give an incorrect semantics to a sequence of SIMP commands (compared with the intuitive meaning of sequential composition, or with the semantics obtained by using the abstract machine).

6. Prove that the small-step semantics of SIMP is deterministic, that is, $\langle P, s \rangle \to \langle P_1, s_1 \rangle$ and $\langle P, s \rangle \to \langle P_2, s_2 \rangle$ implies $\langle P_1, s_1 \rangle = \langle P_2, s_2 \rangle$.

7. Using the big-step semantics of SIMP, prove by rule induction that if E is an integer expression in SIMP that uses only locations in m, then $\langle E, m \rangle \Downarrow n$ holds for a unique value n.

   Prove that also the values of Boolean expressions working in a memory m are uniquely determined if the values of arithmetic expressions are uniquely determined.

8. Assume that in the definition of the big-step semantics of SIMP we replace the rule (seq) defining sequential composition by the following rule:

   $$\frac{\langle C_1, s \rangle \Downarrow \langle skip, s' \rangle \quad \langle C_2, s \rangle \Downarrow \langle skip, s'' \rangle}{\langle C_1; C_2, s \rangle \Downarrow \langle skip, s'' \rangle}$$

   where both C_1 and C_2 are evaluated in the state s. How is the semantics of the language affected by this change?

9. Assume that in the definition of the big-step semantics of SIMP without reference expressions, we replace the rule for the evaluation of integer expressions:

$$\frac{\langle E_1, s \rangle \Downarrow \langle n_1, s' \rangle \quad \langle E_2, s' \rangle \Downarrow \langle n_2, s'' \rangle}{\langle E_1 \ op \ E_2, s \rangle \Downarrow \langle n, s'' \rangle} \ if \ n_1 \ op \ n_2 = n$$

by

$$\frac{\langle E_1, s \rangle \Downarrow \langle n_1, s \rangle \quad \langle E_2, s \rangle \Downarrow \langle n_2, s \rangle}{\langle E_1 \ op \ E_2, s \rangle \Downarrow \langle n, s \rangle} \ if \ n_1 \ op \ n_2 = n$$

Explain the consequences of this change on the semantics of SIMP.

10. Show, using the big-step semantics of SIMP, that the command

$$if \ False \ then \ C \ else \ C'$$

is equivalent to C' (i.e. both have the same semantics).

11. Prove that for any SIMP program P and memory state s, if $\langle P, s \rangle \rightarrow^* \langle P', s' \rangle$ such that $\langle P', s' \rangle$ is a final and non-blocked configuration, then $\langle P, s \rangle \Downarrow \langle P', s' \rangle$. Hint: use induction on the length of the reduction sequence $\langle P, s \rangle \rightarrow^* \langle P', s' \rangle$, that is, prove that the property holds for sequences of length 0 (base case), then prove that it holds if the reduction sequence $\langle P, s \rangle \rightarrow^* \langle P', s' \rangle$ has $k + 1$ steps, assuming that it holds for sequences with k steps or less (induction hypothesis).

12. We add to the syntax of the language SIMP a post-test logically controlled loop:

```
repeat C until B
```

where the loop-body C will be repeated until the Boolean expression B evaluates to True.

(a) Give a formal definition of the semantics of this command, by specifying the rules that should be added to the big-step semantics of SIMP.

(b) Show that this extension does not change the computational power of the language by giving a translation of

```
repeat C until B
```

in terms of the constructs that already exist in SIMP.

References

1. G. Plotkin, *A structural approach to operational semantics*. Technical Report DAIMI FN-19 (Aarhus University, 1981)
2. H.R. Nielson, F. Nielson, *Semantics with Applications: An Appetizer. Undergraduate topics in computer science* (Springer, Berlin, 2007)
3. A.M. Pitts, *Semantics of programming languages*, Lecture Notes and Slides (Cambridge University, 2002)
4. G. Winskel, *The Formal Semantics of Programming Languages*, Foundations of Computing (MIT Press, 1993)
5. R. Harper, *Practical Foundations for Programming Languages* (Cambridge University Press, Cambridge, 2013)
6. A.P. Parkes, *Introduction to languages, machines and logic—computable languages, abstract machines and formal logic*, Undergraduate topics in computer science (Springer, 2002)
7. W. Kluge, *Abstract Computing Machines, A Lambda Calculus Perspective* Texts in Theoretical Computer Science: An EATCS Series (Springer, 2004)

Part III
Functional Languages

Chapter 5
General Features of Functional Languages

The imperative programming languages we discussed in the previous part all share a common design idea: to make easier and more efficient use of Von Neumann computers, basically by providing

- abstractions for the storage of data and programs, so that programmers do not need to keep track of memory addresses, and
- control structures that make programs more readable and easier to write.

Although the level of abstraction provided by imperative languages varies, there are common features in the design of all imperative languages: they reflect the underlying machine architecture, which makes it easier for compilers to generate efficient code.

However, when developing software applications, efficiency is not always a priority. Depending on the application, properties such as low maintenance cost, easy debugging, or formally provable correctness, might have higher priority. For example, in safety-critical domains (such as medical, telecommunications, or transport systems) it is important to develop programs whose *correctness* can be certified (i.e., formally proved). Declarative languages, and in particular functional languages, can be a good alternative in this case.

Programs in functional languages are in general shorter, easier to understand, easier to design, debug and maintain than their imperative counterparts. For these reasons, functional programming languages are becoming increasingly popular in the industrial sector.

The main domains of application of functional languages are artificial intelligence (for example, for the implementation of expert systems), text processing (for instance, the UNIX editor Emacs is implemented in LISP), natural language, telephony, music composition, graphical interfaces, symbolic mathematical systems, theorem provers and proof assistants.

LISP, which was introduced by McCarthy in the 1950s, is considered to be the first functional programming language. The syntax of LISP is based on lists (as the name of the language suggests: *LISt Processing*), where the atomic elements are numbers and characters.

M. Fernández, *Programming Languages and Operational Semantics*,   93
Undergraduate Topics in Computer Science, DOI: 10.1007/978-1-4471-6368-8_5,
© Springer-Verlag London 2014

Although LISP is essentially an untyped language, and the first versions were dynamically scoped, its conciseness and elegance made it very popular. Since both data and programs are represented as lists, it is easy to define in LISP *higher-order functions*, that is, functions that take other functions as arguments, or produce a function as a result. This gives rise to a very different style of programming, and is one of the main features of functional languages. Several versions of LISP are in use, including Scheme [1], which is a small statically scoped language, and is also untyped.

In recent years, several functional languages appeared, which radically changed the syntax and introduced sophisticated type systems with type inference capabilities. Modern functional languages are *strongly typed* (which guarantees that no type errors can arise at run time), statically scoped, and have built-in memory management. ML and Haskell are examples of these, however they differ in their semantics: ML is *strict*, whereas Haskell is *lazy*, which means that only computations that are needed to evaluate the program will be performed. We will discuss this point in more detail in the following sections. Another difference is that ML includes some imperative features (for efficiency reasons), whereas Haskell is a pure functional language enjoying *referential transparency*: the evaluation of an expression depends only on its components, and is therefore independent of its context.

The common feature of all functional languages is that programs consist of *functions* (as in the mathematical theory of functions, which is different from the notion of function used in imperative languages). A mathematical function is a mapping between elements of two sets (see Chap. 2). For example, the function $f : A \rightarrow B$ associates each element in the set A (the *domain* of the function) with at most one element in the set B (the *codomain* of the function). We say that the function f *has type* $A \rightarrow B$ (or f *is of type* $A \rightarrow B$).

In this part of the book, we adopt the notations that are usual in functional languages; for instance, we write $(f\ x)$ instead of $f(x)$ to denote the result of applying the function f to the element x.

If a function f has type $A \rightarrow B$, it means that it transforms an input x of type A into a result $(f\ x)$ of type B. With this approach, the focus is in *what* is to be computed (the mapping between A and B), not *how* it should be computed. Functional languages are *declarative*.

To define a function, programmers can give a direct definition of the mapping or define it in terms of other, previously defined, functions (i.e., functions that have already been specified by the programmer, taken from libraries, or provided as language primitives).

For the examples in this part of the book we will use a notation similar to Haskell's syntax. Haskell is a pure functional language freely available from the internet: it can be downloaded, including the language report and user manual, from http://www.haskell.org. There are several interpreters and compilers available; for example, Hugs (the Haskell Users' Gofer System) is a small, portable Haskell interpreter written in C, and GHC (the Glasgow Haskell Compiler) is an optimising compiler, less portable than Hugs but produces programs that run much faster. It is also possible to run Haskell code via a browser (see http://tryhaskell.org).

5.1 Defining Functions

The syntax of Haskell, ML, Clean, and most modern functional languages, is inspired by the definitions of functions in mathematics, using *equations* and *pattern-matching*.

Patterns are expressions made out of variables and constructors. The latter can be predefined (such as the pair or list constructors) or can be defined by the programmer.

We start by giving some examples in Haskell.

Example 5.1 (Square)

We can compute the square of a number using a function `square` defined by the equation:

```
square x = x * x
```

where we have used one of the predefined arithmetic functions (multiplication, written *). The variable x in the left hand side of the equation is a pattern, indicating that we do not require arguments of any specific format. However, this does not mean that the function `square` can be applied to any kind of argument. If we do not include a type declaration, the type inference algorithm will be used and the system will infer that this is a function on numbers because we are using multiplication (more details are given in Sect. 5.4).

Another traditional example is the function factorial, which can be defined in several ways.

Example 5.2 (Factorial)

First we use a conditional, where we test if the argument is 0 (the test for equality in Haskell is written ==).

```
fact :: Integer -> Integer
fact n = if n == 0 then 1 else n * (fact (n-1))
```

The program above consists of one equation, and we have included a type declaration specifying that we are defining a function from integers to integers. We can avoid the conditional and define factorial with two equations, using pattern-matching on the argument:

```
fact :: Integer -> Integer
fact 0 = 1
fact (n + 1) = (n + 1) * (fact n)
```

Or better, we can use *conditional equations* (also called *guarded equations*), where we add guards to specify the conditions under which each equation can be applied; guards are evaluated in the order in which they appear:

```
fact :: Integer -> Integer
fact n
    |n > 0  = n * (fact(n − 1))
    |n == 0 = 1
    |n < 0  = error "negative argument"
```

In the last example we used a predefined function, *error*, that takes a string as argument. When evaluated it causes immediate termination of the program and displays the string.

Another example of the use of guarded equations is in the definition of the function sign below.

Example 5.3 (Sign)
The function `sign` indicates whether its argument is positive, negative or zero.

```
sign : : Integer -> Integer
sign x
    |x < 0 = −1
    |x == 0 = 0
    |x > 0  = 1
```

The definition of `sign` given above is equivalent to, but more readable than:

```
sign x = if x < 0 then − 1 else if x == 0 then 0 else 1
```

One of the distinctive features of modern functional languages is that functions are also values even though we cannot display them or print them. We can therefore use functions as arguments or results for other (higher-order) functions.

In Haskell all functions are typed (although type declarations are optional). A type declaration for a function has the form

```
f : : A -> B
```

where f is the name of the function and A and B are types. Since a function can have another function as argument or result, the types A and B can in turn be functional types of the form A' -> B'. Functional types are sometimes called *arrow types*.

The application of a function to an argument is denoted by juxtaposition, as in the examples above: `fact(n − 1)` denotes the application of the function `fact` to the argument $(n − 1)$. To avoid writing too many brackets in expressions, there are some conventions:

– Application has precedence over other operations.

For example, `square 3 + 1` means `(square 3) + 1`. To change the meaning of this expression we need brackets, as in `square (3 + 1)`.

– Application associates to the left.

For example, `square square 3` is interpreted as `(square square) 3`.

Note that this expression is ill-typed, since the function `square` expects an argument of type integer, not a function. We will show later how the type inference algorithm detects the error. We must use brackets in this case:

`square (square 3)` is correctly typed.

– We will not write the outermost brackets. For example, we will write

`square 3` instead of `(square 3)`

Another distinctive feature of functional programs is the use of recursion: in the definition of a function `f` we can use the function `f` itself. An example of a recursive definition is the definition of the factorial function (see Example 5.2).

Recursion is the counterpart of iteration, which is one of the main control structures in imperative languages.

Before giving more details of the syntax of function definitions, we need to describe the mechanism by which programs are executed. The approach is radically different from that of imperative languages: for functional programming languages the role of the computer is to *evaluate and display the results* of the expressions that the programmer writes, using the functions defined in the program, in libraries or as primitives of the language. As in mathematics, expressions may contain numbers, variables or names of functions. For instance `36`, `square 6`, `6 * 6` are valid expressions. When we write an expression such as `square 6` the computer will display its result: `36`. The process of evaluation is described in the next section.

5.2 Evaluation

The expression `square 6` will be evaluated by using the definition of `square`, that is, `square x = x * x`, with the value 6. More precisely, the evaluator will replace the expression `square 6` by `6 * 6`, and then, using the predefined `*` operation, it will give the result `36`.

The process of evaluating an expression is a *simplification process*, also called the *reduction* or *evaluation* process. The goal is to obtain the *value* or *irreducible form* associated with an expression, by a series of reduction steps. The *meaning* of an expression is its value, also called a *normal form*.

We will write $e \rightarrow e'$ to denote a reduction step from the expression e to e'.

Example 5.4 (Evaluating an Arithmetic Expression)
Consider the expression
$$(3 + 1) + (2 + 1).$$

We can simplify it as follows:

$$(3 + 1) + (2 + 1) \rightarrow (3 + 1) + 3 \rightarrow 4 + 3 \rightarrow 7.$$

Therefore 7 is the value denoted by the expression $(3 + 1) + (2 + 1)$.

There may be several reduction sequences for an expression. The following is also a correct reduction sequence for $(3 + 1) + (2 + 1)$:

$$(3 + 1) + (2 + 1) \rightarrow 4 + (2 + 1) \rightarrow 4 + 3 \rightarrow 7$$

In this example, we obtained the same value in both cases. This is a general property of functional programs.

Unicity of Normal Forms: *In (pure) functional languages the value of an expression is uniquely determined by its components, and is independent of the order of reduction.*

An obvious advantage of this property is the improved readability of programs. It amounts to the referential transparency that was mentioned earlier.

Note also that not all the reduction sequences that start with a given expression lead to a value. This is not in contradiction to the previous property. It is due to non-termination: some reduction sequences for a given expression may be infinite, but all the sequences that terminate reach the same value. This is more clearly seen with an example.

Example 5.5 (Non-Termination)

Let us define the constant function `fortytwo`:

```
fortytwo x = 42
```

and the function `infinity`:

```
infinity x = infinity (x + 1)
```

It is clear that the evaluation of the expression `infinity` n never reaches a normal form, no matter which number n we provide as an argument. The expression

$$fortytwo\ (infinity\ 5)$$

gives rise to some reduction sequences that do not terminate, but those which terminate produce the value 42 (a unique normal form).

The example above shows that although the normal form is unique, the order of reductions is important. Functional programming languages evaluate expressions following a specific *strategy*, which specifies at each point the next position where reduction should take place.

Definition 5.6 (Strategy)

A *strategy of evaluation* specifies the order in which reductions take place; it defines the reduction sequence that the language implements to evaluate an expression.

The most popular strategies of evaluation for functional languages are:

1. *Call-by-Name (Normal order):* if more than one subexpression is reducible, reduce first at the leftmost outermost position available. This means that in the presence of a function application, first the definition of the function is used, then the arguments are evaluated if needed.
2. *Call-by-Value (Applicative order):* if more than one subexpression is reducible, reduce first at the leftmost innermost position available. This means that in the presence of a function application, first the arguments are evaluated, then the definition of the function is used to evaluate the application.

For example, using the call-by-name strategy, the expression

```
fortytwo (infinity5)
```

is reduced in one step to the value 42, since this strategy specifies that the definition of the function `fortytwo` is used, which does not require the argument (it is a constant function). However, using the call-by-value strategy we must first evaluate the argument `(infinity 5)`, and as we already mentioned, the reduction sequence for this expression is infinite, hence we will never reach a normal form.

The call-by-name strategy guarantees that if an expression has a value, it will be reached.

As Example 5.5 shows, different strategies of evaluation require a different number of reduction steps, therefore the efficiency of a program depends on the strategy used.

Some functional languages (for instance, the languages in the ML family) use call-by-value, which in most cases is an efficient strategy. This is because when an argument is used several times in the definition of a function, the call-by-value strategy will only evaluate it once.

Haskell uses a strategy called *lazy evaluation*, which is based on call-by-name and therefore guarantees that if an expression has a normal form, the evaluator will find it. In other words, it eliminates the risk of selecting a non-terminating reduction sequence when a finite one exists. To counter the potential lack of efficiency of a pure call-by-name strategy, Haskell uses *sharing*, that is, when an argument is used many times in a function definition, its evaluation is performed at most once, and the value is shared between all its occurrences.

Even in languages that follow a call-by-value strategy, a bit of laziness is required: if-then-else expressions cannot be evaluated in an innermost fashion, because this would cause non-termination in the case of recursive definitions.

Recursive definitions are also evaluated by simplification. For instance, given the definition

```
fact :: Integer -> Integer
fact n = if n == 0 then 1 else n * (fact (n - 1))
```

and the expression `fact 0`, the following is a possible reduction sequence:

$$\begin{aligned}
\text{fact } 0 &\to \text{if } 0 == 0 \text{ then } 1 \text{ else } 0 * (\text{fact } (0 - 1)) \\
&\to \text{if True then } 1 \text{ else } 0 * (\text{fact } (0 - 1)) \\
&\to 1
\end{aligned}$$

Note that the else branch was not evaluated in this example. In general, conditional (if-then-else) expressions are evaluated as follows:

1. First evaluate the condition.
2. If the result is True then evaluate *only* the expression in the `then` branch.
3. If the result is False then evaluate *only* the expression in the `else` branch.

Therefore the only reduction sequence for the expression `fact 0` is the one shown above, and this expression is terminating (there are no infinite reduction sequences).

However, this definition of `fact` does not treat correctly the case of negative arguments. For example, if we start reducing `fact (−1)` the sequence is infinite and the evaluation process does not terminate.

Using the version of factorial with conditional equations:

```
fact :: Integer -> Integer
fact n
  |n > 0  = n * fact(n − 1))
  |n == 0 = 1
  |n < 0  = error "negative argument"
```

this problem does not arise.

5.3 Building Functional Programs

Functions are the building blocks of functional languages. One way of combining functions is by *composition*, denoted by ·, as in the expression f · g. Composition is itself a function, which is predefined in functional languages. In Haskell it is defined as follows:

$$(\cdot) :: (\beta \rightarrow \gamma) \rightarrow (\alpha \rightarrow \beta) \rightarrow (\alpha \rightarrow \gamma)$$
$$(f \cdot g) \, x = f \, (g \, x).$$

We have used Greek letters in the type of this function to highlight the fact that we are dealing with *type variables* representing arbitrary types. The type of the operator · indicates that we can only compose functions whose types are compatible. The composition operation · expects two functions f and g as arguments, such that the domain of f coincides with the codomain of g: the type of f is $(\beta \rightarrow \gamma)$ and the type of g is $(\alpha \rightarrow \beta)$, where α, β and γ represent arbitrary types.

The result of composing two functions f and g of compatible types $(\beta \rightarrow \gamma)$ and $(\alpha \rightarrow \beta)$ respectively, is a function of type $(\alpha \rightarrow \gamma)$: it accepts an argument x of type α (which will be supplied to g) and produces f (g x) which is in the codomain of f and therefore is of type γ.

Example 5.7 (Composition)
Consider the function `square` of Example 5.1. Since we have

$$\mathtt{square \ :: \ Integer \ -> \ Integer}$$

we can define a function `quad` to compute the 4th power of a number as follows:

$$\mathtt{quad = square \cdot square}$$

Arithmetic operations are also primitive functions, used in infix notation as in the expression 3 + 4. In Haskell, we can use them in prefix notation if we enclose them in brackets, for example: (+) 3 4.

However, the functions (+) and + are different: the latter expects a pair of numbers as input, whereas the first one has type[1]

```
(+) :: Integer -> Integer -> Integer
```

The function (+) is the *Curryfied* version of +, that is, instead of working on *pairs* of numbers (i.e., two numbers provided simultaneously), it expects a number followed by another number. This might seem a small difference at first sight, but Curryfication (the word derives from the name of the mathematician Haskell Curry, after whom the programming language is also named) provides great flexibility to functional languages. For instance, we can use (+) to define new functions, as in the following example.

```
successor :: Integer -> Integer
successor = (+) 1
```

Note that the expression + 1 is untypeable since + expects a pair of numbers as arguments. If we replace (+) by + in the previous definition of successor, the program is untypeable.

Another example along the same lines is the definition of the function double, which doubles its argument:

```
double :: Integer -> Integer
double = (*) 2
```

Recall that there are some notational conventions to avoid writing too many brackets in arithmetic expressions:

- Application has priority over arithmetic operations.

  For example, square 1 + 4 * 2 should be read as (square 1) + (4 * 2).
- Subtraction associates to the left.

  For example, $3 - 1 - 2$ is interpreted as $(3 - 1) - 2$.

5.3.1 Local Definitions

As in mathematics, we can write:

```
f x = a * a where a = x/2
```

or equivalently,

```
f x = let a = x/2 in a * a
```

The words let and where are used to structure the program, introducing local definitions that are valid just on the right-hand side of the equation where they appear.

---

[1] In fact, it has a more general type in Haskell, since it can accept inputs from any numerical type: (+) :: Num a => a -> a -> a; we discuss this point in Sect. 5.5.

We can write several local definitions in one equation, as in the following example:

```
f x = square (successor x) where
          square z = z * z ; successor  = (+) 1
```

If e is an expression that contains occurrences of a, which we denote as $e[a]$, the evaluation of expressions of the form

```
e[a] where a = e'
```

or

```
let a = e'in e[a]
```

can be done in a call by value manner as follows:

1. evaluate the expression e', obtaining a result r;
2. replace the occurrences of a in e by r, obtaining an expression $e\{a \mapsto r\}$;
3. evaluate $e\{a \mapsto r\}$, that is, the expression e where every occurrence of a has been replaced by r, obtaining a result r'.

The value associated with the initial expression is r'.

Since the value of a is computed only once, the use of local definitions not only helps making programs more readable, but also more efficient.

5.4 Types: General Concepts

Types help not only to catch errors in the program code, but also during the design phase: they can be seen as a partial specification of the program. In fact, in some very expressive type systems, types *are* complete specifications, containing enough detail for executable programs to be extracted from them. These powerful type systems are used in sophisticated proof assistants, to develop certified programs. However, in most programming languages, types are used as a *complement* to the program: they are concise descriptions of programs that serve primarily to detect errors at an early stage in the software development process. Types can also help the programmer in other ways, for instance they allow the compiler to perform code optimisations (some operations can be performed more efficiently if the types of the operands are known at compile time), and types can speed up the search for functions in libraries (for example, if we know we need a function on integers, we will search only in the corresponding part of the library).

In a typed language, values are divided into classes according to the operations that can be performed on them, and each of these classes is called a type. Actually, in a typed functional language every valid expression (not only values) must have a type. Moreover, if an expression has a value (a normal form) the type of the expression should be the same as the type of its normal form.

Usually, typed programming languages come with a set of predefined types, which in most languages include basic types, such as numbers, Booleans and characters. For example, in Haskell the set of predefined types includes:

- Basic data types: `Bool`, `Char`, `Int`, `Integer`, `Float`, `Double`, ... corresponding respectively to Booleans, characters, small integers (single precision), big integers (arbitrary precision), single precision floating point numbers, and double precision floating point numbers (there are also other numeric types in Haskell).
- Structured types: tuples, strings, lists. Pairs are a particular case of tuples. The notation for tuples is $(a_1, \ldots, a_n)$. A list type is denoted in Haskell as $[\alpha]$, where α is the type of the elements of the list; for instance, `[Integer]` is the type of lists of integers. Strings are lists of characters, such as "Hello".
- Function types: `Integer -> Integer`, `Integer -> Float`, `[a] -> Integer`, `(Integer -> Integer) -> Integer`, are all examples of function types, or *arrow types*. By convention, arrows associate to the right, that is,

$$\texttt{Integer -> Integer -> Integer}$$

should be read as

$$\texttt{Integer -> (Integer -> Integer)}.$$

This is the type of a higher-order function that takes an integer and produces a function from integers to integers as a result. In functional languages, functions can be used as arguments as well. For instance, a function of type

$$\texttt{(Integer -> Integer) -> Integer}$$

has one argument, a function from integers to integers, and produces a number as a result.

Haskell is a static, strongly-typed language, that is, types are checked at compile time and only expressions that will not generate type errors at run time are accepted for evaluation. Expressions that cannot be typed are considered erroneous and are rejected by the compiler or interpreter, prior to evaluation (of course a program that passes the type controls might not solve correctly the problem for which it has been built: the type system only guarantees that typeable programs are free of type errors at run time).

Since it is impossible to decide exactly which expressions are safe and which are not (i.e., the set of programs that may produce a type error at run time is not decidable), every static type checker will reject some programs that do not generate run time errors. Therefore a good type system for a statically typed programming language is one that offers a reasonable level of flexibility without compromising its correctness (i.e., without accepting programs that are unsafe). Modern functional languages have succeeded in this respect: they offer flexible type systems while filtering out all the programs with type errors before execution. This feature, together with the clarity and conciseness of the code, makes the software development process for functional languages shorter than for imperative languages in general.

One of the strengths of the type systems in modern functional languages is that they offer powerful type constructors, allowing the programmer to add new types to the language to suit the application that is being developed. This can be done by introducing *type definitions* in programs.

Moreover, types may contain *type variables* that represent arbitrary types: they can be instantiated to (i.e., replaced by) arbitrary types, in other words, the type system is *polymorphic*. Another useful feature of modern functional languages is that they have a *type inference mechanism*, which frees the programmer from the need of writing type declarations for data and functions. We will discuss polymorphism and type inference in the remaining sections.

5.5 Polymorphism

Type systems can be classified as *monomorphic* or *polymorphic* depending on the number of types that an expression can have. In a monomorphic language every expression has at most one type (the word monomorphic derives from Greek and means "one, single form"), whereas in a polymorphic language some expressions may have more than one type (polymorphic actually means many forms).

There are several ways of defining a polymorphic type system for a programming language:

1. we can use *generic types*, with type variables that can be instantiated to obtain several different types;
2. we can use *overloading*, where several different functions with different types share the same name;
3. we can use a *subtyping relation* and allow a program to be used with different subtypes of a given type.

The use of subtypes is typical of object-oriented languages. We will not discuss this technique in this book. In the rest of the section we will define and compare generic polymorphism and overloading.

Functional languages achieve polymorphism by using generic types. For example, the functional composition operator defined in Sect. 5.3 has type:

$$(\cdot)::(\beta \to \gamma) \to (\alpha \to \beta) \to (\alpha \to \gamma)$$

where α, β, γ are type variables. This means that we can use the same composition operator in different situations, as the examples below show. One of the main advantages of this kind of polymorphism is that it allows the programmer to *reuse* code.

Example 5.8

1. Consider again the function `quad` defined by:

   quad = square · square

   Since `square` is a function on integers as indicated by its type

   $$\text{square} :: \text{Integer} \to \text{Integer}$$

   the operator · is used in the definition of `quad` with type:

   (·) :: (Integer -> Integer) -> (Integer -> Integer) -> (Integer -> Integer)

   Therefore we can deduce that `quad` is a function from integers to integers:

   $$\text{quad} :: \text{Integer} \to \text{Integer}.$$

   But we can also define a function `sqrt` :: `Integer -> Float` to compute square roots of integers, and compose it with `square` using the *same* composition operator:

   $$\text{sqrt} \cdot \text{square}$$

   In this expression, the type of the composition operator is:

   (·) :: (Integer -> Float) -> (Integer -> Integer) -> (Integer -> Float)

2. The `error` function used in the definition of factorial in Example 5.2:

   ```
   fact n

     |n > 0   = n * (fact(n − 1))

     |n == 0 = 1

     |n < 0   = error "negative argument"
   ```

   is also polymorphic: `error` :: `String -> a`. In the definition of `fact` it is used with type `String -> Integer`.

   Formally, the language of generic polymorphic types (we will call them just polymorphic types in the following) is defined as a set of *terms* (see Definition 2.7 in Chap. 2).

Definition 5.9 (Polymorphic Types)

The set of terms representing polymorphic types is built out of *type variables* (α, β, γ, ...), and *type constructors*, each with a given arity. It is defined inductively:

– The basic polymorphic types are type variables and 0-ary type constructors (e.g., Integer, Float, String, ...).
– If C is a type constructor of arity n, and $T_1, \ldots, T_n$ are polymorphic types, then $C(T_1, \ldots, T_n)$ is a polymorphic type. For example, $\rightarrow$ is a binary type constructor, written infix, so String$\rightarrow \alpha$ is a polymorphic type; the type constructor for lists requires just one argument, as in $[\alpha]$ (the polymorphic type of lists).

A polymorphic type represents the set of all its *instances*, obtained by substituting type variables by types.

In functional programs, instead of α we write simply a, but here we use Greek letters to emphasise that they are type variables.

Polymorphic types provide a very concise and elegant notation for a possibly infinite set of types. For example, $[\alpha]$ represents the set of all the types of lists, including [Integer], which corresponds to lists of integers, [[Integer]], which denotes lists of lists of integers, [Integer $\rightarrow$ Integer], which corresponds to lists of functions from integers to integers, etc.

Although generic polymorphism is typical of modern functional languages, imperative languages can also be designed to include this feature. For example, C++ uses type variables in *templates* to achieve polymorphism. However, C++ requires the programmer to write type declarations, whereas ML and Haskell can *infer* polymorphic types. We study type inference in the next section.

Implementing generic polymorphism in a programming language is not trivial, and it may cause some overheads at run time. For instance, the memory space required to store a polymorphic data structure depends on the actual type of the components; if this is not known at compile time, the compiler may solve the problem by introducing pointers (but this will make the access less efficient). Most imperative languages use only *overloading*, which is sometimes called *ad-hoc polymorphism*.

Typical examples of overloaded operations are the arithmetic operations, which can be used both with integers or floating point numbers. However, the function that adds integers is different from the function that adds floating point numbers even if both are denoted by + (because the internal representation of these data differ: integers are represented as binary numbers, whereas floating point numbers are represented as exponent and mantissa). The compiler selects the function to be used according to the types of the operands, and generates code for the corresponding function (in contrast with generic polymorphism, where the *same* code is used with arguments of different types). Therefore, in the case of overloading, we do not achieve the goal of code reuse. Moreover, using the same name for two different operations may lead to errors and less clear programs. Although there is no final solution to this problem, several alternatives have been proposed:

1. We could use different symbols for addition of integers and floating point numbers. For example, in the language Caml (a dialect of ML) we write + for addition of integers and + . for floating point addition.

2. We can enrich the language of types. For example, we could write type expressions such as

$$+::(Integer \rightarrow Integer \rightarrow Integer) \wedge (Float \rightarrow Float \rightarrow \texttt{Float})$$

with the intended meaning that + has both of these types.

3. We can define a notion of a *type class*, as it is done in Haskell. For example, we can write:

$$(+) \quad :: \quad \texttt{Num a => a -> a -> a}$$

which indicates that `(+)` has type `a -> a -> a` where `a` is in the class `Num`, that is, `a` is a type variable that can only be instantiated with numeric types. Writing simply `(+) :: a -> a -> a` would not be correct, because it would allow addition to be used with arguments of *any* type.

5.6 Type Checking and Type Inference

Languages that are statically typed usually implement either a type checking or a type inference algorithm to detect type errors in programs at compile time.

Most modern functional languages offer type inference mechanisms. In a language with type inference the programmer does not need to write types for the expressions used. If a type declaration is given, then it can be used to check the program, but if there is no type declaration, then the type inference algorithm will try to "guess" (*infer*) a type for the program, based on the types of the primitive values and operations that appear in the program.

In contrast, a type checker requires type declarations for all the functions. It reads the program and verifies that the types declared are compatible with the use of the different constructs in the language.

The first type inference algorithms were proposed by Milner [2] for ML, based on the notion of types introduced by Curry for the λ-calculus. The λ-calculus provides a very elegant notation for function definition (λ-abstraction) and application, and serves as a theoretical model of computation for functional languages. The type system of ML not only introduced type inference, but also a form of generic polymorphism. Haskell's type system is based on similar ideas.

The type inference algorithm works roughly as follows. Given an expression to type:

– First the expression is decomposed into smaller subexpressions, and when a basic atomic expression is found (such as a constant, a variable, or a primitive operation), the information available is used (if it is a primitive of the language) or otherwise it is assigned the most general type possible (using type variables).

For example, if the number 3.14 occurs in an expression, it will be assigned the type Float.

- Using the information gathered in the previous part, a set of type constraints is generated. Constraints are equations involving type variables. For example, if an expression contains the function f applied to the number 3.14, and f was given type α and 3.14 type Float, then we know that $\alpha = $ Float $\rightarrow \beta$ for some type β, since the domain of the function must contain the number 3.14. The type of the application (f 3.14) should be β, the codomain of f.

The rules to generate types for functions and applications are the following:

(Function)

Given a function definition $fx_1 \ldots x_n = t$, we assume that the formal arguments have arbitrary types $\sigma_1, \ldots, \sigma_n$ and try to obtain a type for the expression t. This is written:

$$x_1 \; : \; : \; \sigma_1, \ldots, x_n \; : \; : \; \sigma_n \vdash t \; : \; : \; \tau$$

which means that under the assumptions $x_1 \; : \; : \; \sigma_1, \ldots, x_n \; : \; : \; \sigma_n$, the expression t has type τ. From this we deduce a type for the function f:

$$\vdash f \; : \; : \; \sigma_1 \rightarrow \ldots \rightarrow \sigma_n \rightarrow \tau$$

Note that there are no assumptions for the type of f, since $\sigma_1, \ldots, \sigma_n$ are part of the arrow type (it is usual to omit the symbol $\vdash$ in this case).

(Application)

For any arbitrary set Γ of type assumptions, if $\Gamma \vdash s \; : \; : \; \sigma \rightarrow \tau$ and $\Gamma \vdash t \; : \; : \; \sigma$ then

$$\Gamma \vdash (s \, t) \; : \; : \; \tau$$

This means that the domain of the function s should be the same as the type of t, and the result of the application should be in the codomain of the function.

In the same way, we can give rules describing how each kind of expression is typed. We need a rule for each predefined constant, function and operation, and also rules to type expressions including local definitions (we will study typing rules in Chap. 6).

- Finally, the type constraints are solved, using a unification algorithm (the details of this algorithm, which also has applications in logic programming languages, are given in Chap. 8). If no solution to the type constraints can be found, the expression is not typeable. Otherwise the most general solutions to the constraints are used in order to obtain the most general type for the given expression. Note that the type of the expression depends on the types of its components only.

The implementation of the type inference algorithm is out of the scope of this book. A detailed description of the type inference algorithm and its implementation in Caml can be found in [3]; see Sect. 5.9 for more references.

We now give some simple examples of type inference.

Example 5.10

With the definition:

$$square\ x = x * x$$

we can infer

$$square\ ::\ Integer\ ->\ Integer$$

assuming `*` is a predefined operation of type `(Integer, Integer)->` `Integer`.

We proceed as follows:

First the rule to type functions (see **(Function)** above) says that we need to obtain a type τ for `x  *  x` assuming `x : : ` σ, in order to deduce `square : :` $\sigma -> \tau$. The operation `*` requires two arguments of type `Integer` (recall that the infix notation `x` `*  x` is an abbreviation for `* (x, x)`). Therefore, according to the rule **(Application)**, we need $\sigma = $ `Integer`, and $\tau = $ `Integer`. These constraints are trivially solvable, and we obtain

$$square\ ::\ Integer\ ->\ Integer$$

If we now try to infer a type for the expression

$$square\ square3$$

we obtain a set of unsolvable constraints: Since application associates to the left, the expression above is parsed as

$$(square\ square)3$$

and since both occurrences of `square` are associated with the type `Integer ->` `Integer`, in order to obtain a type for the expression `(square  square)` we need a solution for the equation `Integer  =  Integer  ->  Integer`. Note that we are using the typing rule for application here, which says that the domain of the function must coincide with the type of the argument.

The equation `Integer  =  Integer  ->  Integer` is obviously unsolvable. The type inference algorithm will then give an error message, indicating that the expression

$$square\ square3$$

cannot be typed since the function `square` requires a number as argument, not a function.

If a function is defined by several equations, we proceed as in the example above, generating a type from each equation. Since all the equations define the same function, a final constraint is added to force all the generated types to coincide.

Example 5.11

Consider the definition of factorial using guarded equations:

```
fact n
   |n > 0   = n * (fact(n − 1))
   |n == 0  = 1
   |n < 0   = error "negative argument"
```
Since 0 is a primitive constant of type Integer, from these equations we deduce that n is an integer, and moreover from the first and second equations we get:

$$n \quad :: \quad Integer$$
$$fact \quad :: \quad Integer \rightarrow Integer$$

Similarly, since error is a predefined function of type String $\rightarrow$, and 0 is a primitive constant of type Integer, from the third equation we obtain

$$n \quad :: \quad Integer$$
$$fact \quad :: \quad Integer \rightarrow \alpha$$

Since the three equations define the same function, we must obtain a common type for fact. In other words, we need to add a constraint:

$$Integer \rightarrow \alpha = Integer \rightarrow Integer$$

The solution for this constraint is α = Integer, therefore the type of fact is

$$Integer \rightarrow Integer.$$

We give more examples of typing in Chap. 6 where we formally define the operational semantics and type system of a small language of recursive equations.

5.7 Data Structures and Data Type Definitions

In modern functional languages we can declare a new type by giving its name together with the *constructors* that are used to build the values in the type. These are *data constructors*, not to be confused with the type constructors mentioned in Definition 5.9. Data constructors may be monomorphic or polymorphic, and it is possible to define several constructors for a type. Moreover some of these constructors might use elements of the type being defined to build new elements. In the latter case we say that the type defines a *recursive* data structure.

We give examples of non-recursive data types first.

Example 5.12
We can define a type by enumerating its elements. A simple case is the type of Booleans, which is monomorphic and has only two constructors:
```
data Bool = True | False
```

The keyword `data` is used to introduce a type definition in Haskell. There is also a keyword `type`, which is used to give a new name to an existing type. For example, if we wanted to implement the abstract machine for **SIMP** using Haskell, we could decide to use strings to represent variable labels. Since the type string already exists in Haskell, we could define

```
type Label = String
```

Example 5.13
We can define new types to represent the abstract syntax of arithmetic expressions in **SIMP** (given in Sect 4.1). For instance, we could start by defining the types `Op` and `BOp` for the operators:

```
data Op = Plus | Minus | Mult | Div
data BOp = Sup | Inf | Equ
```

Here, the constructors correspond to the different operators available in **SIMP** $(+, -, *, /, >, <, =)$.

Any type with a finite number of values can be defined in this way. For example, we can define a type of colours, with seven constructors, as shown below.

Example 5.14
The following data type is used to represent colours.

```
data Colours = Red | Orange | Yellow | Green | Blue |
Indigo | Violet
```

We can now define functions on colours using pattern-matching. For instance, the function that given a colour indicates its composition in terms of primary colours (in art, these are red, blue and yellow) can be defined as follows:

```
decomposition :: Colours -> [Colours]
decomposition Violet = [Red, Blue]
decomposition Indigo = [Red, Blue]
decomposition Green = [Blue, Yellow]
decomposition Orange = [Red, Yellow]
decomposition x = [x]
```

We can apply the function `decomposition` to any colour. For example, the expression `decomposition Violet` gives the result `[Red,Blue]` and `decomposition Red` gives the result `[Red]`.

The definition by pattern-matching given above relies on the fact that patterns are considered in the order in which they appear in the program. If an argument for `decomposition` does not match any of the first four equations, then the fifth one will be used.

Data types can also be polymorphic, as the following example shows.

Example 5.15
In Haskell we have a type

```
data Maybe a = Nothing | Just a
```

where a is a type variable. `Nothing, Just 3`, and `Just 'b'` are values. The intuitive meaning of this definition is that an expression of type `Maybe a` is *either* `Nothing` *or* `Just x`, with x of type a.

We can then write a function by pattern-matching as follows

```
foo Nothing = 0
foo (Just n) = n
```

The inferred type for foo is Maybe Int -> Int.

This is useful to handle the case when a value may be undefined. For example, consider again the implementation of the abstract machine for SIMP: we could represent the memory as a function Label -> Int that maps variable labels to values. However, this is a partial function since some variables do not have a value in memory. In this case, we can use the Maybe type:

```
type Memory = Label -> Maybe Int.
```

If we ask for the value of an undefined variable, the result will be Nothing instead of generating an error, thus allowing the calling function to cleanly handle the problem.

A data type definition may be recursive. A well-known example is the set of natural numbers.

Example 5.16 (Natural Numbers)

We define the type Nat with two constructors: Zero and Succ. The latter takes an argument of type Nat (thus making the definition of the type recursive).

```
data Nat = Zero | Succ Nat
```

The following expressions are values of type Nat: Zero, Succ Zero, Succ (Succ Zero), ...

In this case the constructors are not polymorphic, but we can define types with polymorphic constructors in the same way, as in the following example.

Example 5.17 (Sequences)

The type of sequences can be defined as follows:

```
data Seq a = Empty | Cons a (Seq a)
```

The constructors are Empty and Cons. The latter takes two arguments, the first one is of type a (a type variable), and the second is a sequence of elements of the type a. This is a polymorphic type since a can be replaced by any type. For instance, we can define sequences of integers by instantiating a to Integer. The following expressions are values of type Seq Integer:

– Cons 3 Empty, a sequence containing just the element 3;
– Cons 3 (Cons 2 Empty), a sequence containing the elements 3 and 2.

The expression Cons 'a' (Cons 'b' Empty) has type Seq Char.

We can define functions on sequences using pattern-matching. For instance, the function that computes the number of elements in a sequence can be written as follows.

```
seqLength :: (Seq a) -> Integer
seqLength Empty = 0
seqLength (Cons x s) = 1 + (seqLength s)
```

As expected

```
seqLength(Cons 3 (Cons 2 Empty)) = 2
seqLength(Cons 'a' (Cons 'b' Empty)) = 2
```

The type of sequences defined above is isomorphic to the type of lists, which is predefined in most modern functional languages. In Haskell, the empty list is denoted by [], and a non-empty list has the form (h:l) where h is the first element of the list (i.e., the *head*), and l is the list of the remaining elements (the *tail* of the list). It is usual to write values of the predefined type list using a shorthand notation: we can simply enumerate the elements of the list between square brackets, e.g. [1,2,3,4] instead of 1:(2:(3:(4:[]))).

Example 5.18 (Transforming sequences into lists)

Any sequence can be transformed into a list (and vice-versa) simply by changing the constructors:

```
toList :: (Seq a) -> [a]
toList Empty = []
toList (Cons x s) = (x:(toList s))
toSeq :: [a] -> (Seq a)
toSeq [] = Empty
toSeq (x:l) = (Cons x (toSeq l))
```

As the examples above show, constructors are used to build data structures. What distinguishes a constructor from a function is that there is no definition associated with a constructor, and constructors can be used in patterns.

We give more examples of recursive data types below.

Example 5.19 (SIMP abstract syntax)

To represent the abstract syntax of expressions and commands in the language SIMP, we define a type for integer expressions (which we call IExpr), a type for Boolean expressions (which we call BExpr) and a type for commands (which we call Comm). The constructors in the definitions of the types are in one-to-one correspondence with the elements of the grammar given in Sect. 4.1.

```
data IExpr=NatNumber Int | Deref Label | Oper
IExpr Op IExpr
data BExpr=IF Bool | BOper IExpr BOp IExpr | Not
BExpr | And BExpr BExpr
data Comm=Skip | Assign Label IExpr | Seq Comm
Comm | IfThEl BExpr Comm Comm | While BExpr Comm
data Prog=C Comm | E IExpr | B BExpr
```

The definitions of the types for expressions and commands are recursive, as expected: they are derived directly from the grammar.

We end this section with some examples of higher-order functions. The first is a function on sequences, defined by pattern-matching, to filter the elements that satisfy a condition. The second is a recursive function that implements Newton's method to compute square roots.

Example 5.20 (Filter)

The function `seqfilter` extracts from a given sequence all the elements that satisfy a certain predicate[2]:

```
seqfilter : : (a -> Bool) -> (Seq a) -> (Seq a)
seqfilter p Empty = Empty
seqfilter p (Cons x s) =  if p x then (Cons x
(seqfilter p s))else (seqfilter p s)
```

Given a sequence of s of numbers, we can obtain all its even numbers by evaluating the expression

```
seqfilter even s
        where even n = (mod n 2) == 0
```

If we want the even numbers that are smaller than 100, we can write

```
seqfilter small (seqfilter even s)
        where small n = n < 100
```

or better

```
seqfilter smalleven s
        where smalleven n = (n < 100) && ((mod n 2) == 0)
```

Note that sequences can have an infinite number of elements. For instance, we can define the sequence of natural numbers:

```
nats = from 0
        where from n = Cons n (from (n+1))
```

Although we cannot expect to be able to build the sequence `nats` in finite time, we can still use this sequence in a lazy language such as Haskell. For instance, `toList (seqfilter smalleven nats)` is the list of all the even natural numbers smaller than 100, and using the predefined function `take` on lists we can extract the first n even numbers:

```
myevens n = take n (toList(seqfilter smalleven nats))
```

For example, the expression `myevens 10` evaluates to

```
[0,2,4,6,8,10,12,14,16,18].
```

Example 5.21 (Computing square roots)

The function `sqrt` computes the non-negative square root of a non-negative number. The mathematical specification is:

$$For \ x \geq 0 : (sqrt \ x) \geq 0 \ and \ square(sqrt \ x) = x$$

However, this requires working with real numbers (e.g., sqrt 2 = 1.41421...) We will weaken the specification to work with approximations. More precisely, we want to define a function

```
              sqrtN : : Float -> Float
```

such that

---

[2] `filter` is a predefined function on lists in most modern functional languages.

```
for x ≥  0 : (sqrtN x) ≥ 0 and (abs(square(sqrtN x) − x)) < eps
```

where `eps` is a suitable small number, greater than zero.

We will use Newton's method to compute the square root of x by successive approximations:

$$y_{n+1} = (y_n + x/y_n)/2$$

For example, to compute the square root of 2, starting from $y_0 = 2$, we get:

$y_0 = 2$

$y_1 = 1.5$

$y_2 = 1.4167$

$y_3 = 1.4142157$

$\vdots$

Therefore, if `eps` = 0.01, then y_2 is already a good approximation.

We can implement this method as follows:

```
sqrtN x = until  done improve x
           where
                until p f x = if p x then x
                                else until p f (f x);
                done y = (abs (y * y − x)) < 0.001;
                improve y = (y + x/y)/2
```

Here, the recursive, higher-order function `until` is used to improve the value, until it is within the accepted error range.

5.8 Reasoning About Programs

All the values in a recursive data type are built using the constructors indicated in the data type definition. For this reason, to prove universal properties about programs involving recursive data types we can use the Principle of Structural Induction described in Chap. 2.

In the case of the type `Nat` defined in Example 5.16, the Structural Induction Principle coincides with the Principle of Mathematical Induction:

To prove a property P for all the values of type `Nat` we have to

1. Prove $P(Zero)$. This is the basis of the induction.
2. Prove that if $P(n)$ holds then $P(Succ\ n)$ holds. This is the induction step.

Example 5.22 (Proving Properties of `Nat` Programs)

The following is a definition of addition on `Nat` by pattern-matching on the first argument:

```
add Zero x = x
add (Succ x) y = Succ (add x y)
```

1. We can prove by induction that Zero is a neutral element, that is, for every value n in Nat:

$$\text{add Zero } n = n = \text{add } n \text{ Zero}$$

The first equality, add Zero n = n, is part of the definition of add (it is the first equation). To prove n = add n Zero we use induction.

   (a) *Basis:* We obtain add Zero Zero = Zero directly, using the definition of add.
   (b) *Induction:* By definition of add:

$$\text{add (Succ } n) \text{ Zero} = \text{Succ (add } n \text{ Zero)}$$

   and the latter is equal to Succ n as required, using the induction hypothesis.

2. We can also prove that add is commutative, that is, for every n and m in Nat:

$$\text{add } n \text{ } m = \text{add } m \text{ } n$$

We proceed by induction on n:

   (a) *Basis:* Since we have just proved that Zero is a neutral element,

$$\text{add Zero } m = \text{add } m \text{ Zero} = m.$$

   (b) *Induction:* By definition of add:

$$\text{add (Succ } n) \text{ } m = \text{Succ (add } n \text{ } m)$$

   and by the induction hypothesis,

$$\text{Succ (add } n \text{ } m) = \text{Succ (add } m \text{ } n).$$

   Using the second equation in the definition of add (from right to left!) we obtain Succ (add m n) = add (Succ m) n. To finish the proof we need a lemma:

$$\text{add (Succ } m) \text{ } n = \text{add } m \text{ (Succ } n)$$

   which we will also prove by induction (on m):
   i. *Basis:* Note that

$$\text{add (Succ Zero) } n = \text{Succ (add Zero } n) = \text{Succ } n,$$

   and also add Zero (Succ n) = Succ n, using the equations in the definition of add.

ii. *Induction:* We have to prove that

$$\text{add (Succ (Succ m)) n} = \text{add (Succ m) (Succ n)}.$$

Using the second equation for add:

$$\text{add (Succ (Succ m)) n} = \text{Succ (add (Succ m) n)}$$

and we can now apply the induction hypothesis:

$$\text{Succ (add (Succ m) n)} = \text{Succ (add m (Succ n))}$$

and again use the second equation for add:

$$\text{Succ (add m (Succ n))} = \text{add (Succ m) (Succ n)},$$

which completes the proof.

5.9 Further Reading

Bird's book [4] gives a nice introduction to functional programming, without assuming any previous knowledge. Readers interested in functional programming techniques can find detailed descriptions in [3, 5], amongst others.

The theoretical foundations of functional programming languages can be traced back to the work done by Alonzo Church on abstract computation models. Church's λ-calculus can be seen as the abstract model of computation underlying functional programming languages such as LISP, Scheme, ML and Haskell. More information on the λ-calculus can be found in [6]. Barendregt's book [7] is a comprehensive reference.

The polymorphic type system used in the languages of the ML family, which is also the basis for Haskell's system, is based on the ideas introduced independently by Hindley and Milner in the 1960s and 1970s. The first type inference algorithm, called algorithm W, was presented in [8] (see also [2]). For more details about the implementation of functional programming languages and type inference algorithms, see [9, 10]; more advanced readers can refer to [11, 12].

More examples of the use of induction to prove properties of functional programs can be found in [4].

5.10 Exercises

1. Define, using a syntax similar to Haskell's,

    (a) a function min and a function max to compute the minimum and the maximum of two numbers, respectively;

(b) a function `fibonacci` that takes a natural number n as input and gives the nth Fibonacci number as a result. Fibonacci numbers are generated by the recursive equation:

$$Fib_n = Fib_{n-1} + Fib_{n-2}, \text{ with } Fib_0 = 0 \text{ and } Fib_1 = 1.$$

2. Write the definitions of `quad` (the function that computes the 4th power of a number), and `double` (the function that doubles its argument). Describe the reduction sequences for the expression:

$$\text{quad (double } (3+1))$$

using the call-by-name (normal order) and the call-by-value (applicative order) strategies.

3. What happens if we try to evaluate the expression

```
take 10 (toList (seqfilter smalleven nats))
```

mentioned at the end of Example 5.20, in a language that uses a call-by-value strategy?

Write a functional program to list the first n even numbers assuming a call-by-value evaluation strategy will be used.

4. (a) Assume the function `mult` on natural numbers is defined by

```
mult x y = if (x == 0) then 0 else x * y
```

where `==` is the equality test. Assume that $e_1 == e_2$ is evaluated by reducing e_1 and e_2 to normal form, and then comparing the normal forms.

Is `mult` commutative?

(b) Let `infinity` be the function defined by

```
infinity = infinity + 1
```

What is the value of `mult infinity 0`?

And `mult 0 infinity`?

5. What is the type of `until` in Example 5.21?

6. Imperative languages have pre-test and post-test loops, such as *while B do C* and *do C while B*. Both can be simulated in a functional language using recursion.

(a) Write a recursive function `while-do` that takes as arguments:
   - a predicate b of type $\alpha \rightarrow$ `Bool`,
   - a function c of type $\alpha \rightarrow \alpha$ and

- an element x of type α.

If x does not satisfy b then the result should be x, otherwise, `while-do` iterates the function c on x until a value x' is obtained which does not satisfy b.

(b) Write a recursive function `do-while` to simulate a post-test loop. This function takes the same arguments as the function `while-do`, and it also iterates the function c on x until a value x' is obtained which does not satisfy b, but the test is performed after the application of c. Therefore, even if the given x does not satisfy b, the function c will be applied at least once.

(c) Give a polymorphic type for `while-do` and `do-while`.

7. Consider the following functional program:

```
apply f x = f x
```

(a) Give a polymorphic type for the function `apply`.
(b) We define now a function `selfapply` as follows.

```
selfapply f = f f
```

Can Haskell find a type for the function `selfapply`?

8. Give a recursive definition of the function g such that

$$g\,n = \sum_{i=1}^{n} i$$

and prove by induction that, for any natural number n,

$$g\,n = n(n+1)/2$$

9. In Haskell we can define the type of polymorphic stacks as follows:

```
data Stack a = Empty | Push a (Stack a)
```

Write the usual functions `peek` and `pop` on stacks (peek gives the first element in the stack and pop eliminates the first element). Give a polymorphic type declaration for each function.

10. (†) Write an implementation of the transition function for the abstract machine defined for SIMP in Chap. 4, using the data types already defined for expressions and commands (see Example 5.19). To represent the control and results stacks, use the types:

```
data Control = P Prog | O Op | CAssign | CIf | CWhile
| CNot | CAnd | BO BOp
```

```
data Result = RP Prog | RL Label

type ControlStack = [Control]

type ResultStack = [Result]
```

For the memory, use the type already described (see Example 5.15).

```
type Memory = Label -> Maybe Int
```

Configurations have the type `State`:

```
type State = (ControlStack,ResultStack,Memory)
```

11. (†) A beginner Haskell programmer wrote the following program to add all the elements in a sequence of numbers:

```
sum Empty = 0

sum (Cons x s) = sum s
```

Even though there was no type error message, seeing the type that Haskell had inferred the programmer immediately realised that there was a bug in the program. Can you explain why?

References

1. G. Sussman, G. Steele, Scheme: an interpreter for extended lambda calculus. MIT AI Memo **349** (1975)
2. R. Milner, A theory of type polymorphism in programming. J. Comput. Syst. Sci. **17** (1978)
3. G. Cousineau, M. Mauny, *The Functional Approach to Programming* (Cambridge University Press, 1998)
4. R. Bird, *Introduction to Functional Programming Using Haskell* (Prentice-Hall, 1998)
5. S. Thompson, *The Craft of Functional Programming* (Addison-Wesley, 1999)
6. C. Hankin, *An Introduction to Lambda Calculi for Computer Scientists, volume 2 of Texts in Computing* (King's College Publications, 2004)
7. H.P. Barendregt, *The Lambda Calculus: Its Syntax and Semantics*, Revised edition. (North-Holland, 1984)
8. L.M.M. Damas, R. Milner, Principal type schemes for functional programs, in *Conference Record of the Ninth Annual ACM Symposium on the Principles of Programming Languages* (1982), pp. 207–212
9. J.C. Mitchell, *Concepts in Programming Languages* (Cambridge University Press, 2003)
10. B.C. Pierce, *Types and Programming Languages* (MIT Press, 2002)
11. S.L.P. Jones, *The Implementation of Functional Programming Languages* (Prentice-Hall, 1987)
12. P. Sestoft, *Programming Language Concepts*. Undergraduate topics in computer science (Springer, Berlin, 2012)

Chapter 6
Operational Semantics of Functional Languages

In this chapter, we will give a precise, formal description of the main features of functional programming languages. For this we will use the same tools that we applied in the study of the operational semantics of imperative languages in Chap. 4: *transition systems*.

In order to isolate the important issues in the semantics of functional languages and avoid irrelevant details, we will define a small functional programming language working on integers and Booleans, called **SFUN**.

Programs in **SFUN** are simply sets of recursive equations; each equation defines a function, using variables, numbers, Booleans, operations on numbers and Booleans (including a conditional), and other functions.

We will first define the (abstract) syntax of **SFUN**, and give a type system to filter out programs that are syntactically correct but contain type errors. We will use axioms and rules to specify the typing relation. Then we will give two alternative definitions of the operational semantics of **SFUN**, using the Structural Operational Semantics approach. More precisely, assuming programs are well-typed, we specify an evaluation relation between well-typed terms and values (integers and Booleans) using first a call-by-value strategy, which we then modify to obtain a call-by-name language.

Finally, we will extend the language **SFUN** in two ways: we will include a `let` construct, which will allow us to write local definitions in expressions and programs, and we will consider higher-order function definitions, that is, functions that take functional values as inputs or produce a function as output. We will show how the type system and the operational semantics can be extended to deal with this general class of programs.

6.1 Abstract Syntax of SFUN

Since our goal is to provide a formal specification of the operational semantics of **SFUN** programs, from now on we will only consider **SFUN** programs that are syntactically correct. We will not define a concrete syntax for **SFUN**, instead, we

M. Fernández, *Programming Languages and Operational Semantics*,
Undergraduate Topics in Computer Science, DOI: 10.1007/978-1-4471-6368-8_6,
© Springer-Verlag London 2014

assume that a parser is available to transform syntactically correct programs into abstract syntax trees and simply give below the definition of the abstract syntax trees that are used to represent SFUN programs (see Chap. 1 for definitions and properties of concrete and abstract syntax).

To define the abstract syntax of SFUN, we assume that the lexical analyser produces tokens representing numbers and Boolean values (n and b respectively), and variables (we assume that a set $\mathcal{V}$ of variables $\{x, y, z, x_1, x_2, \ldots\}$ is used). In addition, we use a set $\mathcal{F}$ of function symbols $\{f_1, \ldots, f_k\}$ with fixed arities. Functions will be defined in SFUN programs by means of recursive equations. The arity of a function corresponds to the number of arguments it takes. For instance, the function $\neg$, which will be used for negation on Booleans is unary, whereas $\wedge$ (and) is binary. In general, we assume that the arity of f_i, denoted by $ar(f_i)$, is $a_i \geq 0$.

Definition 6.1 (SFUN terms)

The abstract syntax trees used to represent expressions in the language SFUN will be called *terms*. They are defined by the grammar:

$$t ::= n \mid b \mid x \mid t_1 \; op \; t_2 \mid t_1 \; bop \; t_2 \mid \neg t_1 \mid t_1 \wedge t_2 \mid$$
$$\text{if } t_0 \text{ then } t_1 \text{ else } t_2 \mid f_i(t_1, \ldots, t_{a_i})$$
$$op ::= + \mid - \mid * \mid /$$
$$bop ::= > \mid < \mid =$$

where

- n represents integer numbers (constants), we will refer to n simply as a number;
- b represents Boolean values ($True$, $False$), we will refer to b simply as a Boolean;
- x represents variables in $\mathcal{V}$; and
- f_i denotes a function, to be defined in a program.

Note that for terms of the form $f_i(t_1, \ldots, t_{a_i})$, a_i could be 0, in which case we will omit the brackets and write just f_i.

We emphasise that the grammar above is defining the abstract syntax of the language, therefore the expressions in the grammar rules should be understood as labelled *trees*. The leaf nodes are labelled by numbers, Booleans, variables and 0-ary function symbols. Non-leaf nodes are labelled by function symbols of arity greater than 0, by arithmetic or Boolean operators, or by if-then-else (which can be seen as a primitive function symbol of arity 3).

Example 6.2

The following are examples of terms in SFUN.

- $2 * 3$ is a term, and so is $(2 * 3) + 4$. Note that these are string representations of the corresponding syntax trees; we use brackets to avoid ambiguities.
- If $ar(f_1) = 0$ then f_1 is a term, and so is $f_1 + 1$.

- $x > 0$ is a term, and if $ar(f_2) = ar(f_3) = 1$ then

$$\text{if } x > 0 \text{ then } f_2(x) \text{ else } f_3(x)$$

is a term.

We can now define programs in SFUN. Programs are used to define functions, by giving an equation for each function symbol $f_1, \ldots, f_k$. In the definition below, we will use the notation $Var(t)$ to represent the variables that occur in the term t. For instance, $Var(x) = \{x\}$, $Var(f_1(y, z)) = \{y, z\}$. If a term does not contain any occurrences of variables, we say that it is *closed*. For example, $f_2(True)$ is a closed term and so is $f_1 + 2$, but $x > 0$ is not closed.

Definition 6.3 (SFUN Program)

A program in SFUN is a set of equations of the form:

$$f_1(x_1, \ldots, x_{a_1}) = t_1$$
$$\vdots$$
$$f_k(x_1, \ldots, x_{a_k}) = t_k$$

such that

- $t_1, \ldots, t_k$ are terms;
- for each t_i $(1 \le i \le k)$, $Var(t_i) \subseteq \{x_1, \ldots, x_{a_i}\}$;
- there is only one equation $f_i(x_1, \ldots, x_{a_i}) = t_i$ for each function f_i (where $1 \le i \le k$).

The equations may be recursive, the terms t_i might contain occurrences of $f_1, \ldots, f_k$.

Example 6.4

The following program P defines three functions, the first one has arity 0 and is recursive, the others are unary and non-recursive.

$$f_1 = f_1 + 1$$
$$f_2(x) = 1$$
$$f_3(x) = x * x$$

The function *factorial* can be defined in SFUN with one recursive equation, as follows:

$$\text{fact}(x) = \text{if } x = 0 \text{ then } 1 \text{ else } x * \text{fact}(x - 1)$$

Comparing the syntax of function definitions in SFUN and the syntax *à la* Haskell that we used in the previous chapter, we notice that several simplifications have been made:

- patterns in SFUN are restricted to variables, therefore one equation is enough for each function;
- every function in SFUN works on tuples (with zero or more elements), there is no Curryfication;
- there are no local definitions in SFUN.

In the rest of this chapter, when we talk about "a SFUN program" or "a SFUN expression", we will always mean "an abstract syntax tree representing a SFUN program (resp. a SFUN expression)".

6.2 A Type System for SFUN

The grammar defining the syntax of SFUN allows us to build terms such as $5 \wedge True$, which does not make sense if $\wedge$ is the Boolean "and" operator. To filter out expressions that are syntactically correct but will produce type errors at run time, programming languages use *type systems*. As mentioned in Chap. 3, some languages check types before the execution of the program (i.e., at compile time; these languages have *static* type systems), while other languages check types at run time (using *dynamic* type systems).

We will now define a type system for SFUN, which will be used to statically check terms and programs. Our goal is to obtain a *strongly typed* language, that is, a language in which every typeable term can be successfully evaluated. In other words, the type system should ensure that type errors cannot arise during the evaluation of well-typed terms.

Definition 6.5 (SFUN Types)

The set of *types* for SFUN is defined by the following grammar:

$$bt ::= \text{int} \mid \text{bool}$$
$$\tau ::= bt \mid (bt_1, \ldots, bt_n) \to bt$$

The first rule in the grammar defines the basic types (int for integers and bool for Booleans). There is only one type constructor in SFUN, the arrow, written infix, which builds function types. In the last rule, $n > 0$. A type of the form $(bt_1, \ldots, bt_n) \to bt$ is interpreted as the type of a function that takes n arguments of types $bt_1, \ldots, bt_n$ and gives a result of type bt. If $n = 1$ we will omit the brackets and simply write $bt_1 \to bt$.

Terms may contain variables, so to type terms we need information about the types of the variables. We will type terms in a *variable environment*, which provides type assumptions for variables.

Definition 6.6 (Well-Typed Terms)

The set of *well-typed terms* will be defined using a relation between terms, types and variable environments, written:

$$\Gamma \vdash_\varepsilon t : \tau$$

where

- Γ is a *variable environment* or simply an environment, associating variables with types. More precisely, Γ is a finite partial function from variables to types (that is, there is at most one type for each variable). We represent it as a list $x_1 : \sigma_1, \ldots, x_n : \sigma_n$ of pairs of variables and types, such that $\Gamma(x_i) = \sigma_i$.
- ε is a *function environment* assigning a type to each function, respecting its arity: If $arity(f_i) = a_i$ then $\varepsilon(f_i) = (\sigma_1, \ldots, \sigma_{a_i}) \to \sigma$.
- t is a SFUN term.
- τ is a SFUN type.

The relation $\Gamma \vdash_\varepsilon t : \tau$ can be read as: *The term t has type τ under the assumptions in Γ and ε.* That is, assuming that each variable x in $dom(\Gamma)$ has type $\Gamma(x)$, and the functions $f_1, \ldots, f_k$ have types $\varepsilon(f_1), \ldots, \varepsilon(f_k)$, then the term t has type τ.

This relation is inductively defined by the system of axioms and rules shown in Fig. 6.1.

The axioms (or more precisely, axiom schemes) (n) and (b), simply specify that number tokens have type int and Boolean tokens have type bool, in any environment. The axiom for variables, (var), assigns to x the type associated with x in the given environment Γ.

There is one rule for each arithmetic and comparison operator, requiring the arguments to be of type int, as expected. These rules are represented by the rule schemes (op) and (bop) in Fig. 6.1, where the operators *op* and *bop* are defined by the grammar in Definition 6.1.

We also have rules to type terms with a Boolean operator at the root (rules (and) and (not)); these require the arguments to be of type bool as expected.

The rule to type conditional expressions, called (if) in Fig. 6.1, specifies that the condition in an if-then-else must be of type bool and both of the alternative expressions must be of the same type.

Finally, the rule scheme (fn) specifies how to type function applications $f_i(t_1, \ldots, t_{a_i})$. The function environment ε is used in this rule to check that the types of the actual arguments $t_1, \ldots, t_{a_i}$ are compatible with the type given for the function in the environment ε. The type of the expression $f_i(t_1, \ldots, t_{a_i})$ is the type declared in ε as output for f_i. So, if f has been declared to be of type (int, bool) $\to$ int, then f must be applied to two arguments of type int and bool, respectively, and the result of the application will be of type int. More generally, the rule says that if f_i is a function of arity a_i and the type declared for f_i in ε is $(\sigma_1, \ldots, \sigma_{a_i}) \to \sigma$ then each each t_i must have type σ_i and the type of the result is σ.

We will assume that the types for all the functions in a SFUN program are declared by the programmer, so the environment ε is always given (instead of inferring the

Axioms:

$$\frac{}{\Gamma \vdash_\varepsilon b: \text{bool}} \text{(b)} \qquad \frac{}{\Gamma \vdash_\varepsilon n: \text{int}} \text{(n)}$$

$$\frac{}{\Gamma \vdash_\varepsilon x: \sigma} \text{(var)} \quad \text{if } \Gamma(x) = \sigma$$

Rules:

$$\frac{\Gamma \vdash_\varepsilon t_1: \text{int} \quad \Gamma \vdash_\varepsilon t_2: \text{int}}{\Gamma \vdash_\varepsilon t_1 \ op \ t_2: \text{int}} \text{(op)}$$

$$\frac{\Gamma \vdash_\varepsilon t_1: \text{int} \quad \Gamma \vdash_\varepsilon t_2: \text{int}}{\Gamma \vdash_\varepsilon t_1 \ bop \ t_2: \text{bool}} \text{(bop)}$$

$$\frac{\Gamma \vdash_\varepsilon t_1: \text{bool} \quad \Gamma \vdash_\varepsilon t_2: \text{bool}}{\Gamma \vdash_\varepsilon t_1 \wedge t_2: \text{bool}} \text{(and)} \qquad \frac{\Gamma \vdash_\varepsilon t: \text{bool}}{\Gamma \vdash_\varepsilon \neg t: \text{bool}} \text{(not)}$$

$$\frac{\Gamma \vdash_\varepsilon t_0: \text{bool} \quad \Gamma \vdash_\varepsilon t_1: \sigma \quad \Gamma \vdash_\varepsilon t_2: \sigma}{\Gamma \vdash_\varepsilon \text{if } t_0 \text{ then } t_1 \text{ else } t_2: \sigma} \text{(if)}$$

$$\frac{\Gamma \vdash_\varepsilon t_1: \sigma_1 \quad \cdots \quad \Gamma \vdash_\varepsilon t_{a_i}: \sigma_{a_i}}{\Gamma \vdash_\varepsilon f_i(t_1, \ldots, t_{a_i}): \sigma} \text{(fn)} \quad \text{if } \varepsilon(f_i) = (\sigma_1, \ldots, \sigma_{a_i}) \to \sigma$$

Fig. 6.1 Typing SFUN terms

types of functions, we use the types declared by the programmer). However, for variables we will not require type declarations: the variable environment Γ could be inferred.

We will say that a term t is *typeable* if there is an environment Γ and a type σ such that $\Gamma \vdash_\varepsilon t : \sigma$ can be derived using the axioms and rules given in Fig. 6.1.

Example 6.7

We give several examples of typeable terms below.

1. The term $x * x$ is typeable, with type int, in any environment that associates the variable x with the type int. The following is a type derivation for this term, using the axioms and rules in Fig. 6.1.

$$\frac{\dfrac{}{x: \text{int} \vdash_\varepsilon x: \text{int}} \text{(var)} \qquad \dfrac{}{x: \text{int} \vdash_\varepsilon x: \text{int}} \text{(var)}}{x: \text{int} \vdash_\varepsilon x * x: \text{int}} \text{(op)}$$

2. Assuming we have a function environment ε where $\varepsilon(f_1) = \text{int}$, the term $f_1 + 1$ is typeable (with type int). In particular, this term is typeable in an empty variable environment since it is closed (no assumptions for variables are needed). We can prove it as follows.

$$\cfrac{\cfrac{}{\vdash_\varepsilon f_1 : \text{int}} \text{(fn)} \quad \cfrac{}{\vdash_\varepsilon 1 : \text{int}} \text{(n)}}{\vdash_\varepsilon f_1 + 1 : \text{int}} \text{(op)}$$

3. The term $x * \text{fact}(x - 1)$ is typeable under the assumption $x : \text{int}$ in a function environment ε such that $\varepsilon(\text{fact}) = \text{int} \rightarrow \text{int}$. First we show that $\text{fact}(x - 1)$ is typeable:

$$\cfrac{\cfrac{\cfrac{}{x : \text{int} \vdash_\varepsilon x : \text{int}} \text{(var)} \quad \cfrac{}{x : \text{int} \vdash_\varepsilon 1 : \text{int}} \text{(n)}}{x : \text{int} \vdash_\varepsilon x - 1 : \text{int}} \text{(op)}}{x : \text{int} \vdash_\varepsilon \text{fact}(x - 1) : \text{int}} \text{(fn)}$$

Since x is trivially typeable under the assumption $x : \text{int}$ (using axiom (var)), then using the rule (op) we obtain:

$$x : \text{int} \vdash_\varepsilon x * \text{fact}(x - 1) : \text{int}$$

4. The term

$$\text{if } x = 0 \text{ then } 1 \text{ else } x * \text{fact}(x - 1)$$

is typeable if $\varepsilon(\text{fact}) = \text{int} \rightarrow \text{int}$ and $\Gamma(x) = \text{int}$. First we show that $x = 0$ is typeable in the environment $x : \text{int}$.

$$\cfrac{\cfrac{}{x : \text{int} \vdash_\varepsilon x : \text{int}} \text{(var)} \quad \cfrac{}{x : \text{int} \vdash_\varepsilon 0 : \text{int}} \text{(n)}}{x : \text{int} \vdash_\varepsilon x = 0 : \text{bool}} \text{(bop)}$$

We have also shown (above) that $x * \text{fact}(x - 1)$ is typeable in the same environment, and using the axiom (n) we can derive:

$$x : \text{int} \vdash_\varepsilon 1 : \text{int}$$

Therefore, we can use the rule (if) to obtain a type derivation for our initial term:

$$\cfrac{x : \text{int} \vdash_\varepsilon x = 0 : \text{bool} \quad x : \text{int} \vdash_\varepsilon 1 : \text{int} \quad x : \text{int} \vdash_\varepsilon x * \text{fact}(x - 1) : \text{int}}{x : \text{int} \vdash_\varepsilon \text{if } x = 0 \text{ then } 1 \text{ else } x * \text{fact}(x - 1) : \text{int}} \text{(if)}$$

Programs in **SFUN** will be type-checked to ensure that each function definition is compatible with the type declared for the function in the environment ε: both sides of each equation should have the same type.

Definition 6.8 (Typing SFUN Programs)

A program P in **SFUN**:

$$f_1(x_1, \ldots, x_{a_1}) = t_1$$

$$\vdots$$

$$f_k(x_1, \ldots, x_{a_k}) = t_k$$

is *typeable* in the function environment ε if for each equation $f_i(x_1, \ldots, x_{a_i}) = t_i$ there is a type τ_i and an environment Γ_i containing type assumptions for $x_1, \ldots, x_{a_i}$ such that

$$\Gamma_i \vdash_\varepsilon f_i(x_1, \ldots, x_{a_i}) : \tau_i \quad \text{and} \quad \Gamma_i \vdash_\varepsilon t_i : \tau_i.$$

Example 6.9

We give examples of typeable programs below.

1. The program P of Example 6.4:

$$f_1 = f_1 + 1$$

$$f_2(x) = 1$$

$$f_3(x) = x * x$$

is typeable in an environment ε where

$$\varepsilon(f_1) = \text{int}$$

$$\varepsilon(f_2) = \text{int} \rightarrow \text{int}$$

$$\varepsilon(f_3) = \text{int} \rightarrow \text{int}$$

To prove that P is correctly typed, we must type-check each equation.

The left-hand side of the first equation is the term f_1 of type int; in our system this is written

$$\vdash_\varepsilon f_1 : \text{int}.$$

The right-hand side is the term $f_1 + 1$, which also has type int (see Example 6.7, where we proved $\vdash_\varepsilon f_1 + 1 : \text{int}$). Therefore the first equation is well-typed.

Similarly, we can show that the second equation type-checks: using the axiom (var) and the rule (fn) we obtain $x :$ int $\vdash_\varepsilon f_2(x) :$ int, and using the axiom (n) we obtain $x :$ int $\vdash_\varepsilon 1 :$ int.

To see that the third equation is correctly typed, recall that

$x :$ int $\vdash_\varepsilon x * x :$ int (see Example 6.7),

and given $\varepsilon(f_3) =$ int $\to$ int we can easily deduce $x :$ int $\vdash_\varepsilon f_3(x) :$ int.
2. The program

$$\mathtt{fact}(x) = \mathtt{if}\, x = 0 \,\mathtt{then}\, 1 \,\mathtt{else}\, x * \mathtt{fact}(x - 1)$$

is typeable if $\varepsilon(\mathtt{fact}) =$ int $\to$ int: we have already proved (see Example 6.7) that
$$x :\, \mathsf{int} \vdash_\varepsilon \mathtt{if}\, x = 0 \,\mathtt{then}\, 1 \,\mathtt{else}\, x * \mathtt{fact}(x - 1):\, \mathsf{int}$$

and we obtain $x :$ int $\vdash_\varepsilon \mathtt{fact}(x) :$ int using rule (fn) and axiom (var).

The type system of SFUN is syntax-directed: the form of the term indicates the rules that need to be applied in order to type-check it. It also has the property of *unicity of types*: there is at most one type for a given term t in a given Γ and ε.

Property 6.10 (Unicity of Types)

For any SFUN term t, variable environment Γ and function environment ε, if $\Gamma \vdash_\varepsilon t : \sigma$ and $\Gamma \vdash_\varepsilon t : \tau$ then $\sigma = \tau$.

We can prove this property by induction (see Exercise 6 at the end of this chapter).

This property indicates that the system is monomorphic. In order to define a polymorphic type system, we can include type variables in the definition of types and generalise the typing rules so that functions could be applied to arguments with types that are instances of the types declared in the environment. We will not develop the system further in this direction, instead, in Sect. 6.4 we will extend it in order to type additional language constructs.

6.3 Operational Semantics of SFUN

In this section we assume that programs and terms are well-typed. We will give two alternative definitions for the semantics of SFUN: first we will model a *call-by-value* evaluation strategy (also called *applicative order* of reduction), then we will modify the transition system to follow a *call-by-name* strategy (*normal order* of reduction).

First, note that open terms do not have a meaning in themselves, since they contain variables whose values are not defined. Also, it is clear that we cannot give a meaning to SFUN terms in isolation. We need to take into account the program, which gives meanings to the function symbols that appear in terms. We will therefore define the semantics of *closed* terms in the context of a given program P:

$$f_1(x_1, \ldots, x_{a_1}) = d_1$$
$$\vdots$$
$$f_k(x_1, \ldots, x_{a_k}) = d_k$$

We will specify two *evaluation relations* for closed terms in SFUN. In other words, we will define two alternative *big-step semantics* for the language SFUN. In both cases *configurations* will simply be terms, and values will be constants (numbers and Booleans). The evaluation relations will be denoted by $\Downarrow_P^V$ and $\Downarrow_P^N$, respectively, to emphasise the fact that the value of a term depends on the given program P and the strategy that we follow: call-by-value for $\Downarrow_P^V$ and call-by-name for $\Downarrow_P^N$.

6.3.1 Call-by-Value Semantics of SFUN

In Fig. 6.2 we give an inductive definition, using a set of axioms and rules, of the evaluation relation $\Downarrow_P^V$ for a given SFUN program P. The expression $t \Downarrow_P^V v$ can be read as "the term t evaluates to v under the call-by-value strategy using the program P".

In SFUN, the basic terms represented by n and b (integer and Boolean constants) are already values, as the axioms (n) and (b) indicate.

The rules (op) and (bop) for arithmetic and Boolean operators are standard.

We have two rules for if-then-else terms, because depending on the value of the condition we need to evaluate either the then branch or the else branch.

The rule (fn) indicates how function applications are evaluated, and it is here that we see that a call-by-value strategy is in place: the arguments of the function are evaluated first, and then the definition of the function is used (d_i is the right-hand side of the equation that defines f_i in the program P). Note that the formal arguments in the equation are replaced with the values of the actual arguments. We use the notation $d_i\{x_1 \mapsto v_1, \ldots, x_{a_i} \mapsto v_{a_i}\}$ to represent the term obtained after replacing (simultaneously) in d_i each occurrence of x_1 by v_1, x_2 by v_2, etc. For example, if a function f is defined by the equation $f(x) = 2 * x$, then to evaluate $f(5)$ using rule (fn) we need to find the value of $2 * x\{x \mapsto 5\}$, that is, evaluate $2 * 5$.

Again, we observe that the system is syntax-directed: given a term to evaluate (i.e., a labelled syntax tree), the labels in the tree indicate the rules or axioms that should be applied.

We now give some examples of evaluation.

Example 6.11

First we evaluate terms with respect to the program P consisting of the three equations:

$$\frac{}{n \Downarrow_P^V n} \text{ (n)} \qquad \frac{}{b \Downarrow_P^V b} \text{ (b)}$$

$$\frac{t_1 \Downarrow_P^V n_1 \quad t_2 \Downarrow_P^V n_2}{t_1 \; op \; t_2 \Downarrow_P^V n \quad \text{if } n = (n_1 \; op \; n_2)} \text{ (op)}$$

$$\frac{t_1 \Downarrow_P^V n_1 \quad t_2 \Downarrow_P^V n_2}{t_1 \; bop \; t_2 \Downarrow_P^V b \quad \text{if } b = (n_1 \; bop \; n_2)} \text{ (bop)}$$

$$\frac{t_1 \Downarrow_P^V b_1 \quad t_2 \Downarrow_P^V b_2}{t_1 \wedge t_2 \Downarrow_P^V b \quad \text{if } b = (b_1 \; and \; b_2)} \text{ (and)} \qquad \frac{t \Downarrow_P^V b}{\neg t \Downarrow_P^V b' \quad \text{if } b' = not \; b} \text{ (not)}$$

$$\frac{t_0 \Downarrow_P^V True \quad t_1 \Downarrow_P^V v_1}{\text{if } t_0 \text{ then } t_1 \text{ else } t_2 \Downarrow_P^V v_1} \text{ (If}_T)$$

$$\frac{t_0 \Downarrow_P^V False \quad t_2 \Downarrow_P^V v_2}{\text{if } t_0 \text{ then } t_1 \text{ else } t_2 \Downarrow_P^V v_2} \text{ (If}_F)$$

$$\frac{t_1 \Downarrow_P^V v_1 \quad \cdots \quad t_{a_i} \Downarrow_P^V v_{a_i} \quad d_i\{x_1 \mapsto v_1, \ldots, x_{a_i} \mapsto v_{a_i}\} \Downarrow_P^V v}{f_i(t_1, \ldots, t_{a_i}) \Downarrow_P^V v} \text{ (fn)}$$

Fig. 6.2 Call-by-value evaluation

$$f_1 = f_1 + 1$$
$$f_2(x) = 1$$
$$f_3(x) = x * x$$

1. The term $f_2(0)$ has the value 1, more precisely: $f_2(0) \Downarrow_P^V 1$. This can be shown as follows, using the axioms and rules in Fig. 6.2:

$$\frac{\dfrac{}{0 \Downarrow_P^V 0} \text{ (n)} \quad \dfrac{}{1\{x \mapsto 0\} \Downarrow_P^V 1} \text{ (n)}}{f_2(0) \Downarrow_P^V 1} \text{ (fn)}$$

2. With the same program, the term $f_2(f_1)$ does not have a value: there is no v such that $f_2(f_1) \Downarrow_P^V v$. This is because to evaluate $f_2(f_1)$ we must use rule **(fn)**, which requires the evaluation of f_1 first. But to find a value for f_1 we must use again rule **(fn)**, which requires a value for $f_1 + 1$, leading to an infinite evaluation process.

3. With the same program, $f_3(2 + 1)$ has the value 9. This is shown as follows:

$$\cfrac{\cfrac{}{2 \Downarrow_P^V 2}\text{(n)} \quad \cfrac{}{1 \Downarrow_P^V 1}\text{(n)}}{\cfrac{2 + 1 \Downarrow_P^V 3}{}}\text{(op)} \qquad \cfrac{\cfrac{}{3 \Downarrow_P^V 3}\text{(n)} \quad \cfrac{}{3 \Downarrow_P^V 3}\text{(n)}}{x * x\{x \mapsto 3\} \Downarrow_P^V 9}\text{(op)}$$
$$\cfrac{}{f_3(2 + 1) \Downarrow_P^V 9}\text{(fn)}$$

Example 6.12

In the previous chapter we gave an informal description of call-by-value and call-by-name evaluation, and showed an evaluation sequence for (fact 0), obtaining the value 1 (see Sect. 5.2). Using the SFUN program P defining the factorial function

$$\texttt{fact}(x) = \texttt{if } x = 0 \texttt{ then } 1 \texttt{ else } x * \texttt{fact}(x - 1)$$

we can prove that fact(0) evaluates to 1 under call-by-value:

$$\cfrac{\cfrac{}{0 \Downarrow_P^V 0}\text{(n)}}{} \quad \cfrac{\cfrac{\cfrac{}{0 \Downarrow_P^V 0}\text{(n)} \quad \cfrac{}{0 \Downarrow_P^V 0}\text{(n)}}{0 = 0 \Downarrow_P^V True}\text{(bop)} \quad \cfrac{}{1 \Downarrow_P^V 1}\text{(n)}}{\texttt{if } 0 = 0 \texttt{ then } 1 \texttt{ else } 0 * \texttt{fact}(0 - 1) \Downarrow_P^V 1}\text{(If}_\mathsf{T}\text{)}}{\texttt{fact}(0) \Downarrow_P^V 1}\text{(fn)}$$

6.3.2 Properties of SFUN

First of all we remark that the operational semantics of SFUN and the type system are consistent: the evaluation relation preserves types.

Property 6.13 (Type Preservation)

If t is a closed term of type σ in SFUN, and $t \Downarrow_P^V v$, then v is a value of type σ.

This property (also called Subject Reduction) can be proved by rule induction. The proof is left as an exercise (see Exercise 7 at the end of this chapter). It relies on the following substitution lemma (for the case of function application), which states that in any typeable term, it is safe to replace a variable of type σ with a closed term of type σ.

Lemma 6.14 (Substitution Lemma)

If $x_1 : \sigma_1, \ldots, x_n : \sigma_n \vdash_\varepsilon t : \tau$ and $t_1, \ldots, t_n$ are closed terms such that $\vdash_\varepsilon t_i : \sigma_i$ for $1 \leq i \leq n$, then $\vdash_\varepsilon t\{x_i \mapsto t_i\} : \tau$.

Another important property of SFUN is that there is *at most one* value associated to a closed term in the context of a given program. In other words, the semantics of SFUN is *deterministic*. Moreover, if a closed term is typeable then the evaluation process cannot produce type errors: **SFUN** is a *strongly typed language*. However, since recursive functions may be undefined for certain arguments, we cannot guarantee that any closed typeable term has a value.

Property 6.15 (Strong Typing and Determinism)

The evaluation of a closed, typeable term t, with respect to a typeable program P, cannot produce type errors.

Moreover, if $t \Downarrow_P^V v_1$ and $t \Downarrow_P^V v_2$ then $v_1 = v_2$.

Proof

This property can be proved by rule induction, using the substitution lemma.

Basis:

- If t is a number n then $n \Downarrow_P^V n$ using the axiom **(n)**, and this is the only axiom or rule that applies.
- If t is a Boolean b then $b \Downarrow_P^V b$ using the axiom **(b)**, and this is the only axiom or rule that applies.

In both cases the evaluation is successful and there is only one possible result. The case of a 0-ary function is treated later. There are no other base cases to consider because t is closed (it cannot be a variable). So the basis of the induction is proved.

Induction:

We distinguish cases according to the rule applied (which is determined by the term t, since the system is syntax directed).

- If there is an operator at the root of t, then we will apply one of the rules **(op)**, **(bop)**, **(and)**, **(not)**, depending on the operator (only one rule applies in each case). We will only show the case where t is a term of the form $t_1 + t_2$ (the other cases are similar). In this case t_1, t_2 and t are all of type **int**. By induction, the evaluation of t_1 and t_2 cannot produce type errors, and there is at most one value v_1 such that $t_1 \Downarrow_P^V v_1$, and at most one value v_2 such that $t_2 \Downarrow_P^V v_2$. Since evaluation preserves types (Property 6.13), v_1 and v_2 are integer values. Hence $v_1 + v_2$ is defined, and $t \Downarrow_P^V v$ where $v = v_1 + v_2$, using the rule for $+$.
- In the case of a conditional if t_1 then t_2 else t_3, since the term is typeable by assumption, then t_1 is a term of Boolean type and t_2, t_3 have both a certain type σ. By induction, the evaluation of the terms t_1, t_2, and t_3 does not produce type errors, and t_1, t_2, t_3 have at most one value each: v_1, v_2 and v_3. Since the evaluation relation preserves types (Property 6.13), v_1 is a Boolean constant. If v_1 is $True$, we can only apply the rule **(If$_T$)**, and the value of t is v_2. Otherwise, we apply the rule **(If$_F$)** and the value of t is v_3. In both cases the value is uniquely determined.
- Finally, if t is a function application $f_i(t_1, \ldots, t_{a_i})$, then using the rule **(fn)**:
$f_i(t_1, \ldots, t_{a_i}) \Downarrow_P^V v$ if and only if
$t_1 \Downarrow_P^V v_1, \ldots, t_{a_i} \Downarrow_P^V v_{a_i}, d_i\{x_1 \mapsto v_1, \ldots, x_{a_i} \mapsto v_{a_i}\} \Downarrow_P^V v$.
Note that here a_i could be 0, in which case we have simply $d_i \Downarrow_P^V v$.
By the induction hypothesis, there is at most one value v_j for each term t_j

$(1 \leq j \leq n)$, and also there is at most one value for $d_i\{x_1 \mapsto v_1, \ldots, x_{a_i} \mapsto v_{a_i}\}$. Therefore the value of t is uniquely determined.

Now it remains to prove that the evaluation of $f_i(t_1, \ldots, t_{a_i})$ does not produce type errors. By induction, we know that the evaluation of the terms $t_1, \ldots, t_{a_i}$ does not produce type errors, but we need to show that $d_i\{x_1 \mapsto v_1, \ldots, x_{a_i} \mapsto v_{a_i}\}$ is also safe, and to apply the induction hypothesis here, we must show first that this is a typeable term.

Note that, since $f_i(t_1, \ldots, t_{a_i})$ is well-typed, and its type is derived using rule (fn) (see Fig. 6.1), the terms $t_1, \ldots, t_{a_i}$ must have the type required by the type declaration for f_i in ε. In other words, if $\varepsilon(f_i) = (\sigma_1, \ldots, \sigma_{a_i}) \rightarrow \sigma$ then $\vdash_\varepsilon f_i(t_1, \ldots, t_{a_i}): \sigma$ and $\vdash_\varepsilon t_j: \sigma_j$ (for $1 \leq j \leq a_i$). By Property 6.13, also $\vdash_\varepsilon v_j: \sigma_j$ (for $1 \leq j \leq a_i$). Now, since the program is well-typed, the equation $f_i(x_1, \ldots, x_{a_i}) = d_i$ defining f_i is well-typed (see Definition 6.8), and therefore its right-hand side d_i must have type σ. More precisely: $x_1: \sigma_1, \ldots, x_{a_i}: \sigma_{a_i} \vdash_\varepsilon d_i: \sigma$.

Now, using the substitution lemma (Lemma 6.14), we deduce $\vdash_\varepsilon d_i\{x_1 \mapsto v_1, \ldots, x_{a_i} \mapsto v_{a_i}\}: \sigma$. We can now apply the induction hypothesis: we have a closed typeable term, which cannot produce a type error. This completes the proof.

$\square$

6.3.3 Call-by-Name Semantics of SFUN

The evaluation relation defined in the previous section implements a call-by-value strategy: when a function call is processed, the actual arguments are evaluated first, and their values are passed to the function. In order to implement a call-by-name strategy, we have to change the rule (fn) that defines the behaviour of application in Fig. 6.2. Instead of passing to the function the values of the actual arguments, we will pass the arguments themselves.

As in the previous section, we assume that a SFUN program P is given. We specify a binary relation between closed terms and values in the context of the program P, denoted $t \Downarrow_P^N v$, meaning that the term t evaluates to v under call-by-name using the program P. We use the super-index N to distinguish this evaluation relation from the one studied in the previous sections.

To define the relation $\Downarrow_P^N$ we use the rules and axioms of Fig. 6.2 (replacing $\Downarrow_P^V$ by $\Downarrow_P^N$), except for rule (fn), which is replaced by the following rule:

$$\frac{d_i\{x_1 \mapsto t_1, \ldots, x_{a_i} \mapsto t_{a_i}\} \Downarrow_P^N v}{f_i(t_1, \ldots, t_{a_i}) \Downarrow_P^N v} \ (fn_N)$$

where d_i is the right-hand side of the equation defining f_i in the program P:

$$f_i(x_1, \ldots, x_{a_i}) = d_i$$

According to rule (fn$_N$), the result of the application of the function f_i to the arguments $t_1, \ldots, t_{a_i}$ is obtained by using the equation defining f_i in P where the formal parameters $x_1, \ldots, x_{a_i}$ are replaced by the actual arguments $t_1, \ldots, t_{a_i}$. In contrast, in the call-by-value evaluation relation the formal parameters of the function are replaced by the values of the actual arguments.

The system is still deterministic, and the language remains strongly typed.

Property 6.16 (Strong Typing and Determinism)

The call-by-name evaluation of a closed, typeable term t, in the context of a typeable program P, does not produce type errors. Moreover, if $t \Downarrow_P^N v_1$ and $t \Downarrow_P^N v_2$ then $v_1 = v_2$.

The proof is similar to the one given in the previous section for $\Downarrow_P^V$.

We now give some examples of call-by-name evaluation.

Example 6.17

Consider again the program P:
$$f_1 = f_1 + 1$$
$$f_2(x) = 1$$
$$f_3(x) = x * x$$

1. With this program, the term $f_2(0)$ has the value 1, that is, $f_2(0) \Downarrow_P^N 1$. To see this, we use the definition of the evaluation relation:

$$\frac{\cfrac{}{1\{x \mapsto 0\} \Downarrow_P^N 1} \; \text{(n)}}{f_2(0) \Downarrow_P^N 1} \; \text{(fn}_N)$$

2. With the same program, $f_2(f_1)$ also has the value 1. This is in contrast with the call-by-value semantics (see Example 6.11) in which this term does not have a value. We prove that $f_2(f_1) \Downarrow_P^N 1$ as follows:

$$\frac{\cfrac{}{1\{x \mapsto f_1\} \Downarrow_P^N 1} \; \text{(n)}}{f_2(f_1) \Downarrow_P^N 1} \; \text{(fn}_N)$$

Note that the function f_2 does not use its argument. In this case, $1\{x \mapsto f_1\} = 1$ and hence the actual argument f_1 is not evaluated (avoiding in this way an infinite computation). This is a general property of the call-by-name semantics: if a term has a value, the call-by-name strategy will find it.

3. With the same program, the term $f_3(2 + 1)$ has the value 9 (compare with the call-by-value semantics in Example 6.11). We show it as follows:

$$\dfrac{\dfrac{}{2 \Downarrow_P^N 2}\,(n) \quad \dfrac{}{1 \Downarrow_P^N 1}\,(n)}{\dfrac{2 + 1 \Downarrow_P^N 3}{\,}}\,(op) \quad \dfrac{\dfrac{}{2 \Downarrow_P^N 2}\,(n) \quad \dfrac{}{1 \Downarrow_P^N 1}\,(n)}{2 + 1 \Downarrow_P^N 3}\,(op)$$

$$\dfrac{\dfrac{\cdots}{x * x\{x \mapsto 2 + 1\} \Downarrow_P^N 9}\,(op)}{f_3(2 + 1) \Downarrow_P^N 9}\,(fn_N)$$

Here, according to rule (fn$_N$) we have to evaluate $x * x\{x \mapsto 2 + 1\}$, which represents the term $(2 + 1) * (2 + 1)$. We see that the argument $(2 + 1)$ is copied and then evaluated twice. The call-by-value semantics is more efficient in this case, because instead of copying the argument, it copies the value 3. This is a general property of the call-by-value strategy: arguments are evaluated only once, even if they are used several times.

Under the call-by-name semantics, if an argument is used more than once in a function definition, then the actual parameter will be evaluated several times. To avoid this source of inefficiency, languages that implement a call-by-name strategy (e.g. Haskell) use *sharing*. Call-by-name with sharing is known as *lazy evaluation*. The basic idea is to represent terms in the right-hand side of equations as graphs, where repeated occurrences of variables are represented via pointers to a unique variable node. In this way, actual arguments are not copied: a substitution operation replaces the unique variable node by the actual argument, and when it is evaluated (if it is needed), the value obtained is shared. Things are more complicated in higher-order languages, see the references at the end of the chapter for more details.

6.4 Extensions of SFUN

In the previous sections we assumed that programs consist of equations defining a set of *global* functions, which are all available to be used in terms. We will now define an extension of the language SFUN in which it will be possible to introduce *local* definitions, using the keyword `let`. Moreover, functions will be allowed to take other functions as input, or to produce functions as a result. Functions will become first class values.

Recall the standard syntax for local definitions in functional languages (see Chap. 5):

```
let x = expression1 in expression2
```

Using a `let` construct, we can write terms containing local identifiers, for example:

```
let y = x * x in y * y
```

and use them in equations, such as

$$f\,x = \texttt{let}\ y = x * x\ \texttt{in}\ y * y$$

We will also add a let fun construct to define local functions. For instance, we can write

$$\texttt{let fun square}\ x = x * x\ \texttt{in}\ (\texttt{square}\ 3)$$

Actually, the same let construct could be used to define local identifiers or local functions, however, to make programs easier to understand we prefer to use two different keywords. We will assume that definitions using let are *not* recursive, whereas a function defined via a let fun may be recursive.

We will extend the abstract syntax of SFUN to take into account these changes. The extended language will be called FUN. We will also adapt the type system and operational semantics to deal with the new language constructs.

6.4.1 Abstract Syntax of FUN

The following grammar defines the abstract syntax of FUN.

Definition 6.18 (Terms in FUN)

The set of terms is generated by the grammar below, where n and b correspond to tokens representing integer numbers and Boolean values, respectively, and x denotes a variable and f a function.

$$
\begin{aligned}
t ::=\ & n \mid b \mid x \mid f \mid op \mid bop \mid \neg \mid \wedge \mid \\
& \texttt{if}\ t_0\ \texttt{then}\ t_1\ \texttt{else}\ t_2 \mid Ap(t_1, t_2) \mid \\
& \texttt{let}\ x = t_1\ \texttt{in}\ t_2 \mid \texttt{let fun}\ f\ x_1 \ldots x_n = t_1\ \texttt{in}\ t_2 \\
op ::=\ & + \mid - \mid * \mid / \\
bop ::=\ & > \mid < \mid =
\end{aligned}
$$

The set of basic terms includes functions (denoted by f in the grammar above) and operators, in addition to integer and Boolean constants, and variables. This reflects the fact that functions are now values on their own. A term of the form $Ap(t_1, t_2)$ represents the application of t_1 to t_2. The let expressions are as discussed above, and conditionals have the same syntax as in SFUN.

Applications $Ap(t_1, t_2)$ will often be written simply as $(t_1 t_2)$, omitting the application operator. For example, in FUN we have a term $Ap(\neg, True)$ (or simply $\neg True$) instead of the term $\neg(True)$ available in SFUN. Note that these are different trees:

$$
\begin{array}{ccc}
Ap & vs. & \neg \\
/\ \backslash & & | \\
\neg \quad True & & True
\end{array}
$$

According to the grammar, functions and primitive operators are written in Curryfied form (see Chap. 5). The Ap operator is used to pass arguments to functions one by one. Since in the language **FUN** a term can produce a function as a result, Ap builds a syntax tree $Ap(t_1, t_2)$ out of any two terms t_1 and t_2.

For example, in **FUN** the conjunction $True \; and \; y \; and \; z$ is represented by the term $Ap(Ap(Ap(\wedge, True), y), z)$, or $(((\wedge \; True) \; y) \; z)$.

As usual in functional languages, we will omit brackets whenever possible in our examples, writing $\wedge True \, yz$ instead of $(((\wedge True) y) z)$. Generally, we write $s \; t_1 \ldots t_n$ instead of $(\ldots (s \; t_1) \; t_2) \ldots t_n)$. The convention is that *application associates to the left*. So a function f applied to n arguments $x_1, \ldots, x_n$ will be written $f \; x_1 \ldots x_n$.

We need to introduce the notion of a free variable, in order to define programs. If a variable x occurs in a term t and there is no local definition for x, we say that x is a *free variable* (or a global variable). Otherwise, if x is defined by a `let` construct or it is an argument for a function defined by a `let fun` construct, then x is a bound variable. A formal definition of the set $FVar(t)$ of free variables of t can be given by induction (see Exercise 9 at the end of the chapter).

Definition 6.19

Programs in **FUN** are sets of equations defining global functions, which are Curryfied:

$$f_1 \; x_1 \ldots x_{a_1} = t_1$$
$$\vdots$$
$$f_k \; x_1 \ldots x_{a_k} = t_k$$

where

- $t_1, \ldots, t_k$ are **FUN** terms (see Definition 6.18);
- for each t_i ($1 \le i \le k$), $FVar(t_i) \subseteq \{x_1, \ldots, x_{a_i}\}$;
- there is only one equation for each global function f_i ($1 \le i \le k$).

The terms t_i may contain occurrences of $f_1, \ldots, f_k$, i.e., the equations may be mutually recursive, and in addition t_i may contain occurrences of the parameters $x_1, \ldots, x_{a_i}$ of the function being defined, as well as local definitions. But note that t_i may not contain free variables; all the variables used in the definition of a global function should be either parameters or locally defined variables.

To make **FUN** programs more readable, we will write the predefined operators in infix notation when they are applied to two arguments, as in **SFUN**. Thus, we write $(t_1 + t_2)$ instead of $+ \; t_1 \; t_2$.

For example, we can write the following program in **FUN** to compute the 4th power of a number:

```
quad x = let y = (x * x) in (y * y)
```

In the next sections, we extend the type system and the operational semantics given for **SFUN**, to take into account the new constructs.

6.4.2 A Type System for FUN

To type terms and programs containing local definitions and higher-order functions, the set of types has to include general arrow types.

Definition 6.20 (Types for FUN terms)

The set of types is defined by the following grammar:

$$\tau ::= \text{int} \mid \text{bool} \mid \tau \rightarrow \tau$$

As usual, we use brackets in the textual notation to avoid ambiguities, for instance we write (int $\rightarrow$ int) $\rightarrow$ int for the type of functions that take a function from integers to integers as input and produce an integer as a result. To avoid writing too many brackets, we assume arrows associate to the right (as indicated in Chap. 5).

We will assume that local function definitions in FUN are explicitly typed (type inference in this general setting is out of the scope of this book). For this, we add type declarations in `let fun` constructs, using the syntax:

$$\text{let fun } f x_1 : \sigma_1 \ldots x_n : \sigma_n = t_1 : \sigma \text{ in } t_2$$

We will define a typing relation $\Gamma \vdash t : \tau$ where

- Γ is an environment associating identifiers (variables and functions) with types;
- t is a FUN term (see Definition 6.18); and
- τ is a type as defined by the grammar in Definition 6.20 above.

Note that, in contrast with the type system for SFUN, the environment Γ now contains type assumptions for functions as well as variables. We could keep a separate environment for functions as we did for SFUN, but since terms in FUN may contain local functions, we will need to update the assumptions of types for functions during the typing of the term, as we do with variables. For simplicity, we use just one environment. Moreover, since the language is higher-order and operators can be used in a Curryfied way, we will assume that the environment contains also type information for arithmetic and Boolean operators; that is, Γ contains declarations of the form $f_i : \tau$ for global functions, $op : \tau$ for Boolean and integer operations, $x : \tau$ for variables, and $f : \tau$ for local functions. In general, elements of Γ are pairs consisting of an identifier and a type, written id: τ.

The structure of the environment Γ becomes important now, because we might have several local definitions for an identifier. Therefore Γ will be treated as a stack. We will write

$$\Gamma, \text{id}: \tau$$

for the stack obtained by pushing id: τ onto Γ, that is, we represent the top of the stack at the right. We will write $\Gamma(\text{id})$ to denote the rightmost declaration for the identifier id in Γ. Formally:

Axioms:

$$\frac{}{\varGamma \vdash b\colon \mathsf{bool}}\ \text{(b)} \qquad \frac{}{\varGamma \vdash n\colon \mathsf{int}}\ \text{(n)} \qquad \frac{}{\varGamma \vdash \mathsf{id}\colon \sigma}\ \text{(id)}\quad \text{where } \sigma = \varGamma(\mathsf{id})$$

Rules:

$$\frac{\varGamma \vdash t_1\colon \mathsf{int} \quad \varGamma \vdash t_2\colon \mathsf{int}}{\varGamma \vdash t_1\ op\ t_2\colon \mathsf{int}}\ \text{(op)}$$

$$\frac{\varGamma \vdash t_1\colon \mathsf{int} \quad \varGamma \vdash t_2\colon \mathsf{int}}{\varGamma \vdash t_1\ bop\ t_2\colon \mathsf{bool}}\ \text{(bop)}$$

$$\frac{\varGamma \vdash t_1\colon \mathsf{bool} \quad \varGamma \vdash t_2\colon \mathsf{bool}}{\varGamma \vdash t_1 \wedge t_2\colon \mathsf{bool}}\ \text{(and)} \qquad \frac{\varGamma \vdash t\colon \mathsf{bool}}{\varGamma \vdash \neg t\colon \mathsf{bool}}\ \text{(not)}$$

$$\frac{\varGamma \vdash t_0\colon \mathsf{bool} \quad \varGamma \vdash t_1\colon \sigma \quad \varGamma \vdash t_2\colon \sigma}{\varGamma \vdash \mathsf{if}\ t_0\ \mathsf{then}\ t_1\ \mathsf{else}\ t_2\ \colon \sigma}\ \text{(if)}$$

$$\frac{\varGamma \vdash t_1\colon \sigma \to \tau \quad \varGamma \vdash t_2\colon \sigma}{\varGamma \vdash (t_1\ t_2)\colon \tau}\ \text{(Ap)}$$

$$\frac{\varGamma \vdash t_1\colon \sigma \quad \varGamma, x\colon \sigma \vdash t_2\colon \tau}{\varGamma \vdash \mathsf{let}\ x = t_1\ \mathsf{in}\ t_2\ \colon \tau}\ \text{(let)}$$

$$\frac{\varGamma, x_1\colon \sigma_1, \ldots, x_n\colon \sigma_n, f\colon \rho \vdash t_1\colon \sigma \quad \varGamma, f\colon \rho \vdash t_2\colon \tau}{\varGamma \vdash \mathsf{let\ fun}\ f\ x_1\colon \sigma_1\ \ldots x_n\colon \sigma_n = t_1\colon \sigma\ \mathsf{in}\ t_2\ \colon \tau}\ \text{(letfun)}$$
$$\text{where}\quad \rho = \sigma_1 \to \ldots \to \sigma_n \to \sigma$$

Fig. 6.3 Type system for FUN

$\varGamma(\mathsf{id}) = \tau$ if and only if $\varGamma = \varGamma_1, \mathsf{id}\colon \tau, \varGamma_2$ and $\varGamma_2$ does not contain a declaration for id.

Definition 6.21 (Typing Relation for FUN)

The axioms and rules in Fig. 6.3 define the typing relation $\varGamma \vdash t\colon \tau$ in FUN.

The axioms (b) and (n), and the rule (if), were already used in the type system for SFUN (see Fig. 6.1). The axiom (id) and the rules (Ap), (let) and (letfun) are new and deserve some explanations.

We have replaced the axiom (var) in the type system for SFUN with a more general axiom, (id), which allows us to extract information from the environment in order to assign a type to a variable, a local or global function, or a primitive operator.

The rule **(Ap)** requires the left component in an application $(t_1\ t_2)$ to have an arrow type $\sigma \to \tau$. The right component (which will be used as an argument for t_1) must then be of type σ, and since t_1 returns an element of type τ, the application $(t_1\ t_2)$ has type τ.

In the rule **(let)** we see that Γ has to be treated as a stack rather than a set: we can have nested definitions for the same identifier, in which case Γ will contain several declarations for the same variable. Also note that we type t_1 in the environment Γ, and t_2 in Γ augmented with $x : \sigma$ since t_2 may contain occurrences of the newly defined local variable x, but t_1 cannot (the `let` construct is not recursive).

The rule **(letfun)** allows us to type recursive function definitions: we type t_1 in an environment containing type information for the formal arguments $x_1, \ldots, x_n$ and for the newly defined function f. In t_2 we can use f but not the formal arguments.

The rules **(op)**, **(bop)**, **(and)**, **(not)** are no longer needed, because we can type expressions containing operators using **(Ap)** and the information provided in the environment (recall that Γ now contains type assumptions for functions and primitive operators). However, we prefer to include these rules in the type system to make the typing of arithmetic and Boolean expressions more clear.

We now give some examples of typeable terms in **FUN**.

Example 6.22 (Typing Terms in FUN)

We will show that the term

$$\texttt{let fun } square\ x : \textsf{int} = (x * x) : \textsf{int in } (square\ 3) + (square\ 2)$$

has type **int**. In the type derivations below, Γ represents an environment containing the declaration $square : \textsf{int} \to \textsf{int}$.

First we show that $(square\ 3)$ has type **int**, as follows:

$$\cfrac{\cfrac{}{\Gamma \vdash square : \textsf{int} \to \textsf{int}} \text{(id)} \quad \cfrac{}{\Gamma \vdash 3 : \textsf{int}} \text{(n)}}{\Gamma \vdash (square\ 3) : \textsf{int}} \text{(Ap)}$$

In the same way we can show $\Gamma \vdash (square\ 2) : \textsf{int}$, and using rule **(op)** we derive:

$$\cfrac{\Gamma \vdash (square\ 3) : \textsf{int} \quad \Gamma \vdash (square\ 2) : \textsf{int}}{\Gamma \vdash (square\ 3) + (square\ 2) : \textsf{int}} \text{(op)}$$

We can also derive the type **int** for $x * x$ assuming $\Gamma'(x) = \textsf{int}$:

$$\cfrac{\cfrac{}{\Gamma' \vdash x : \textsf{int}} \text{(id)} \quad \cfrac{}{\Gamma' \vdash x : \textsf{int}} \text{(id)}}{\Gamma' \vdash (x * x) : \textsf{int}} \text{(op)}$$

Therefore we can use the rule (letfun), where Γ' is the environment $x:$ int, $square:$ int $\rightarrow$ int.

$$\frac{\Gamma' \vdash (x * x): \text{int} \quad \Gamma \vdash (square\ 3) + (square\ 2): \text{int}}{\vdash \texttt{let fun}\ square\ x: \text{int} = (x * x): \text{int}\ \texttt{in}\ (square\ 3) + (square\ 2): \text{int}}\ \text{(letfun)}$$

Similarly, we can show that the term

$$\texttt{let fun}\ square\ x: \text{int} = (x * x): \text{int}\ \texttt{in}\ (square\ 3) > (square\ 2)$$

has type bool.

To type check a **FUN** program

$$f_1\ x_1 \ldots x_{a_1} = t_1$$
$$\vdots$$
$$f_k\ x_1 \ldots x_{a_k} = t_k$$

we use the type information provided by the programmer for the global functions $f_1, \ldots, f_k$, in the same way as we did for **SFUN**.

Definition 6.23 (Typing Programs in FUN)

Let Γ be an environment containing a type declaration $f_i : \sigma_1 \rightarrow \ldots \rightarrow \sigma_{a_i} \rightarrow \tau_i$ for each global function $f_1, \ldots, f_k$ in a program P.

The program P is correctly typed in the environment Γ if for each equation $f_i\ x_1 \ldots x_{a_i} = t_i$ in P, where $\Gamma(f_i) = \sigma_1 \rightarrow \ldots \rightarrow \sigma_{a_i} \rightarrow \tau_i$, we have

$$\Gamma, x_1 : \sigma_1, \ldots, x_{a_i} : \sigma_{a_i} \vdash t_i : \tau_i$$

In other words, a **FUN** program is well-typed if the equations are compatible with the types declared by the programmer for the global functions. The term t_i in the right hand side of the ith equation should have the type of $f_i\ x_1 \ldots x_{a_i}$, that is, τ_i. Note that a_i may be 0. In contrast with **SFUN**, here τ_i may be any type, for instance it could be an arrow type if the result of f_i is a function. To type the term t_i we use the type system given in Fig. 6.3.

We now give examples of programs that are well-typed.

Example 6.24

Consider the program P defining a global function f_1 as follows:

$$f_1\ x = \texttt{let}\ y = (x * x)\ \texttt{in}\ (y * y)$$

and assume $\Gamma(f_1) = \text{int} \rightarrow \text{int}$.

The program P is correctly typed, because $\texttt{let}\ y = (x * x)\ \texttt{in}\ (y * y)$ has type int in the environment $\Gamma, x: \text{int}$, as the following type derivation shows. The environment Γ' is $\Gamma, x:$ int, $y:$ int.

$$\cfrac{\cfrac{\Gamma, x: \text{int} \vdash x: \text{int} \quad \Gamma, x: \text{int} \vdash x: \text{int}}{\Gamma, x: \text{int} \vdash (x * x): \text{int}} \text{(op)} \quad \cfrac{\Gamma' \vdash y: \text{int} \quad \Gamma' \vdash y: \text{int}}{\Gamma' \vdash (y * y): \text{int}} \text{(op)}}{\Gamma, x: \text{int} \vdash \texttt{let } y = (x * x) \texttt{ in } (y * y): \text{int}} \text{(let)}$$

Note that the program

$$f_1\, x = \texttt{let } x = (x * x) \texttt{ in } (x * x)$$

is also well-typed, although less readable.

Consider now the program

$$succ = + 1$$

which is an example of a program defining a higher-order function. This program is typeable in an environment Γ such that $\Gamma(succ) = \text{int} \to \text{int}$, and $\Gamma(+) = \text{int} \to \text{int} \to \text{int}$. To show this, we build a type derivation for $\Gamma \vdash (+\, 1): \text{int} \to \text{int}$.

$$\cfrac{\cfrac{}{\Gamma \vdash +: \text{int} \to \text{int} \to \text{int}} \text{(id)} \quad \cfrac{}{\Gamma \vdash 1: \text{int}} \text{(n)}}{\Gamma \vdash +\, 1: \text{int} \to \text{int}} \text{(Ap)}$$

6.4.3 *Operational Semantics of* FUN

We now give a meaning to FUN programs and terms using a transition system. We define a call-by-value evaluation relation, which we denote by $\Downarrow_P$ to emphasise the fact that the value of a term depends on a given program P. A call-by-name semantics can be obtained by a simple modification of the rules defining $\Downarrow_P$; we leave it as an exercise (see Exercise 12 at the end of the chapter).

In order to take into account the local definitions that might occur in FUN terms, we will define $\Downarrow_P$ as a ternary relation between:

- An environment Γ that maps identifiers to values and stores function definitions: Γ will be represented as a list of pairs, which can be of the form $id = v$, i.e., an identifier and a value, or $f = \lambda x_1 \ldots x_n.t$ for a function definition $f\, x_1 \ldots x_n = t$. The notation $\lambda x_1 \ldots x_n.t$ makes it clear that f has n arguments; the variables $x_1 \ldots x_n$ are bound in t.
- A well-typed FUN term t, which may contain local definitions (see Definition 6.18).
- A value v (since FUN is a higher-order language, values are integers, Booleans and irreducible functions).

We write $\Gamma \vdash t \Downarrow_P v$ to indicate that the term t has the value v in the context of the program P under the assumptions in Γ.

All type declarations are erased from the `let fun` constructs before the evaluation: we assume the terms to be evaluated are well-typed, but we do not need to know their type.

Again, Γ will be structured as a stack, and we will write

$$\Gamma, u = w$$

to denote the stack obtained by pushing the pair $u = w$ onto Γ, that is, the top of the stack is the rightmost pair. The notation $\Gamma(x)$ will be used to extract from Γ the last value associated with x (i.e., the value v in the rightmost pair $x = v$). Similarly, $\Gamma(f)$ will denote the term $\lambda x_1 \ldots x_n.t$ associated with f in the last definition processed for the function f.

In Fig. 6.4 we give an inductive definition, using a set of axioms and rules, for the evaluation relation $\Downarrow_P$.

Some explanations are in order:

As in **SFUN**, the axioms **(n)** and **(b)** show that integers and Booleans are already values.

Additionally, in **FUN** we also have the axiom **(fnVal)**, for functions whose arity is greater than 0 (i.e., functions that have a definition of the form $f_i\, x_1 \ldots x_{a_i} = d_i$) but are not applied to any arguments. These are values in **FUN**. The axiom **(fnVal)** also applies to the predefined arithmetic operators (op), comparisons (bop) and Boolean operators $\wedge$ and $\neg$.

Rule **(Ap)** deals with partial applications; it is used to collect and evaluate the arguments of Curryfied functions (local and global) and operators. If the number of arguments that we have is smaller than the arity of the function we do not apply it; in this case we just evaluate the arguments and return the application. If all the arguments are provided, the term can be evaluated using the rule **(fn)**. In this rule, the definition of the function, denoted **def**(f_i), is used after all the arguments have been evaluated.

We have to specify how the definition of the function is obtained:

$$\mathsf{def}(f_i) = \begin{cases} \Gamma(f_i) & \text{if } f_i \in dom(\Gamma) \\[2ex] \lambda x_1 \ldots x_{a_i}.d_i & \text{if } f_i \notin dom(\Gamma) \text{ and} \\ & f_i\, x_1 \ldots x_{a_i} = d_i \text{ is in } P \\[2ex] \lambda x_1\, x_2.\, x_1\, f_i\, x_2 & \text{if } f_i \text{ is an arithmetic or} \\ & \text{Boolean operator} \end{cases}$$

In other words, we search for the definition of the function f_i first in the environment Γ and then in the program P (i.e., local definitions have priority over global ones); for arithmetic and Boolean operators we have ad-hoc evaluation rules.

$$\frac{}{\Gamma \vdash n \Downarrow_P n} \text{ (n)} \qquad \frac{}{\Gamma \vdash b \Downarrow_P b} \text{ (b)} \qquad \frac{}{\Gamma \vdash f \Downarrow_P f} \text{ if } ar(f) > 0 \text{ (fnVal)}$$

$$\frac{}{\Gamma \vdash x \Downarrow_P v} \text{ if } \Gamma(x) = v \text{ (id)}$$

$$\frac{\Gamma \vdash t_1 \Downarrow_P n_1 \quad \Gamma \vdash t_2 \Downarrow_P n_2}{\Gamma \vdash t_1 \ op \ t_2 \Downarrow_P n} \text{ if } n = n_1 \ op \ n_2 \text{ (op)}$$

$$\frac{\Gamma \vdash t_1 \Downarrow_P n_1 \quad \Gamma \vdash t_2 \Downarrow_P n_2}{\Gamma \vdash t_1 \ bop \ t_2 \Downarrow_P b} \text{ if } b = n_1 \ bop \ n_2 \text{ (bop)}$$

$$\frac{\Gamma \vdash t_1 \Downarrow_P b_1 \quad \Gamma \vdash t_2 \Downarrow_P b_2}{\Gamma \vdash t_1 \wedge t_2 \Downarrow_P b} \text{ if } b = b_1 \ and \ b_2 \text{ (and)} \qquad \frac{\Gamma \vdash t \Downarrow_P b}{\Gamma \vdash \neg t \Downarrow_P b'} \text{ if } b' = not \ b \text{ (not)}$$

$$\frac{\Gamma \vdash t_0 \Downarrow_P True \quad \Gamma \vdash t_1 \Downarrow_P v_1}{\Gamma \vdash \text{ if } t_0 \text{ then } t_1 \text{ else } t_2 \Downarrow_P v_1} \text{ (If}_\mathsf{T})$$

$$\frac{\Gamma \vdash t_0 \Downarrow_P False \quad \Gamma \vdash t_2 \Downarrow_P v_2}{\Gamma \vdash \text{ if } t_0 \text{ then } t_1 \text{ else } t_2 \Downarrow_P v_2} \text{ (If}_\mathsf{F})$$

$$\frac{\Gamma \vdash t_1 \Downarrow_P v_1 \quad \Gamma, x = v_1 \vdash t_2 \Downarrow_P v}{\Gamma \vdash \text{ let } x = t_1 \text{ in } t_2 \Downarrow_P v} \text{ (let)}$$

$$\frac{\Gamma, f = \lambda x_1 \ldots x_n . t_1 \vdash t_2 \Downarrow_P v}{\Gamma \vdash \text{ let fun } f \ x_1 \ldots x_n = t_1 \text{ in } t_2 \Downarrow_P v} \text{ (letfun)}$$

$$\frac{\Gamma \vdash s \Downarrow_P (f \ t_1 \ldots t_i) \quad \Gamma \vdash t \Downarrow_P v}{\Gamma \vdash (s \ t) \Downarrow_P (f \ t_1 \ldots t_i \ v)} \text{ if } ar(f) > i + 1 \text{ (Ap)}$$

$$\frac{\Gamma \vdash s \Downarrow_P f_i \ v_1 \ldots v_{a_i - 1} \quad \Gamma \vdash t \Downarrow_P v_{a_i} \quad \Gamma \vdash d_i \{\overline{x_j \mapsto v_j}\} \Downarrow_P v}{\Gamma \vdash (s \ t) \Downarrow_P v} \text{ if } def(f_i) = \lambda x_1 \ldots x_{a_i} . d_i \text{ (fn)}$$

$$\frac{\Gamma \vdash d_i \Downarrow_P v}{\Gamma \vdash f_i \Downarrow_P v} \text{ if } def(f_i) = d_i \text{ (fn0)}$$

Fig. 6.4 Call-by-value evaluation in FUN

The notation $d_i\{\overline{x_j \mapsto v_j}\}$ used in rule (fn) is shorthand for

$$d_i\{x_1 \mapsto v_1, \ldots, x_{a_i} \mapsto v_{a_i}\}$$

which represents the term obtained after replacing (simultaneously) in d_i each *free* occurrence of x_1 by v_1, x_2 by v_2, etc.

Rule (fn0) deals with the particular case of 0-ary functions, for which we do not need to evaluate any arguments. In this case, $\mathsf{def}(f_i) = \Gamma(f_i)$ if f_i is a locally defined function, otherwise, if $f_i = d_i$ is in P, $\mathsf{def}(f_i) = d_i$.

Note that the axiom (fnVal), together with rules (Ap), (fn) and (fn0) indicate that FUN is a higher-order language, in contrast with SFUN.

The rules (op), (bop), (and) and (not) are standard, and we have two rules for the if-then-else, as usual.

In the rule (let) we see that Γ has to be treated as a stack: we may have nested evaluations for the same identifier, in which case Γ will contain several values for the same variable. Also note that we evaluate t_1 in the environment Γ, and t_2 in Γ augmented with $x = v_1$ since t_2 may contain occurrences of the new variable x, but t_1 cannot (the let construct is not recursive).

In the rule (letfun) we evaluate t_2 in an environment in which the function f is associated with its most recent definition.

We need an axiom for identifiers (which was not present in the system given for SFUN, see Fig. 6.2) in order to extract from the environment Γ the values defined for variables (these are added to Γ when the rule let is used, in the case of locally defined variables; otherwise, if the variable is free in the term, then its value must be provided in the initial environment Γ in which the term is evaluated).

We end this section with some examples of evaluation.

Example 6.25

We can show that the term

$$\texttt{let fun } square\; x\colon \mathsf{int} = (x * x)\colon \mathsf{int} \texttt{ in } (square\; 3) + (square\; 2)$$

has the value 13 (independently of the given program P) as follows.

First we show that $(square\; 3)$ has the value 9 in an environment Γ that contains the definition $square\; x = x * x$ (i.e. $\Gamma(square) = \lambda x.x * x$). We omit the derivation of $\Gamma \vdash 3 * 3 \Downarrow_P 9$.

$$\dfrac{\dfrac{}{\Gamma \vdash square \Downarrow_P square}\;(\mathsf{fnVal}) \qquad \dfrac{}{\Gamma \vdash 3 \Downarrow_P 3}\;(\mathsf{n}) \quad \Gamma \vdash 3 * 3 \Downarrow_P 9}{\Gamma \vdash (square\; 3) \Downarrow_P 9}\;(\mathsf{fn})$$

In the same way we can show $\Gamma \vdash (square\; 2) \Downarrow_P 4$.

We use these derivations below, where again Γ is the environment containing the definition $square\; x = x * x$. Note that we evaluate the term obtained after erasing all type annotations.

$$\frac{\Gamma \vdash (square\ 3) \Downarrow_P 9 \quad \Gamma \vdash (square\ 2) \Downarrow_P 4}{\Gamma \vdash (square\ 3) + (square\ 2) \Downarrow_P 13} \ (op)$$

$$\frac{}{\vdash \texttt{let fun } square\ x = x * x \texttt{ in } (square\ 3) + (square\ 2) \Downarrow_P 13} \ (letfun)$$

Consider now the program P defining the higher-order (0-ary) function $succ$:

$$succ = +1$$

We can show that the term $(succ\ 3)$ evaluates to 4 as follows (we omit the derivation for $\vdash 1 + 3 \Downarrow_P 4$).

$$\frac{\dfrac{\dfrac{\vdash + \Downarrow_P +}{}\ (fnVal) \quad \dfrac{\vdash 1 \Downarrow_P 1}{}\ (n)}{\dfrac{\vdash +1 \Downarrow_P +1}{\vdash succ \Downarrow_P +1}}\ (Ap)\ (fn0) \quad \dfrac{\vdash 3 \Downarrow_P 3}{}\ (n) \quad \vdash 1 + 3 \Downarrow_P 4}{\vdash (succ\ 3) \Downarrow_P 4}\ (fn)$$

6.4.4 Properties of FUN

The language FUN with the type system and the semantics defined above is not strongly typed. We can give examples of correctly typed terms which fail to produce a value due to a type error at run time.

Example 6.26

Consider the term:

```
let  x = 0  in
    let fun f y: int = (x + y): int in
        let  x = True in (f 3)
```

To see that this is a typeable term:
First we show that $\Gamma' \vdash \texttt{let } x = True \texttt{ in } (f\ 3) : \mathsf{int}$, where Γ' is the type environment $x: \mathsf{int}, f: \mathsf{int} \to \mathsf{int}$.

$$\frac{\dfrac{\vdash True: \mathsf{bool}}{}\ (b) \quad \dfrac{\dfrac{\Gamma', x: \mathsf{bool} \vdash f: \mathsf{int} \to \mathsf{int}}{}\ (id) \quad \dfrac{\vdash 3: \mathsf{int}}{}\ (n)}{\Gamma', x: \mathsf{bool} \vdash (f\ 3): \mathsf{int}}\ (Ap)}{\Gamma' \vdash \texttt{let } x = True \texttt{ in } (f\ 3) : \mathsf{int}}\ (let)$$

Using the type derivation above, we can show that our original term has type int. Below, Γ is the type environment $x:$ int, $y:$ int, $f:$ int $\to$ int, and t represents the term let $x = True$ in $(f\ 3)$.

$$\cfrac{\cfrac{0:\text{int}}{\vdash 0:\text{int}}\ (\text{n}) \qquad \cfrac{\cfrac{\cfrac{\Gamma \vdash x:\text{int}}{}\ (\text{id}) \qquad \cfrac{\Gamma \vdash y:\text{int}}{}\ (\text{id})}{\Gamma \vdash x+y:\text{int}}\ (\text{op}) \qquad \Gamma' \vdash t:\text{int}}{x:\text{int} \vdash \text{let fun } f\ y:\text{int} = (x+y):\text{int in } t:\text{int}}\ (\text{letfun})}{\vdash \text{let } x = 0 \text{ in let fun } f\ y:\text{int} = (x+y):\text{int in } t:\text{int}}\ (\text{let})$$

Now, during the evaluation of this term according to the semantics of **FUN** we reach a point in which we have to obtain a value for $(f\ 3)$ in an evaluation environment Γ' where $x = True$. We show the derivation below. Γ represents the evaluation context $x = 0$, $f = \lambda y.x + y$, and Γ' represents $x = 0$, $f = \lambda y.x + y, x = True$. As before the term t represents let $x = True$ in $(f\ 3)$.

$$\cfrac{\cfrac{0 \Downarrow_P 0}{\vdash 0 \Downarrow_P 0}\ (\text{n}) \qquad \cfrac{\cfrac{\cfrac{\Gamma \vdash True \Downarrow_P True}{}\ (\text{b}) \qquad \Gamma' \vdash (f\ 3) \Downarrow_P?}{\Gamma \vdash t \Downarrow_P?}\ (\text{let})}{x = 0 \vdash \text{let fun } f\ y = (x+y) \text{ in } t \Downarrow_P?}\ (\text{letfun})}{\vdash \text{let } x = 0 \text{ in let fun } f\ y = (x+y) \text{ in } t \Downarrow_P?}\ (\text{let})$$

Therefore to complete the evaluation we must derive a value for $(f\ 3)$ in Γ'. The only evaluation rule that can be applied is **(fn)**, but it requires the evaluation of $x + 3$ in Γ':

$$\cfrac{\cfrac{\Gamma' \vdash f \Downarrow_P f}{}\ (\text{fnVal}) \qquad \cfrac{\Gamma' \vdash 3 \Downarrow_P 3}{}\ (\text{n}) \qquad \Gamma' \vdash x+3 \Downarrow_P?}{\Gamma' \vdash (f\ 3) \Downarrow_P?}\ (\text{fn})$$

Only one rule can apply to $x + 3$: we must use **(op)**. But when we try to add $True$ and 3 a type error arises.

$$\cfrac{\cfrac{\Gamma' \vdash x \Downarrow_P True}{}\ (\text{id}) \qquad \cfrac{\Gamma' \vdash 3 \Downarrow_P 3}{}\ (\text{n})}{\Gamma' \vdash x+3 \Downarrow_P?}\ (\text{op})$$

The problem is that our evaluation rules for local definitions specify a *dynamic binding* for identifiers, as the previous example shows. More precisely, in the evaluation of the term $(f\ 3)$, where $f\ y = x + y$, the value of x is the one available at the calling point, rather than the one available when the function f was defined (see Chap. 3 for a discussion and examples of static and dynamic scope).

To obtain a semantics with static scope, in rule (letfun) we should store in the evaluation environment Γ not only the definition of the function but also its own environment (providing the values of the local identifiers and functions at that point). A functional value should be represented as a pair, including an environment. We will not develop a version of SFUN with static scope here, interested readers can find details in [1, 2].

6.5 Further Reading

The operational semantics of functional languages is described in many textbooks (see, for example, [1–3]), often using the λ-calculus [4], PCF [5, 6] (a typed λ-calculus extended with numbers, Booleans and a fixed point operator) or a minimalistic version of an ML-like language. A language similar to SFUN is presented in [7].

More details about type checking and inference can be found for instance in [2, 3, 8, 9].

6.6 Exercises

1. Write a SFUN program defining the functions min and max that take a pair of numbers as arguments and compute their minimum and maximum respectively.
2. Write a SFUN program defining a function fibonacci that takes a natural number n as argument and produces the nth Fibonacci number as a result (see Exercise 1 in Chap. 5).
3. Show that the SFUN program

$$square(x) = x * x$$
$$double(x) = 2 * x$$

and the term $square(double(3))$ are well-typed in an environment ε such that

$\varepsilon(square) = \text{int} \rightarrow \text{int}$

$\varepsilon(double) = \text{int} \rightarrow \text{int}$

4. Show the evaluation of the SFUN term $square(double(3))$ with respect to the program:

$$square(x) = x * x$$
$$double(x) = 2 * x$$

using first the call-by-value semantics, then the call-by-name semantics.

5. Give more examples of programs in SFUN that have different results under call-by-value and call-by-name evaluation.

6. Prove the *unicity of types* in SFUN (Property 6.10), that is, show that for any SFUN term t, if $\Gamma \vdash_\varepsilon t : \sigma$ and $\Gamma \vdash_\varepsilon t : \tau$ then $\sigma = \tau$.

7. Prove the following substitution lemma:
   If $x_1 : \sigma_1, \ldots, x_n : \sigma_n \vdash_\varepsilon t : \tau$ and $t_1, \ldots, t_n$ are closed terms such that $\vdash_\varepsilon t_i : \sigma_i$ for $1 \leq i \leq n$, then $\vdash_\varepsilon t\{x_i \mapsto t_i\} : \tau$.

   Using this result and the call-by-value semantics of the language SFUN, show that the evaluation relation preserves types (Property 6.13). That is, if P is a SFUN program that is typeable in an environment ε, and t is a closed term, then the following property holds: If $t \Downarrow_P^V v$ and $\Gamma \vdash_\varepsilon t : \tau$ then $\Gamma \vdash_\varepsilon v : \tau$.

8. Consider the SFUN program:

$$double(x) = 2 * x$$

   • Show by induction that for any natural number n, $double(n)$ is equivalent to $n + n$ (i.e., show that $double(n)$ and $n + n$ produce the same value, for any natural number n). You can use either call-by-value or call-by-name semantics.
   • Explain why for terms of the form $double(t)$ where t is an arithmetic expression, the call-by-value and call-by-name strategies have the same behaviour and are equally efficient.

9. Define the set $FVar(t)$ of free variables of the term t in FUN, by induction on the structure of t.

10. Explain what the following FUN functions do

$$f_1 \, x = \texttt{let } y = x * x \texttt{ in } y * y$$
$$f_2 \, x = \texttt{let } x = x * x \texttt{ in } x * x$$

   Show that this program is typeable in an environment Γ where

$$\Gamma(f_1) = \Gamma(f_2) = \mathsf{int} \to \mathsf{int}$$

11. Show that the FUN term

$$\texttt{let fun } square \, x : \mathsf{int} = (x * x) : \mathsf{int} \texttt{ in } (square \, 3) > (square \, 2)$$

   has type bool, and derive its value using the semantics of FUN (Fig. 6.4).

12. Give a call-by-name semantics for FUN.

References

1. R. Harper, *Practical Foundations for Programming Languages* (Cambridge University Press, Cambridge, 2013)
2. G. Dowek, J.-J. Lévy, *Introduction to the Theory of Programming Languages*. Undergraduate topics in computer science (Springer, Berlin, 2011)
3. J.C. Mitchell, *Concepts in Programming Languages* (Cambridge University Press, Cambridge, 2003)
4. H.P. Barendregt, *The Lambda Calculus: Its Syntax and Semantics* (North-Holland, Amsterdam, 1984). Revised edition
5. G.D. Plotkin, LCF considered as a programming language. Theor. Comput. Sci. **5**, 223–255 (1977)
6. G.D. Plotkin, Full abstraction, totality and PCF. Math. Struct. Comput. Sci. **9**(1), 1–20 (1999)
7. G. Winskel, *The Formal Semantics of Programming Languages. Foundations of Computing* (MIT Press, Cambridge, 1993)
8. B.C. Pierce, *Types and Programming Languages* (MIT Press, Cambridge, 2002)
9. P. Sestoft, *Programming Language Concepts*. Undergraduate topics in computer science (Springer, Berlin, 2012)

Part IV
Logic Languages

Chapter 7
General Features of Logic Programming Languages

We have already discussed two approaches to programming: the imperative and the functional programming paradigms. If we had to single out one major difference between functional and imperative programs, we could perhaps say that functional programs are concerned with *what* needs to be computed whereas imperative programs specify *how* to compute it. For this reason, functional languages are classified as *declarative* languages. There is another interesting family of declarative languages, which has its roots in logic: *logic programming languages*.

Roughly speaking, a program in a logic programming language consists of logic formulas describing a problem. The execution of a program is a process of proof searching, during which solutions for the problem are generated. Since programs are just descriptions of problems, this is a knowledge-based programming style, which has many applications in artificial intelligence (for example, to build expert systems).

The language of logic is very powerful. The same formalism can be used to specify a problem, write a program, and prove properties of the program. The same program can be used in many different ways. Based on this idea, several programming languages have been developed, which differ in the kind of logic that is used for the description of the problem and the method employed to find proofs.

The most well-known logic programming language is *Prolog*, which is based on first-order logic and uses the Principle of Resolution [1] to build proofs. Actually, first-order logic and resolution are too general to be used directly as a programming language, but in the 1970s, Kowalski, Colmerauer and Roussel defined and implemented a suitable restriction, based on the clausal fragment of classical first-order logic. This resulted in the first version of Prolog [2].

Nowadays, several versions of Prolog exist. The basic framework has been enriched to make it more efficient and easier to use. Extensions include primitive data types for integers and real numbers, advanced optimisation techniques, file-handling facilities, graphical interfaces, control mechanisms, etc. Some of these features are non-declarative, and programs that use them are called *impure* because, to achieve efficiency, the problem description and the implementation details are mixed (i.e., the *what* and the *how* are mixed). Constraint logic programming languages, which

M. Fernández, *Programming Languages and Operational Semantics*,
Undergraduate Topics in Computer Science, DOI: 10.1007/978-1-4471-6368-8_7,
© Springer-Verlag London 2014

were developed from Prolog, achieve efficiency by incorporating optimised proof search methods for specific domains.

In this book, we will only consider the pure fragment of Prolog. We will see how logic can be used to express knowledge and describe problems, and how this knowledge can be processed to compute solutions to problems, using the Principle of Resolution as inference rule.

In this chapter we give an overview of the logic programming paradigm. We start by defining the domain of computation of logic programs, and then describe how Prolog programs are built and how they are used to solve problems. We study the operational semantics of Prolog in Chap. 8.

For the examples in this part of the book, we use a generic notation inspired by the syntax of SWI-Prolog—a free Prolog compiler that can be downloaded, together with the reference manual, from http://www.swi-prolog.org.

7.1 The Herbrand Universe

The domain of computation of logic programs is the *Herbrand universe*, named after Jacques Herbrand, who studied logical deduction as a computation mechanism in the 1930s.

The Herbrand universe is a set of *terms* defined over an *alphabet* of

- *variables*, such as X, Y, etc.; and
- *function symbols* with fixed arities (the arity of a symbol is, as usual, the number of arguments associated with it).

Function symbols are usually denoted by f, g, h, ... or a, b, c, ... for constants (that is, function symbols of arity 0). In our examples, we will often use more meaningful names for function symbols.

Definition 7.1 (Herbrand Terms)

The set of terms in the Herbrand universe is inductively defined. A *Herbrand term* is either a variable, or an expression of form $f(t_1, \ldots, t_n)$, where f is a function symbol of arity $n \geq 0$ and $t_1, \ldots, t_n$ are Herbrand terms. If n is 0 we simply write f, omitting the brackets as usual.

In the rest of the book, we will simply refer to Herbrand terms as terms.

Example 7.2

If a is a constant, f a binary function symbol, g a unary function symbol, and X and Y are variables, then $f(f(X, g(a)), Y)$ is a term.

Function symbols in logic programs correspond to the constructors used to build data structures in functional languages. They are used to give structure to the domain of computation. For example, if our algorithm deals with an array of five elements, a suitable data structure can be defined using a function symbol `array` of arity 5. The array containing the elements $0, 1, 2, 3, 4$ is then represented by the term `array(0,1,2,3,4)`.

It is not possible to give a definition for a function symbol in a logic program; terms are not evaluated. However, in Prolog there are some built-in functions, such as arithmetic operations, for which there are specific evaluation mechanisms.

In logic programming languages, the alphabet is not fixed. The programmer can freely choose the names of variables and functions needed to represent the problem domain (aside from a few reserved keywords). However, Prolog's syntax requires that names of variables start with upper-case letters and names of functions start with lower-case letters. Also, function names should be different from built-in operations.

7.2 Logic Programs

Once the domain of computation is established, a problem can be described by means of logical formulas involving *predicates*.

Predicates represent properties of terms, and are used to build atomic formulas that are then composed using operators such as *and, or* and *not*, for which we write $\land$, $\lor$ and $\neg$, respectively (see Sect. 2.2 in Chap. 2 for a short overview of first-order logic).

Definition 7.3 (Atomic Formulas and Literals)

Let $\mathcal{P}$ be a set of *predicate symbols*, each with a fixed arity. If p is a predicate symbol of arity n and $t_1, \ldots, t_n$ are terms, then $p(t_1, \ldots, t_n)$ is an *atomic formula*, or simply an *atom*. Again, n may be 0, and in this case we omit the brackets.

A *literal* is an atomic formula or a negated atomic formula.

Example 7.4

The following are two literals (the second is a negated atom), where we use the predicates `valueSIMP` of arity 2 and `raining` of arity 0, as well as the unary function symbol `number`, and the constant 1.

```
valueSIMP(number(1),1)
¬raining
```

We have followed another syntactic convention of Prolog: names of predicates start with a lower-case letter.

Definition 7.5 (Programs)

Prolog programs are sets of *definite clauses*, also called *Horn clauses*, which are a restricted class of first-order formulas. A *definite clause* is a disjunction of literals with at most one positive literal.

We now introduce some notational conventions for clauses.

We write $P_1, P_2, \ldots$ to denote atoms.

A definite clause $P_1 \lor \neg P_2 \lor \ldots \lor \neg P_n$ (where P_1 is the only positive literal) is written:

$$P_1 \coloneqq P_2, \ldots, P_n.$$

and we read it as:

$$\text{``}P_1 \text{ if } P_2 \text{ and } \ldots \text{ and } P_n\text{''}$$

We call P_1 the *head* of the clause, and $P_2, \ldots, P_n$ the *body* of the clause.
   If the clause contains just P_1 and no negative literals, then we simply write

$$P_1.$$

Both kinds of clauses (with and without negative literals) are called *program clauses*, the first is a *rule* and the second is a *fact*.
   If the clause contains only negative literals, we call it a *goal* or *query* and write

$$:\text{-} \ P_2, \ldots, P_n.$$

A Prolog program consists of one or more clauses, defining one or more relations. The scoping rules are simple: the scope of each relation is the whole program (it is not possible to write local definitions in Prolog); within a clause, the scope of each variable is the whole clause.
   Program clauses can be seen as defining a database: facts specify information to be stored and rules specify how to deduce more information from previously defined data.
   Goals are questions to be answered using the information about the problem in the database. This can be better seen with some examples.

Example 7.6

In the following Prolog program, the first four clauses are facts and the last one is a rule.

```
based(prolog,logic).¹
based(haskell,maths).
likes(claire,maths).
likes(max,logic).
likes(X,L)  :- based(L,Y), likes(X,Y).
```

We use two binary predicates: based and likes, function symbols prolog, logic, haskell, maths, claire, max of arity 0, and variables X, Y, L.
   The first two clauses in the program can be read as "Prolog is based on logic and Haskell on mathematics". More precisely, these are facts about the predicate based; they define a relation to be stored in the database.
   The next three clauses define the predicate likes. There are two facts, which can be read as "Claire likes mathematics and Max likes logic", and a rule which

---

[1] In some versions of Prolog the word prolog is reserved, therefore to run this example you might need to replace prolog by myprolog for instance.

allows us to deduce more information about people's tastes. We can read this rule as "X likes L if L is based on Y and X likes Y".

Once this information is specified in the program as shown above, we can ask questions such as "is there somebody (some Z) who likes Prolog?" which corresponds to the goal

```
:- likes(Z,prolog).
```

With the information given in the program, we can deduce that Max likes Prolog: we know that Max likes logic and Prolog is based on logic, and therefore the last rule allows us to conclude that Max likes Prolog.

Prolog reaches this conclusion using an inference rule called *resolution*. It will be described in Chap. 8.

Example 7.7

We can use arithmetic operations in program clauses. To compute the value of an arithmetic expression, we use the built-in predicate `is`. For instance, we can define the predicate `mean` by

```
mean(A,B,C)  :- C is (A+B)/2.
```

This rule specifies that the mean of A and B is C, if C is the result of $(A + B)/2$.

If we provide two numbers to instantiate the variables A and B, we can obtain their mean by writing a query as in the following example.

```
:- mean(4,6,X).
```

Prolog evaluates the expression $(4 + 6)/2$ and produces the answer $X = 5$.

7.3 Finding Answers

Answers to goals are represented in Prolog by *substitutions*, which map unknowns (i.e., the variables in the goal) to *values*, that is, terms in the domain of computation (the Herbrand universe, see Sect. 7.1).

Definition 7.8 (Substitution)

A *substitution* is a partial function from variables to terms, with a finite domain. If the domain of the substitution σ, which we denote by $dom(\sigma)$, is $\{X_1, \ldots, X_n\}$, and σ maps each variable X_i to a term t_i, we represent σ by the pairs

$$\{X_1 \mapsto t_1, \ldots, X_n \mapsto t_n\}$$

Substitutions are extended to terms and literals in the natural way: We apply a substitution σ to a term t (resp. to a literal l) by simultaneously replacing each variable X_i in $dom(\sigma)$ occurring in t (resp. in l) by the corresponding term t_i. The resulting term is denoted by $t\sigma$ (we give examples below).

Since substitutions are functions, *composition of substitutions* is simply functional composition. For example, $\sigma \cdot \rho$ denotes the composition of σ and ρ.

Example 7.9

The application of the substitution

$$\sigma = \{X \mapsto g(Y), Y \mapsto a\}$$

to the term

$$f(f(X, g(a)), Y)$$

yields the term

$$f(f(g(Y), g(a)), a)$$

Note the simultaneous replacement of X by $g(Y)$ and Y by a in the term $f(f(X, g(a)), Y)$ given above.

Consider now the substitution

$$\rho = \{Y \mapsto b, Z \mapsto a\}$$

We can compose ρ and σ, and apply the resulting substitution $\rho \cdot \sigma$ to the same term $f(f(X, g(a)), Y)$. The result is the term

$$f(f(g(b), g(a)), a)$$

obtained by applying first σ to $f(f(X, g(a)), Y)$, then ρ to the resulting term $f(f(g(Y), g(a)), a)$.

The behaviour of logic programs can be described in two ways: there is a *declarative interpretation*, in which the semantics of a program is defined with respect to a mathematical model (the Herbrand Universe), and a *procedural interpretation*, which explains how the program is used in computations. The first corresponds to a *denotational semantics* of programs and the second gives an *operational semantics*.

The operational semantics of Prolog is based on the use of SLD-resolution, a specific version of the Principle of Resolution, which we will describe in Chap. 8.

Using SLD-resolution, Prolog tries to find the answers to a given goal by considering different alternatives in the context of a given program. These alternatives are organised as branches in a tree, called the *SLD-resolution* tree, or simply the SLD-tree. In order to find all the solutions, the whole SLD-tree should be explored. However, the tree could be infinite, and some of the branches may not lead to a solution. After arriving at the end of such a branch, which is called a *failure*, Prolog *backtracks* to the nearest point in the tree where there are still alternative branches to explore. It continues traversing the SLD-tree until all the alternatives are exhausted. The examples below illustrate this idea.

Prolog supports interactive programming: the user can submit a query and ask for the first solution, and then for further solutions if desired. Functional programming languages can also work in an interactive mode, but in functional languages the interaction is achieved by submitting expressions to be evaluated using a collection of function definitions, and each expression produces at most one result. Instead, in logic languages the interaction is achieved by means of queries that are resolved using a collection of predicate definitions, and several answers may be found.

To see the analogy (and the differences) between function definitions and predicate definitions, let us look at a Prolog program defining the predicate append for lists[2].

In Prolog, the empty list is denoted by [], and a non-empty list is denoted by [X|L], where X is the first element of the list (also called the *head* of the list) and L is the rest of the list (also called the *tail* of the list). Note that [|] is a binary function symbol, a constructor that is used to build a list structure. We abbreviate [X|[]] (that is, the list that contains only the element X) as [X], and [X|[Y|[]]] as [X,Y]. In general, we write [X1,...,Xn] for the list containing the elements X1,...,Xn.

Example 7.10

Our aim is to write a Prolog program to concatenate lists. For this, we will use a predicate symbol append of arity 3, since we need to represent a relation between three lists: the two lists we want to concatenate and their concatenation. More precisely, our aim is to define append such that the formula append(S,T,U) is true if the result of appending the list T onto the end of the list S is the list U.

We can define the predicate append in Prolog by giving two program clauses (a fact and a rule):

```
append([],L,L).
append([X|L],Y,[X|Z]) :- append(L,Y,Z).
```

The first program clause states that the concatenation of the empty list with a list L is L, that is, if S is empty and U is equal to T then append(S,T,U) holds.

The second program clause, a rule, could be read as: "the concatenation of the lists [X|L] and Y is the list [X|Z], if Z is the concatenation of the lists L and Y". Note that the first element in the list obtained by concatenating [X|L] and Y is X, the head of the first list, as expected.

Now compare this with the functional definition of list concatenation:

append([ ], *l*) = *l*

append(*x* : *l*, *y*) = *x* : *append*(*l*, *y*)

Clauses and equations play similar roles; both programs can be used to concatenate lists. For instance, with the Prolog program given above the solution to the goal

```
:- append([0],[1,2],U).
```

is a substitution associating U with the value [0,1,2] (see Example 7.11 below, where the computation of this answer is described). We obtain the same result by evaluating the expression *append*([0], [1, 2]) in the context of the functional program given above: the result is the list [0, 1, 2].

---

[2] The predicate append is predefined in most Prolog implementations.

However, logic programs do not have a fixed input-output semantics: The predicate append represents a relation, and can be used in different ways. For instance, with the *same* logic program and the goal

```
:- append([0],U,[0,1,2]).
```

we obtain the answer U = [1,2]. In this case, the first and third arguments of the predicate are used as input and the second as output. All combinations are possible.

Answers to goals (i.e., substitutions mapping variables in the goal to values) are automatically generated by the process of resolution, of which the *unification algorithm* is a major component. When Prolog reads a goal, it tries to find in the program the clauses that can be applied. During this process, some equations between terms are generated, and the unification algorithm is called in order to solve these equations. If there is a solution, there is also one that is the most general solution, in the sense that all the others can be derived from it. This is called the *most general unifier*.

We will formally define unification problems and give a unification algorithm in Chap. 8, but we can already give an example.

Example 7.11

To solve the query

```
:- append([0],[1,2],U).
```

in the context of the logic program

```
append([],L,L).
append([X|L],Y,[X|Z]) :- append(L,Y,Z).
```

Prolog will start by using the second program clause (the first one cannot be applied because in our goal the first list is not empty). The substitution

$$\{X \mapsto 0, L \mapsto [], Y \mapsto [1,2], U \mapsto [0|Z]\}$$

unifies the head of the second program clause with the query, that is, if we apply this substitution to the literals

$$\text{append}([X|L], Y, [X|Z]) \text{ and append}([0], [1,2], U)$$

we obtain exactly the same result in both cases: append([0],[1,2],[0|Z]).

Since the clause says that append([X|L],Y,[X|Z]) holds if append (L,Y,Z) holds, to prove the goal it is sufficient to prove that append([], [1,2],Z) holds for some Z.

Now we have an atom in which the first list is empty, and we have a fact append([],L,L) in the program. Applying the substitution

$$\{Z \mapsto [1,2]\}$$

to our atom, we obtain (an instance of) a fact.

Combining both substitutions, i.e., computing the composition of

$$\{X \mapsto 0, L \mapsto [], Y \mapsto [1, 2], U \mapsto [0|Z]\} \text{ and } \{Z \mapsto [1, 2]\},$$

we obtain the substitution

$$\{X \mapsto 0, L \mapsto [], Y \mapsto [1, 2], U \mapsto [0|[1, 2]], Z \mapsto [1, 2]\}$$

and restricting this substitution to the variables in the goal, we get:

$$\{U \mapsto [0, 1, 2]\}$$

which solves the query. It is the most general answer substitution for the given goal.

The process by which we derived this solution is an example of application of the Principle of Resolution.

Goals such as:

```
:- append([0],[1,2],U)
:- append(X,[1,2],U)
:- append([1,2],U,[0])
```

can all be seen as questions to be answered using the definitions given in the program. The first one has only one solution:

$$\{U \mapsto [0, 1, 2]\}$$

The second has an infinite number of solutions, and the third one has none.

In the following chapter we will study in more detail the operational semantics of Prolog.

7.4 Further Reading

During the late 1920s, Jacques Herbrand, a young mathematician, developed a method to check the validity of a class of first-order logic formulas. In his thesis, published in 1931, Herbrand discussed what can be considered the first unification procedure. Unification is at the heart of modern implementations of logic programming languages.

The language Prolog was originally developed in Marseille and Edinburgh by Colmerauer, Kowalski and Roussel in the 1970s [2], based on Robinson's Resolution Principle [1], which provided an efficient mechanism to build proofs of first-order logic formulas in clausal form. Efficient implementations of the unification algorithm were key to the success of Prolog (in the next chapter we describe one of the most well-known unification algorithms).

There are many textbooks that present logic programming techniques and Prolog in particular. For an introduction to the subject, we recommend Hogger's book [3]. For more details and examples of logic programs, the book by Clocksin and Mellish [4] is a standard reference.

7.5 Exercises

1. Assuming that A, B, C are atomic formulas, which of the following clauses are definite clauses?

   a) $\neg A \vee \neg B$
   b) $A \vee B \vee \neg C$
   c) $A \vee \neg A$
   d) A

2. Test the program:

```
based(myprolog,logic).

based(haskell,maths).

likes(claire,maths).

likes(max,logic).

likes(X,L)  :- based(L,Y), likes(X,Y).
```

   with the goals:

```
:- likes(Z,myprolog).

:- likes(X,maths).

:- likes(max,X).
```

   You can do this as follows: Edit the program with your favourite text editor, and save it to a file *name*.pl Then launch SWI-Prolog, and when you see the prompt

   ?-

   load your program by writing the name of the file as shown below.

   ?- ['*name*.pl'].

   Then type each goal (without the symbols ":-") and press return.

In SWI-Prolog, type n to obtain the next answer for a goal with more than one answer.

3. Numbers and arithmetic operations are predefined in Prolog. Assume we define the predicate mean using the clause:

```
mean(A,B,C) :- C is (A+B)/2.
```

Load this program and test it with the following goals:

```
:- mean(2,4,X).
```

```
:- mean(2,4,6).
```

4. Apply the substitution $\{X \mapsto [X, Y], Y \mapsto [X, Y]\}$ to the term $f(X, Y)$.

5. Lists are also predefined in Prolog. In particular, the predicate append is predefined, but in this exercise we will define a new append:

```
myappend([],Y,Y).
```

```
myappend([H|T],Y,[H|U]) :- myappend(T,Y,U).
```

What are the answers to the following goals?

```
:- myappend([1,2],[3,4,5],[1,2,3,4,5]).
```

```
:- myappend([1,2],[3,4,5],[1,2]).
```

```
:- myappend([1,2],[3,4,5],X).
```

```
:- myappend([1,2],X,[1,2,3,4,5]).
```

```
:- myappend(X,[3,4,5],[1,2,3,4,5]).
```

```
:- myappend(X,Y,[1,2,3,4,5]).
```

```
:- myappend(X,Y,Z).
```

Explain the answers.

6. Change the order of the clauses in the previous program, and try again the previous goals.

Can you explain the behaviour of the new program?

References

1. J.A. Robinson, A machine-oriented logic based on the resolution principle. J. ACM **12**(1), 23–41 (1965)
2. P. Roussel, PROLOG: Manuel de référence et d'utilisation. Research report, Artificial Intelligence Team, University of Aix-Marseille, France, 1975
3. C.J. Hogger, *Introduction to Logic Programming*. APIC Studies in Data Processing. Academic Press, Massachusetts, 1984
4. W.F. Clocksin, C.S. Mellish, Programming in Prolog. 4th edn. (Springer, Heidelberg, 1994)

Chapter 8
Operational Semantics of Prolog

In this chapter, we describe the operational interpretation of Prolog programs. More precisely, we describe how a Prolog interpreter solves goals in the context of a given program.

We have already mentioned in the previous chapter that Prolog uses the Principle of Resolution in order to obtain answers for the given goals. We start this chapter by defining unification, which is a key step in the Principle of Resolution. We then define SLD-resolution, the version of Resolution used by Prolog, and describe the strategy used by Prolog's interpreter to search for proofs and find solutions for goals.

8.1 Unification

Although the process of unification was sketched by Herbrand in his thesis in the early 1930s, it was only in the 1960s, after Robinson introduced the Principle of Resolution and gave an algorithm to unify terms, that logic programming became possible. Robinson's unification algorithm was the basis for the implementation of the programming language Prolog.

The version of the unification algorithm that we present in this section is based on the work of Martelli and Montanari, who described unification as a simplification process. Martelli and Montanari proposed a very efficient unification algorithm using multi-equations; however, here we present a simplified version of their algorithm, using just equations between terms.

Definition 8.1 (Unifier)

A *unification problem* $\mathcal{U}$ is a set of equations between terms containing variables. We will use the notation

$$s_1 = t_1, \ldots, s_n = t_n$$

for a unification problem consisting of n pairs of terms to unify.

M. Fernández, *Programming Languages and Operational Semantics*,
Undergraduate Topics in Computer Science, DOI: 10.1007/978-1-4471-6368-8_8,
© Springer-Verlag London 2014

A solution to the unification problem $\mathcal{U}$, also called a *unifier* for the problem $\mathcal{U}$, is a substitution σ (see Definition 7.8 in Chap. 7) such that when we apply σ to all the terms in the equations in $\mathcal{U}$ we obtain syntactical identities: For each equation $s_i = t_i$ in $\mathcal{U}$, the terms $s_i\sigma$ and $t_i\sigma$ coincide.

If there is a unifier for the problem $s = t$, we say that s and t are *unifiable*.

A unifier σ for $\mathcal{U}$ is said to be *most general* if any other unifier for the problem $\mathcal{U}$ can be obtained as an instance of σ.

Although there may be many different substitutions that are most general unifiers for a problem $\mathcal{U}$, they are all equivalent modulo renaming of variables. In other words, if a unification problem $\mathcal{U}$ has a unifier, then there is a unique most general unifier up to renamings, which justifies referring to "the" most general general unifier (mgu) for $\mathcal{U}$.

The algorithm of Martelli and Montanari finds the most general unifier for a unification problem if a solution exists; otherwise it fails, indicating that there are no solutions. To find the most general unifier for a unification problem, the algorithm simplifies the set of equations, until a substitution is generated or a failure is detected.

The simplification rules apply to sets of equations and produce new sets of equations or a failure.

Unification Algorithm.

Input: A finite set of equations between terms (i.e., a unification problem):

$$s_1 = t_1, \ldots, s_n = t_n$$

Output: A substitution that is the most general unifier (mgu) for this problem, or failure.

Transformation Rules: The rules that are given below transform a unification problem into a simpler one or produce a failure. Below, E denotes an arbitrary set of equations between terms.

(1) $f(s_1, \ldots, s_n) = f(t_1, \ldots, t_n), E \;\rightarrow\; s_1 = t_1, \ldots, s_n = t_n, E$
(2) $f(s_1, \ldots, s_n) = g(t_1, \ldots, t_m), E \;\rightarrow\; failure$
(3) $\qquad\qquad\qquad X = X, E \;\rightarrow\; E$
(4) $\qquad\qquad\qquad t = X, E \;\rightarrow\; X = t, E$
$\qquad\qquad\qquad\qquad$ if t is not a variable
(5) $\qquad\qquad\qquad X = t, E \;\rightarrow\; X = t, E\{X \mapsto t\}$
$\qquad\qquad\qquad\qquad$ if X is not in t and X occurs in E
(6) $\qquad\qquad\qquad X = t, E \;\rightarrow\; failure$
$\qquad\qquad\qquad\qquad$ if X occurs in t and $X \neq t$

The unification algorithm applies the transformation rules in a non-deterministic way until no rule can be applied or a failure arises. Note that we are working with *sets* of equations, therefore the order in which they appear in the unification problem is not important.

The test in case (6) is called *occur-check*; for example: $X = f(X)$ fails. This test is time consuming, and for this reason in some systems it is not implemented.

If the algorithm finishes without a failure, we obtain a substitution, which is the *most general unifier* of the initial set of equations.

Note that rules (1) and (2) apply also to equations between constants (i.e., 0-ary function symbols). In the first case, if $n = 0$ then the equation $f = f$ is deleted, and in the second case, the problem does not have any solution (the algorithm stops with failure).

Example 8.2

1. We start with $f(a, a) = f(X, a)$.

    (a) Using rule (1), this problem is rewritten to $a = X, a = a$.
    (b) Using rule (4), the problem $a = X, a = a$ becomes $X = a, a = a$.
    (c) Using rule (1) again the equation $a = a$ is deleted, and we get $X = a$.

    Now no rule can be applied, and therefore the algorithm terminates. The most general unifier is $\{X \mapsto a\}$.
2. In Chap. 7, Example 7.11, we solved the unification problem
    ```
    [X|L] = [0], Y = [1,2], [X|Z] = U
    ```
    Recall that [|] is a binary function symbol (a list constructor; its arguments are the head and the tail of the list respectively). [0] is a shorthand for [0 | []], and [] is a constant (the empty list).
    We apply the unification algorithm, starting with the set of equations above.

    (a) Using rule (1) in the first equation, we get:
    ```
    X = 0, L = [], Y = [1,2], [X|Z] = U
    ```
    (b) Now using rule (5) and the first equation we get:
    ```
    X = 0, L = [], Y = [1,2], [0|Z] = U
    ```
    (c) Using rule (4) and the last equation we get:
    ```
    X = 0, L = [], Y = [1,2], U = [0|Z]
    ```

    Then the algorithm stops. Therefore the most general unifier is
    $\{X \mapsto 0, L \mapsto [], Y \mapsto [1, 2], U \mapsto [0|Z]\}$

8.2 The Principle of Resolution

Resolution is based on *refutation*. In order to solve a query
$$:- A_1,...,A_n$$
with respect to a set P of program clauses, resolution seeks to show that

$$P, \neg A_1, \ldots, \neg A_n$$

leads to a contradiction. That is, the negation of the literals in the goal is added to
the program P; if a contradiction arises, then we know that P did entail the literals
in the query.

Definition 8.3
A contradiction is obtained when a literal and its negation (that is, A and $\neg A$) are
stated at the same time.

   If a contradiction does not arise directly from the program and the goal, new
clauses will be derived by resolution, and the process will continue until a contradiction arises or no more deductions can be made (the search may continue forever).
The derived clauses are called *resolvents*.

   We will describe the generation of resolvents using a restriction of the Resolution
Principle called SLD-resolution; Prolog is based on SLD-resolution.

8.2.1 SLD-Resolution

Let us consider first a simple case, where in the query there is just one atom. If we
have a query

   :- $p(u_1, \dots, u_n)$.

and a program clause (where we rename the variables if necessary, so that all the
variables in the clause are different from those in the query)

   $p(t_1, \dots, t_n)$:- $S_1, \dots, S_m$.

such that the unification problem $p(t_1, \dots, t_n) = p(u_1, \dots, u_n)$ has an mgu σ, then
we obtain a resolvent

   :- $S_1\sigma, \dots, S_m\sigma$.

In the general case, the query may have several literals. Prolog's SLD-resolution
generates a resolvent using the first literal in the goal.

Definition 8.4 (SLD-Resolution)
A *resolvent* for a goal

   :- $A_1, \dots, A_k$.

with respect to a given program P is generated by unifying the *first* atom in the goal
(that is, A_1) and the head of a (possibly renamed) program clause. More precisely,
if there is a clause in P of the form

   $A_1' : -S_1, \dots, S_m$.

such that A_1' and A_1 are unifiable with mgu σ, then we obtain a resolvent

   :- $S_1\sigma, \dots, S_m\sigma, A_2\sigma, \dots, A_k\sigma$.

In other words, the resolvent is generated by replacing in the goal the first atom that
unifies with the head of a clause by the body of the clause, and applying the unifier
to all the atoms in the new goal. Note that when we compute a resolvent using a fact
(i.e., when $m = 0$), the atom simply disappears from the query.

   An empty resolvent indicates a contradiction, which we will denote by the
symbol $\diamond$.

Each SLD-resolution step computes a resolvent between the first atom of the last resolvent obtained and a clause in the program. It is for this reason that this particular form of resolution is called *SLD-resolution*:

'S' stands for *selection rule*: A fixed computation rule is applied in order to select a particular atom to resolve upon in the goal. Prolog always selects the *leftmost* literal in the goal.

'L' stands for *linear*: it indicates that each resolution step uses the most recent resolvent (to start with, it uses the given query) and a program clause. Prolog uses the clauses in the program *in the order they are written*.

'D' stands for *definite*: it indicates that all the program clauses are definite.

Given a program and a query, the idea is to continue generating resolvents until an empty one (a contradiction) is generated. When an empty resolvent is generated, the composition of all the substitutions applied at each SLD-resolution step leading to the contradiction is computed. This is also a substitution (recall that substitutions are functions from terms to terms and composition here means functional composition, see Chap. 7 for more details). The restriction of this substitution to the variables that occur in the initial goal is an *answer* to the initial query.

Definition 8.5 (SLD-resolution tree)
We represent each SLD-resolution step graphically as follows:

$$\text{Query}$$
$$\mid \; mgu$$
$$\text{Resolvent}$$

Since there may be several clauses in the program that can be used to generate a resolvent for a given query, we obtain a branching structure called a *SLD-resolution tree* (or just SLD-tree).

The SLD-tree for a given query has the query at the root, and a branch for each resolvent generated from the query, which in turn becomes the root of a subtree.

Every branch that leads to an empty resolvent in the SLD-tree produces an answer. All the branches that produce an answer are called *success branches*.

If a finite branch does not lead to an empty resolvent, it is a *failure*.

An SLD-resolution tree may have several success branches, failure branches, and also infinite branches that arise when we can continue generating resolvents but never reach an empty one.

Example 8.6
Consider the program P

```
based (prolog,logic).
based (haskell,maths).
likes (max,logic).
likes (claire,maths).
likes (X,P) :- based (P,Y), likes (X,Y).
```

likes(Z,prolog)

$\mid$ {X $\mapsto$ Z, P $\mapsto$ prolog}

based(prolog,Y), likes(Z,Y)

$\mid$ {Y $\mapsto$ logic}

likes(Z,logic).

{Z $\mapsto$ max} /   \ {X' $\mapsto$ Z, P' $\mapsto$ logic}

◇   based(logic,Y'),likes(Z,Y')
(Failure)

Fig. 8.1 SLD-tree for the query :- likes (Z,prolog). using the clauses in the program P

and the query

    :- likes (Z,prolog).

Using the last clause, and the mgu $\{X \mapsto Z, P \mapsto prolog\}$ we obtain the resolvent

    :- based(prolog,Y), likes(Z,Y).

Now, using the first clause and the mgu $\{Y \mapsto logic\}$, we obtain the new resolvent

    :- likes (Z,logic).

Finally, since we can unify this atom with the fact likes (max,logic) using the substitution $\{Z \mapsto max\}$, we obtain an empty resolvent. This is therefore a success branch in the SLD-tree for the initial query.

The composition of the substitutions used in this branch is:

$\{X \mapsto max, P \mapsto prolog, Y \mapsto logic, Z \mapsto max\}$

Therefore, the answer to the initial query is $\{Z \mapsto max\}$.

There are other branches in the SLD-tree for this query, but this is the only successful one. The SLD-resolution tree for this query is shown in Fig. 8.1. Note that in the branch that leads to failure we use again the last clause of the program but rename its variables as X', P', Y' to avoid confusion with the previous use of this clause (see Definition 8.4).

Consider now the same program with an additional clause:

    likes (claire,logic).

The new program will be called P'. The SLD-resolution tree for the same query in the context of the program P' is shown in Fig. 8.2.

Finally, with the same program and a query

    :- likes (Z,painting).

the SLD-tree consists of just one branch (which ends in failure), as shown in Fig. 8.3.

likes(Z,prolog)

| {X ↦ Z, P ↦ prolog}

based(prolog,Y), likes(Z,Y)

| {Y ↦ logic}

likes(Z,logic).

{Z ↦ max}/   {Z ↦ claire}| \

◇   ◇   based(logic,Y'),likes(Z,Y')
                                (Failure)

Fig. 8.2 SLD-tree for :- likes (Z,prolog). using the program P'

likes(Z,)

| {X ↦ Z, P ↦ painting}

based(painting,Y), likes(Z,Y)
                    (Failure)

Fig. 8.3 SLD-tree for :- likes (Z,painting)

8.3 Prolog's Search in the SLD-tree

Prolog builds the SLD-tree for a given query using the clauses in the program in the order in which they occur, in a depth-first manner; the leftmost branch in the SLD-tree is generated first. If this branch is infinite, Prolog will fail to find an answer even if there are other successful branches. For this reason, the order of the clauses in a Prolog program is very important.

If during the traversal of the tree, Prolog arrives at a failure leaf, it will go back (towards the root of the tree) to explore the remaining branches. This process is called *backtracking*.

Prolog usually stops after finding the first solution for a given query, but it will backtrack and continue traversing the tree (always in a depth-first search, from left to right) if we require more answers.

We could summarise Prolog's operational semantics as SLD-resolution with a depth-first search strategy and backtracking.

Example 8.7
Let us recall the program given in Chap. 7 (Example 7.11) to define the predicate append.

```
append ([],L,L).
append ([X|L],Y,[X|Z]) :- append (L,Y,Z).
```

The goal
```
:- append (X,[1,2],U).
```
produces the answer $\{X \mapsto [\ ],\ U \mapsto [1,\ 2]\}$. However, if we change the order of the clauses in the program, the same goal leads to an infinite computation. In this case, there is no answer for the query, and eventually the interpreter will give an error message (when all the memory space available is consumed). This is because the leftmost branch of the SLD-tree is infinite.

SLD-resolution has interesting computational properties:

1. It is refutation-complete: given a Prolog program and a goal, if a contradiction can be derived, then SLD-resolution will eventually generate an empty resolvent.
2. It is independent of the computation rule: if there is an answer for a goal, SLD-resolution will find it whichever selection rule is employed for choosing the literals resolved upon.

However, the particular tree traversal strategy that Prolog uses is not complete. In the example above, we see that if we change the order of the clauses in the program, Prolog fails to find an answer, even if an empty resolvent can be generated by SLD-resolution. The problem is that this empty resolvent will be generated in a branch of the SLD-tree that Prolog does not build.

There is an easy way to obtain a refutation-complete implementation of SLD-resolution: using breadth-first search instead of depth-first search. However, there is a price to pay. A breadth-first search strategy will in general take more time to find the first answer. For this reason, this strategy is seldom applied in practice.

8.4 Further Reading

Robinson's article [1] introduces the Principle of Resolution. More information on the unification algorithm presented in this chapter can be found in Martelli and Montanari's article [2]. The books [3–5] provide more details about Prolog; [6] is an historical reference document for Prolog.

8.5 Exercises

1. Show that, for the problem $f(X) = f(Y)$, both $\{X \mapsto Y\}$ and $\{Y \mapsto X\}$ are most general solutions. Can you find a different substitution that is also a most general unifier for these terms?
2. Recall that the notation $[A,B,C]$ is short for $[A|[B|[C|[\ ]]]]$.

   (a) Are the terms $[[1, 0], [0, 0], [0, 0]]$ and $[X|[X, Y]]$ unifiable? Use the unification algorithm to answer this question, that is, try to solve the unification problem $[[1, 0], [0, 0], [0, 0]] = [X|[X, Y]]$.

(b) Are the terms $[[1, X], Y, Y]$ and $[X\,|\,[0, 0]]$ unifiable? Use the unification algorithm to answer this question, that is, try to solve the unification problem $[[1, X], Y, Y] = [X\,|\,[0, 0]]$.

3. Give the most general unifier (if one exists) for the following problems

   (a) `append ([1,2],L,[]) = append ([X|Y],Y,[]).`
   (b) `append ([1,2],X,U) = append ([Y|L],0,[Y|R]).`

4. Show that the resolvent of the clauses
   $$P \;:- A_1, \ldots, A_n$$
   and
   $$:- Q_1, \ldots, Q_m$$
   is also a definite clause, for any atoms $A_1, \ldots, A_n, Q_1, \ldots, Q_m$.

5. A Prolog program contains the following clauses:
   ```
   sunny(mon).
   sunny(tue).
   sunny(wed).
   warm(mon).
   warm(wed).
   ```

   (a) Write down all the responses that Prolog will give to the query
   ```
   :- sunny(Day), warm(Day).
   ```
   in their proper order.
   (b) Draw the SLD-tree built by Prolog for the previous query.

6. What is the purpose of the *occur-check* in the unification algorithm?

7. Consider the following program and query:
   Program:
   ```
   grandparent(X,Z) :- parent(X,Y),parent(Y,Z).
   parent(X,Y) :- mother(X,Y).
   parent(X,Y) :- father(X,Y).
   mother(eileen,alice).
   mother(alice,victoria).
   father(stephen,victoria).
   sister(alice,john).
   ```
   Query:
   ```
   :- grandparent(eileen,Z).
   ```
   Draw the SLD-resolution tree for this query.
   What are the answers to this query?

8. Consider the following program and queries:
   Program:
   ```
   even(0).
   even(s(s(X))) :- even(X).
   odd(s(0)).
   odd(X) :- even(s(X)).
   ```
   Queries:

```
:- odd(s(s(0))).
:- odd(s(0)).
```

(a) Draw the SLD-resolution tree for each query.

(b) We now replace the fourth clause in the program by:
```
odd(X) :- greater(X,s(0)), even(s(X)).
```
Write the clauses defining the predicate `greater` such that `greater (m,n)` holds when the number m is greater than n.

Give the SLD-tree for the query:
```
:- odd(s(0)).
```
with the modified program.

9. Consider the following logic program to split a list into two lists.
```
split([],[],[]).
split([X],[X],[]).
split([X,Y|L],[X|M],[Y|N]) :- split(L,M,N).
```

(a) Draw the SLD-resolution tree for the query:
```
:- split ([0,1,2],L1,L2)
```
using the computation rule that always selects the leftmost literal as the one resolved upon.

(b) Indicate all the answers that Prolog finds for the query above.

10. Consider the following logic program
```
witness(john).
neighbour(mary).
hide(john).
suspect(X) :- witness(X).
suspect(X) :- neighbour(X).
charge(X) :- suspect(X), hide(X).
```
and queries
```
:- suspect(john).
:- charge(X).
```
Draw the SLD-resolution tree for each query (using the computation rule that always selects the leftmost literal as the one resolved upon) and give the answers that Prolog will find for each query.

11. Write a logic program to sort a list of numbers (in ascending order), using the insertion sort algorithm.

For this, you will need to define:

– a predicate insertion such that insertion (X,L,L') holds if X is a number, L is a sorted list (sorted in ascending order) and L' is the result of inserting X in the appropriate place in the list L; and

– a predicate sort such that sort (L,L') holds if L' is a list containing the same elements as L but in ascending order.

12. Write a logic program defining a binary predicate `member` such that `member (A,L)` is true if A is an element of the list L.

    What are the answers to the following queries? Draw the SLD-resolution tree for each one.

    (a) `:- member (1,[2,1,3]).`
    (b) `:- member (1,[2,3,4]).`
    (c) `:- member (1,[]).`

References

1. J.A. Robinson, A machine-oriented logic based on the resolution principle. J. ACM **12**(1), 23–41 (1965)
2. A. Martelli, U. Montanari, An efficient unification algorithm. Trans. Program. Lang. Syst. **4**(2), 258–282 (1982)
3. P. Blackburn, J. Bos, K. Striegnitz, *Learn Prolog now, Texts in Computing* (Vol. 7) (College Publications, 2007)
4. C.J. Hogger, *Introduction to Logic Programming*, APIC Studies in Data Processing (Academic Press, London, 1984)
5. W.F. Clocksin, C.S. Mellish, *Programming in Prolog*, 4th edn. (Springer, New York, 1994)
6. P. Roussel, PROLOG: Manuel de Référence et d'utilisation. Research Report, Artificial Intelligence Team, University of Aix-Marseille, France (1975)

Chapter 9
Answers to Selected Exercises

Selected Exercises From Chap. 1

1. Using the grammar that specifies the concrete syntax for arithmetic expressions in Example 1.1:

   (a) Show that $1 - 2 - 3$ and $1 + 2 * 3$ are valid expressions in this language, and list their possible results, assuming that the arithmetic operators have the usual semantics.

   Answer:

   These expressions can be generated as follows:

   $Exp \rightarrow Exp\ Op\ Exp \rightarrow Num\ Op\ Exp \rightarrow Digit\ Op\ Exp \rightarrow 1\ Op\ Exp \rightarrow 1 - Exp \rightarrow 1 - Exp\ Op\ Exp \rightarrow 1 - Num\ Op\ Exp \rightarrow 1 - Digit\ Op\ Exp \rightarrow 1 - 2\ Op\ Exp \rightarrow 1 - 2 - Exp \rightarrow 1 - 2 - Num \rightarrow 1 - 2 - Digit \rightarrow 1 - 2 - 3$

   $Exp \rightarrow Exp\ Op\ Exp \rightarrow Num\ Op\ Exp \rightarrow Digit\ Op\ Exp \rightarrow 1\ Op\ Exp \rightarrow 1 + Exp \rightarrow 1 + Exp\ Op\ Exp \rightarrow 1 + Num\ Op\ Exp \rightarrow 1 + Digit\ Op\ Exp \rightarrow 1 + 2\ Op\ Exp \rightarrow 1 + 2 * Exp \rightarrow 1 + 2 * Num \rightarrow 1 + 2 * Digit \rightarrow 1 + 2 * 3$

   (b) Are $1 + (2 - 3)$ and -1 valid expressions in this language?

   Answer:

   No, the grammar cannot generate expressions with brackets or starting with an operator.

M. Fernández, *Programming Languages and Operational Semantics*,
Undergraduate Topics in Computer Science, DOI: 10.1007/978-1-4471-6368-8_9,
© Springer-Verlag London 2014

(c) Using Haskell evaluate the expressions[1] $1 - 2 - 3$ and $1 + 2 * 3$.

From the results obtained, can you explain how Haskell has parsed these expressions? Identify the main operator (i.e., the root of the syntax tree generated by Haskell) and its arguments, in each of the expressions.

Answer:

In Haskell $*$ has higher precedence than $+$, and operators of equal precedence associate to the left. In the first expression, the root operator is the rightmost $-$, whereas in the second the root operator is $+$. The results therefore are -4 and 7.

3. Using the grammar given in Example 1.2 to specify the abstract syntax of arithmetic expressions:

(a) Show that both $-(-(1, 2), 3)$ and $-(1, -(2, 3))$ are valid. What are their values (assuming that the arithmetic operators have the usual semantics)?

Answer:

To show they are valid, we show they can be generated:
$$E \rightarrow Op(E, E) \rightarrow -(E, E) \rightarrow -(Op(E, E), E) \rightarrow -(-(E, E), E) \rightarrow$$
$$-(-(1, E), E) \rightarrow -(-(1, 2), E) \rightarrow -(-(1, 2), 3)$$

$$E \rightarrow Op(E, E) \rightarrow -(E, E) \rightarrow -(1, E) \rightarrow -(1, Op(E, E)) \rightarrow$$
$$-(1, -(E, E)) \rightarrow -(1, -(2, E)) \rightarrow -(1, -(2, 3))$$

The results are -4 and 2.

(b) Explain why $-(1, 2, 3)$ is not a valid abstract syntax tree according to this grammar.

Answer:

The grammar specifies that each operator has two arguments.

5. Assume we want to design a language L in which variable identifiers are sequences of letters or numbers, starting with a capital letter. Give a grammar for the concrete syntax of identifiers in L.

Answer:

We can use the following grammar.

---

[1] Simply use the interactive evaluator in your browser, see http://tryhaskell.org. To evaluate an expression, type the expression after the prompt and press the return key.

$id ::= Cap \mid Cap\ any$

$Cap ::= A \mid B \mid C \mid \ldots \mid Z$

$any ::= char \mid char\ any$

$char ::= Cap \mid small \mid digit$

$small ::= a \mid b \mid c \mid \ldots \mid z$

$digit ::= 0 \mid 1 \mid 2 \ldots \mid 9$

6. The following grammar defines the concrete syntax of identifiers in Haskell. Non-terminals are written in italics. In the first rule, we use a special notation to represent set difference: (*small rest*)—*keywords* denotes the strings generated by *small rest* minus the ones generated by *keywords*. In the third rule, the symbol ϵ denotes an empty string.

$varid \rightarrow (small\ rest) - keywords$

$small \rightarrow a \mid b \mid c \mid \ldots \mid z$

$rest \rightarrow \epsilon \mid sldq\ rest$

$sldq \rightarrow small \mid large \mid digit \mid\ '$

$large \rightarrow A \mid B \mid C \mid \ldots \mid Z$

$digit \rightarrow 0 \mid 1 \mid 2 \mid \ldots \mid 9$

$keywords \rightarrow$ case | class | data | default | deriving | do | else | if | import | in | infix | infixl | infixr | instance | let | module | newtype | of | then | type | where | _

(a) Explain in English how identifiers are formed.

   Answer:

   Identifiers are sequences of letters, numbers and quotes, starting with a lower-case letter, and excluding keywords.

(b) We extend the grammar with a rule to specify the form of function declarations in Haskell:
   $decl \rightarrow$ let *varid args* = *expr1* in *expr2*
   where *varid* is the name of the function, *args* its arguments, *expr1* its definition and *expr2* the expression where it is used (we omit the grammar rules defining *args, expr1, expr2*).

For example, the following is a valid function declaration for a function called double, with an argument x, defined by the expression 2 * x and used to compute the double of 3.
let double x = 2 * x in double 3

The following Haskell programs have syntax errors. Try to run the programs and explain why they produce error messages.[2] Using the grammar given, can you identify the errors and suggest ways to correct them?

let Double x = 2 * x in Double 3

let double x = 2 * x in double 3

let data = 1 in data + 1

Answer:

In these programs the names used for functions do not satisfy the constraints specified by the grammar: the first one starts with a capital letter, the second one includes a question mark, and the third one uses the reserved keyword data.

Selected Exercises From Chap. 2

1. Show the following properties of the intersection and union operators on sets:

$$A \cup B = B \cup A$$
$$(A \cup B) \cup C = A \cup (B \cup C)$$
$$A \cup A = A$$
$$A \cap B = B \cap A$$
$$(A \cap B) \cap C = A \cap (B \cap C)$$
$$A \cap A = A$$

Answer:

We can prove these properties using the definition of set equality and the properties of the logical connectives. We show the first two properties (commutativity and associativity of union).
To prove $A \cup B = B \cup A$, by definition of set equality we need to show $A \cup B \subseteq B \cup A$ and $B \cup A \subseteq A \cup B$. Let us prove the first inclusion, that is, prove that if $a \in A \cup B$ then $a \in B \cup A$, for any a.

---

[2] Type each of the lines using the interactive evaluator for Haskell in your browser, see http://tryhaskell.org, and explain the errors found.

If $a \in A \cup B$, then, by definition of union, $a \in A$ or $a \in B$. Since the connective *or* is commutative (the formula $a \in A$ or $a \in B$ is true whenever one of the two components is true), then also $a \in B$ or $a \in A$ holds. Therefore $a \in B \cup A$. The other inclusion can be proved in a similar way. To prove the associativity property of union, that is, $(A \cup B) \cup C = A \cup (B \cup C)$ we need to prove $(A \cup B) \cup C \subseteq A \cup (B \cup C)$ and $A \cup (B \cup C) \subseteq (A \cup B) \cup C$ (by definition of set equality).

To show the first inclusion, let us assume $a \in (A \cup B) \cup C$. Then, by definition of union, $a \in A \cup B$ or $a \in C$. Again, using the definition of union, this is equivalent to $a \in A$ or $a \in B$ or $a \in C$. Since a disjunction is true when any of the components is true, this is equivalent to stating $a \in A$ or $a \in B \cup C$, which is the definition of $A \cup (B \cup C)$.

The second inclusion can be proved in a similar way.

3. Prove, by mathematical induction, that for any natural number n:

   (a) $\sum_{i=1}^{n} i = n(n+1)/2$
   (b) $\sum_{i=1}^{n} 2^{i-1} = 2^n - 1$

   Answer:

(a) To show by induction that $\sum_{i=1}^{n} i = n(n+1)/2$ for any natural number n, we start by showing that the equality holds for $n = 0$ (base case). Since $\sum_{i=1}^{0} i = 0$ and $0 * 1/2 = 0$, the basis of the induction is proved. Now, assuming $\sum_{i=1}^{n} i = n(n+1)/2$ (induction hypothesis), we need to prove

$$\sum_{i=1}^{n+1} i = (n+1)(n+2)/2$$

The left-hand side can be written as $(\sum_{i=1}^{n} i) + (n+1)$, and using the induction hypothesis, this is the same as $n(n+1)/2 + (n+1)$, which we can write as $(n+1)(n/2 + 1)$, or $(n+1)(n+2)/2$. The latter is exactly the right-hand side. This completes the proof.

(b) To show by induction that $\sum_{i=1}^{n} 2^{i-1} = 2^n - 1$ for any natural number n, we start by showing that the equality holds for $n = 0$ (base case).

Again in this case if $n = 0$ both sides are 0 and the result is trivial. Now, assuming $\sum_{i=1}^{n} 2^{i-1} = 2^n - 1$ (induction hypothesis), we need to prove

$$\sum_{i=1}^{n+1} 2^{i-1} = 2^{n+1} - 1$$

The left-hand side can be written as $(\sum_{i=1}^{n} 2^{i-1}) + 2^n$, and using the induction hypothesis, this is the same as $2^n - 1 + 2^n$, which we can write as $2^{n+1} - 1$ as required.

4. Describe the set of trees generated by the following inductive definition:

Nil is a tree;
If n is a number and t_1 and t_2 are trees, then $Tree(n, t_1, t_2)$ is a tree.
Answer:

A tree according to this definition is either empty (Nil is the base case) or is a binary tree where the root and all the internal nodes store numbers.

5. Prove that the principle of structural induction corresponds to a particular application of the principle of mathematical induction.

Answer:

The principle of structural induction can be justified by the principle of mathematical induction. This is because we work with *finite* data structures, so we can understand structural induction as induction on the *size* of the structure.
More precisely: Let $P'(n)$ be the property:

For each finite labelled tree t of size at most n, $P(t)$ holds.

Then, $\forall t.P(t)$ is equivalent to $\forall n.P'(n)$.

6. Define the abstract syntax of first-order logic formulas using a grammar.
Using structural induction, define for each formula its set of free variables and bound variables.

Answer:

The following grammar generates first-order formulas (we write the binary connectives $\wedge$, $\vee$ and $\Rightarrow$ in infix notation):

$$F ::= A \mid \neg(F) \mid (F \wedge F) \mid (F \vee F) \mid (F \Rightarrow F) \mid \exists x.F \mid \forall x.F$$

where A is a non-terminal that generates atomic formulas (the grammar for A is omitted) and x denotes a variable.
Let $Var(A)$ denote the set of variables that occur in the atomic formula A.
The set of free variables of a formula F is defined by structural induction as follows.

$$FV(A) = Var(A)$$
$$FV(\neg(F)) = FV(F)$$
$$FV(F_1 \wedge F_2) = FV(F_1) \cup FV(F_2)$$
$$FV(F_1 \vee F_2) = FV(F_1) \cup FV(F_2)$$
$$FV(F_1 \Rightarrow F_2) = FV(F_1) \cup FV(F_2)$$
$$FV(\exists x.F) = FV(F) - \{x\}$$
$$FV(\forall x.F) = FV(F) - \{x\}$$

The set of bound variables of a formula F is defined by structural induction as follows.

$$BV(A) = \emptyset$$
$$BV(\neg(F)) = BV(F)$$
$$BV(F_1 \wedge F_2) = BV(F_1) \cup BV(F_2)$$
$$BV(F_1 \vee F_2) = BV(F_1) \cup BV(F_2)$$
$$BV(F_1 \Rightarrow F_2) = BV(F_1) \cup BV(F_2)$$
$$BV(\exists x.F) = BV(F) \cup \{x\}$$
$$BV(\forall x.F) = BV(F) \cup \{x\}$$

8. Let $R \subseteq A \times A$ be a binary relation on A. Define by rule induction the relation R^*, that is, the reflexive-transitive closure of R.

Answer:

The relation R^* is defined by the following axioms and rule.

$$\frac{}{R^*(a, a)} \ for \ any \ a \in A$$

$$\frac{}{R^*(a, b)} if \ R(a, b)$$

$$\frac{R^*(a, b) \quad R^*(b, c)}{R^*(a, c)} \ for \ any \ a, b, c \in A$$

Selected Exercises From Chap. 3

4. Consider the following Pascal program:

```
program main;
    var a : integer;
```

```
     procedure P1;
     begin
        writeln('a =', a)
     end;
     procedure P2;
     var a : integer;
     begin
        a := 10;
        P1
     end;
begin
a := 4;
P2
end.
```

Pascal uses static scoping rules. What is the value of a printed by P1?
Under dynamic scoping rules, what would be the value printed?

Answer:

The value printed is 4. Under dynamic scope it would be 10.

5. Which kind of scoping rules (static or dynamic) does your favourite programming
   language use?

   (a) Try to find the answer to this question in the documentation available for
       the language.
   (b) Write a test program and use its results to justify your answer to the previous
       question.

      Answer:
      Java, C, C++, Scheme, Haskell, and languages in the ML family are
      all statically scoped. Python, LISP, Perl, JavaScript are dynamically
      scoped.
      The following is a test program for Java.

```
     class Test {

          int x = 3;

          int f (int z) {

            return z+x;

          }
```

```
        public static void main(String[] args) {
        Test t = new Test();

        boolean x = true;

        System.out.println(t.f(6));

      }
    }
```

Below is a similar program in Haskell.

```
let x = 3; f z = z + x in let x = True in f 6
```

Both Java and Haskell are typed languages (Java is imperative, Haskell is functional), but Haskell infers the types so we have not written them in the program (type inference is discussed in Chap. 5).

7. Some programming languages have a post-test logically controlled loop of the form:

$$\text{repeat } C \text{ until } B$$

where the loop-body C will be repeated until the Boolean expression B evaluates to True.

Show that it is possible to simulate this kind of loop in a language that provides a pre-test loop such as while B do C.

Answer:

We could write

```
C; while (not B) do C.
```

which has the same behaviour: it executes C at least once, and stops when the condition B is true.

8. Consider a programming language with a branching statement (goto), and a program containing an instruction goto p.

(a) Suppose that p is the address of an instruction inside the body of a loop statement. Should this be considered a mistake? If not, when and how should the counter (if it is a counter-controlled loop) or the Boolean condition (if it is a logically-controlled loop) be evaluated?

(b) Suppose that p is the address of an instruction inside the body of a sub-program. Should this be considered a mistake? If not, how should the local variables and parameters be treated?

Answer:

If a label p is placed inside the body of a loop statement and the program has an instruction to jump to p, it could be considered a mistake since the intended meaning of a loop construct is to cause the body of the loop to be repeated, starting from the first instruction, until a certain condition becomes true. However, it would also be possible to accept the goto instruction, but jump to the beginning of the loop instead (i.e., execute the full loop). Another alternative would be to execute the instruction labelled by p and all the remaining instructions in the body and then continue directly with the instructions after the loop body. Evaluating the condition to decide whether the body of the loop should be executed again or not is problematic, since it may mention variables that have not been initialised.

If a label is placed in the middle of a subprogram (method, function, etc) and a program executes a jump to this label, one alternative would be to simulate a function call and create copies of local variables for the subprogram. If the function has parameters, then some decision has to be made to assign values to those parameters (perhaps include some default values). Another option would be to consider that the code in the subprogram is executed as if it were part of the main program that made the jump. But then if the local variables are used, there will be an error! Another alternative is to forbid jumps into the middle of a subprogram.

Selected Exercises From Chap. 4

1. Draw the abstract syntax tree of the following SIMP programs:

   (a) $y := 0$;

      $if \ !x = !y \ then \ (x := !x + 1; \ y := !y - 1)$

      $else \ (x := !x - 1; \ y := !y + 1)$

   Answer:

   The abstract syntax tree is:

```
              ;
            /   \
          :=    if then else
         / \    / | \
        y   0  t₁ t₂ t₃
```

where t_1, t_2, t_3 are the trees:

(b) C_1; $(C_2; C_3)$ where C_1, C_2, C_3 are arbitrary programs.
(c) $(C_1; C_2)$; C_3 where C_1, C_2, C_3 are arbitrary programs.

Answer:

The abstract syntax tree for $(C_1; C_2)$; C_3 is:

3. Let C_1, C_2 and C_3 be arbitrary SIMP commands. Using the abstract machine semantics of SIMP, show that the programs C_1; $(C_2; C_3)$ and $(C_1; C_2)$; C_3 are equivalent, that is, they produce the same results when executed in the same state. Therefore the brackets are not needed.

Answer:

Starting from the corresponding initial configurations

$$\langle (C_1; (C_2; C_3)) \cdot nil, nil, m \rangle \quad \text{and} \quad \langle ((C_1; C_2); C_3) \cdot nil, nil, m \rangle$$

the abstract machine performs the following transitions:

$$\langle (C_1; (C_2; C_3)) \cdot nil, nil, m \rangle \to \langle C_1 \cdot (C_2; C_3) \cdot nil, nil, m \rangle$$

and

$$\langle ((C_1; C_2); C_3) \cdot nil, nil, m \rangle \to \langle (C_1; C_2) \cdot C_3 \cdot nil, nil, m \rangle \to$$

$$\langle C_1 \cdot C_2 \cdot C_3 \cdot nil, nil, m \rangle$$

To show that the programs have the same semantics we need to prove that either

 - they are both non-terminating, or
 - they give the same result.

This is a consequence of the following property:

For any program C, control stack c and memory m:

(a) If $\langle C \cdot nil, nil, m \rangle \to^* \langle nil, r, m' \rangle$ then $\langle C \cdot c, nil, m \rangle \to^* \langle c, r, m' \rangle$.
(b) If $\langle C \cdot nil, nil, m \rangle$ does not terminate then $\langle C \cdot c, nil, m \rangle$ does not terminate. This is because to decide whether a transition rule applies or not to a configuration, we only need to look at the first element of its control stack (as well as the results stack).

4. (a) Give the structural induction principle for Boolean expressions in SIMP.
   (b) Consider a configuration $\langle B \cdot c, r, m \rangle$ for the abstract machine, where c, r, m are arbitrary stacks and memory states, and B is a Boolean expression in SIMP, such that any integer expression E occurring in B mentions only valid memory locations.
   Prove by structural induction that for any such B, there is a sequence of transitions for the abstract machine:

$$\langle B \cdot c, r, m \rangle \to^* \langle c, b \cdot r, m \rangle$$

where b is a Boolean value (True or False),

   Answer:

   (a) To prove that a property P is true for all Boolean expressions in SIMP it is sufficient to prove:
       i. Basis:
          $P(True)$

$P(False)$

$P(E\ bop\ E')$, for all integer expressions E, E' and comparison operators $bop \in \{>, <, =\}$.

ii. Induction Step:

$P(B)$ implies $P(\neg B)$, for any Boolean expression B.

$P(B)$ and $P(B')$ implies $P(B \wedge B')$, for any Boolean expressions B, B'.

(b) We can apply this induction principle to prove the property "the value of B is defined", for any expression B, under the assumption that arithmetic expressions satisfy this property (we proved in Chap. 4, Example 4.5, that all arithmetic expressions that use only valid memory locations produce a result).

Basis:

— $P(True)$, $P(False)$ hold by definition (see the transition rules for $b \in \{True, False\}$).

— If an expression of the form $(E\ bop\ E')$ is at the top of the control stack, the machine will move to a configuration in which E and E' are at the top and by assumption E and E' have a value, therefore the transitions of the machine will take us to a configuration where bop is at the top of the control stack and the values of E and E' are in the results stack. Applying the transition rule for bop, we obtain a result for the initial expression.

Induction Step:

— $P(B)$ implies $P(\neg B)$ for any Boolean expression B, using the transition rule for $\neg$.

— If the expression has the form $(B \wedge B')$, we can reason as in the second base case and deduce that $P(B \wedge B')$ holds because, by the induction hypothesis, $P(B)$ and $P(B')$ hold (i.e., the rules of the machine allow us to find values for B and B').

6. Prove that the small-step semantics of **SIMP** is deterministic, that is, $\langle P, s \rangle \rightarrow \langle P_1, s_1 \rangle$ and $\langle P, s \rangle \rightarrow \langle P_2, s_2 \rangle$ implies $\langle P_1, s_1 \rangle = \langle P_2, s_2 \rangle$.

Answer:

The proof is by induction on the structure of P, which can be a command C, an integer expression E or a Boolean expression B. Below we show the cases for C only, the other cases are similar.

– If P is the command $skip$, then $\langle P, s \rangle$ is a final configuration and the property holds trivially since there is no transition out of $\langle P, s \rangle$.
– If P is an assignment $l := E$, then there are two cases:

If E is a number, then $\langle E, s \rangle$ is final, and we have a unique transition $\langle l := n, s \rangle \rightarrow \langle skip, s[l \mapsto n] \rangle$ using the axiom (:=).
Otherwise, since there is at most one transition out of $\langle E, s \rangle$ by the induction hypothesis, there is at most one transition for $\langle P, s \rangle$ using the axiom (:=$_R$).
No other axiom or rule applies.

- We can reason in the same way in the case of a sequence $C_1; C_2$: either C_1 is $skip$, and only the axiom (skip) applies (since $\langle skip, s \rangle$ is final), or there is at most one transition $\langle C_1; C_2, s \rangle \rightarrow \langle C_1'; C_2, s' \rangle$, because by induction hypothesis there is at most one transition $\langle C_1, s \rangle \rightarrow \langle C_1', s' \rangle$, and only rule (seq) applies.
- The case for $P = if\ B\ then\ C_1\ else\ C_1$ is similar. The axioms (if$_T$) and (if$_F$) can only be used if the condition is already a Boolean value, and at most one of them can be applied to $\langle P, s \rangle$. The rule (if) can only be used if there is a transition out of $\langle B, s \rangle$ (which cannot happen if B is a Boolean value). Since, by the induction hypothesis, there is at most one transition $\langle B, s \rangle \rightarrow \langle B', s' \rangle$, the result follows.
- The case where P is a while is easy: only the (while) axiom applies in this case.

12. We add to the syntax of the language SIMP a post-test logically controlled loop:

$$\texttt{repeat C until B}$$

where the loop-body C will be repeated until the Boolean expression B evaluates to True.

(a) Give a formal definition of the semantics of this command, by specifying the rules that should be added to the big-step semantics of SIMP.
(b) Show that this extension does not change the computational power of the language by giving a translation of

$$\texttt{repeat C until B}$$

in terms of the constructs that already exist in SIMP.

Answer:

(a) We add to the big-step semantics of SIMP the following rules:

$$\frac{\langle C, s \rangle \Downarrow \langle skip, s'' \rangle\ \langle B, s'' \rangle \Downarrow \langle False, s''' \rangle\ \langle repeat\ C\ until\ B, s''' \rangle \Downarrow \langle skip, s' \rangle}{\langle repeat\ C\ until\ B, s \rangle \Downarrow \langle skip, s' \rangle}$$

$$\frac{\langle C, s \rangle \Downarrow \langle skip, s'' \rangle\ \ \langle B, s'' \rangle \Downarrow \langle True, s' \rangle}{\langle repeat\ C\ until\ B, s \rangle \Downarrow \langle skip, s' \rangle}$$

(b) The command `repeat C until B` is equivalent to

`C; while ¬ B do C`

To show that they are equivalent, we need to check that for any command *C* and Boolean condition *B* in SIMP, either both programs terminate and reach a configuration with the same memory state, according to the given semantics, or they are both non-terminating.

Selected Exercises From Chap. 5

2. Write the definitions of `quad` (the function that computes the 4th power of a number), and `double` (the function that doubles its argument). Describe the reduction sequences for the expression:

$$quad\ (double\ (3 + 1))$$

using the call-by-name (normal order) and the call-by-value (applicative order) strategies.

Answer:

`quad x = y * y where y = x * x`

`double x = 2 * x`

There are three redexes in `quad (double (3 + 1))`:
3 + 1, double (3 + 1), and quad (double (3 + 1)). Therefore there are three choices for the first reduction step. We show below two reduction sequences:

(a) Normal Order: Leftmost-outermost
quad (double (3 + 1)) → y * y where

$$y = (double\ (3 + 1)) * (double\ (3 + 1)$$

→ y * y where y = 2 * (3 + 1) * (double (3 + 1))

→ y * y where y = 2 * 4 * (double (3 + 1))

→ y * y where y = 8 * (double (3 + 1))

$\rightarrow$ y * y where y = 8 * 2 * (3 + 1)

$\rightarrow$ y * y where y = 16 * (3 + 1)

$\rightarrow$ y * y where y = 16 * 4

$\rightarrow$ y * y where y = 64 $\rightarrow$ 64 * 64 $\rightarrow$ 4096

(b) Applicative Order: Leftmost-innermost

quad (double (3 + 1)) $\rightarrow$ quad (double 4)

$\rightarrow$ quad (2 * 4)

$\rightarrow$ quad 8

$\rightarrow$ y * y where y = 8 * 8

$\rightarrow$ y * y where y = 64 $\rightarrow$ 64 * 64 $\rightarrow$ 4096

4. (a) Assume the function `mult` on natural numbers is defined by

```
mult x y = if (x == 0) then 0 else x * y
```

where == is the equality test. Assume that e_1 == e_2 is evaluated by reducing e_1 and e_2 to normal form, and then comparing the normal forms.
Is `mult` commutative?

(b) Let `infinity` be the function defined by

```
infinity = infinity + 1
```

What is the value of `mult infinity 0`?

And `mult 0 infinity`?

Answer:

For `mult infinity 0` the evaluation process does not terminate, the value is undefined.
For `mult 0 infinity` the value is 0, and can be found with a strategy that uses normal order.

5. What is the type of `until` in Example 5.21?

Answer:

The general type of `until` is

```
until :: (a -> Bool) -> (a -> a) -> a -> a
```

and in this example it is used with type

```
until :: (Float -> Bool) -> (Float -> Float) -> Float
-> Float
```

6. Imperative languages have pre-test and post-test loops, such as *while B do C* and *do C while B*. Both can be simulated in a functional language using recursion.

   (a) Write a recursive function `while-do` that takes as arguments:
       - a predicate b of type $\alpha \rightarrow$ `Bool`,
       - a function c of type $\alpha \rightarrow \alpha$, and
       - an element x of type α.
       If x does not satisfy b then the result should be x, otherwise, `while-do` iterates the function c on x until a value x' is obtained which does not satisfy b.
   (b) Write a recursive function `do-while` to simulate a post-test loop. This function takes the same arguments as the function `while-do`, and it also iterates the function c on x until a value x' is obtained which does not satisfy b, but the test is performed after the application of c. Therefore, even if the given x does not satisfy b, the function c will be applied at least once.
   (c) Give a polymorphic type for `while-do` and `do-while`.

   Answer:

   The functions `while-do` and `do-while` can be defined as follows:

   ```
   while-do b c x = if not (b x) then x else while-do
   b c (c x)
   ```

   ```
   do-while b c x = while-do b c (c x)
   ```

   The types are:

   ```
   while-do :: (a -> Bool) -> (a -> a) -> a -> a
   ```

   ```
   do-while :: (a -> Bool) -> (a -> a) -> a -> a
   ```

7. Consider the following functional program:

   ```
   apply f x = f x
   ```

   (a) Give a polymorphic type for the function `apply`.

(b) We define now a function `selfapply` as follows.

```
selfapply f = f f
```

Can Haskell find a type for the function `selfapply`?

Answer:

```
apply :: (a -> b) -> a -> b
```

The function `selfapply` is not typeable because we need two types for `f` that are not compatible: `a -> b` and `a`.

8. Give a recursive definition of the function g such that

$$g\,n = \sum_{i=1}^{n} i$$

and prove by induction that, for any natural number n,

$$g\,n = n(n+1)/2$$

Answer:
To define g, we use pattern-matching on the natural numbers:

```
g 0 = 0
g (n+1) = (g n) + n + 1
```
We prove `g n = n(n+1)/2` for all n by induction as follows.
Base case:
For n = 0, we have `g 0 = 0` as required.
Induction Step:
Assuming that `g n = n(n+1)/2` we have to prove that `g (n+1) = (n+1)(n+2)/2`
Note that `g (n+1) = (g n) + n + 1` by definition of g. Therefore, using the induction hypothesis,
`g (n+1) = n(n+1)/2 + n + 1` and `n(n+1)/2 + n + 1 = (n+1)(n+2)/2` as required.

11. (†) A beginner Haskell programmer wrote the following program to add all the elements in a sequence of numbers:

```
sum Empty = 0

sum (Cons x s) = sum s
```

Even though there was no type error message, seeing the type that Haskell had inferred the programmer immediately realised that there was a bug in the program. Can you explain why?

Answer:
The type of the function is:

```
sum :: Num a => Seq b -> a
```

so this function works with sequences of any type, which is not right if the intention is to add the elements in the sequence.

Selected Exercises From Chap. 6

3. Show that the SFUN program

$$square(x) = x * x$$
$$double(x) = 2 * x$$

and the term $square(double(3))$ are well-typed in an environment ε such that
$\varepsilon(square) = \text{int} \rightarrow \text{int}$
$\varepsilon(double) = \text{int} \rightarrow \text{int}$

Answer:
To prove that the program is well typed, we need to show that both sides of each equation have the same type (in this case int). The left-hand sides are both of type int in an environment Γ such that $x : \text{int} \in \Gamma$. The right-hand sides use $*$, which takes two arguments of type int and produces a result of type int, so it is easy to see that in both equations the right-hand side has type int (we omit the type derivations).
The type derivation for the term $square(double(3))$ is given below.

$$\cfrac{\cfrac{\cfrac{}{\vdash_\varepsilon 3 : \text{int}}\text{(n)}}{\vdash_\varepsilon \texttt{double(3)}: \text{int}}\text{(fn)}}{\vdash_\varepsilon \texttt{square(double(3))}: \text{int}}\text{(fn)}$$

4. Show the evaluation of the SFUN term $square(double(3))$ with respect to the program:

$$square(x) = x * x$$
$$double(x) = 2 * x$$

using first the call-by-value semantics, then the call-by-name semantics.

Answer:
Call-by-value

$$\cfrac{\cfrac{\quad}{3 \Downarrow_P 3} \quad \cfrac{\cfrac{\quad}{2 \Downarrow_P 2} \quad \cfrac{\quad}{3 \Downarrow_P 3}}{(2 * x)\{x \mapsto 3\} \Downarrow_P 6}}{\cfrac{double(3) \Downarrow_P 6}{\quad}} \quad \cfrac{\cfrac{\cfrac{\quad}{6 \Downarrow_P 6} \quad \cfrac{\quad}{6 \Downarrow_P 6}}{(x * x)\{x \mapsto 6\} \Downarrow_P 36}}{\quad}$$
$$square(double(3)) \Downarrow_P 36$$

Call-by-name:

$$\cfrac{\cfrac{\cfrac{\quad}{2 \Downarrow_P 2} \quad \cfrac{\quad}{3 \Downarrow_P 3}}{(2 * x)\{x \mapsto 3\} \Downarrow_P 6}}{double(3) \Downarrow_P 6} \quad \cfrac{\cfrac{\quad}{2 \Downarrow_P 2} \quad \cfrac{\quad}{3 \Downarrow_P 3}}{\cfrac{(2 * x)\{x \mapsto 3\} \Downarrow_P 6}{double(3) \Downarrow_P 6}}$$
$$\cfrac{(x * x)\{x \mapsto double(3)\} \Downarrow_P 36}{\quad}$$
$$square(double(3)) \Downarrow_P 36$$

Note that the term $double(3)$ is evaluated twice with call-by-name.

6. Prove the *unicity of types* in SFUN (Property 6.10), that is, show that for any SFUN term t, if $\Gamma \vdash_\varepsilon t : \sigma$ and $\Gamma \vdash_\varepsilon t : \tau$ then $\sigma = \tau$.

   Answer:
   We prove this property by induction on the structure of t.
   Base cases: We have to prove that the type is unique if t is a number, a Boolean value or a variable.
   If t is a number n, at most one axiom (axiom (n)) can be used to type t. Similarly, if t is a Boolean b (resp., a variable x) only the axiom (b) (resp., (var)) can be used to type t. Therefore, we can derive at most one type for t, for any Γ.
   Induction:
   Assume that t_1 and t_2 have a unique type under the assumptions in Γ. If $t = t_1 op \; t_2$, then t can only be typed using rule (op). In this case, the only possible type for t is int.
   Similarly, if $t = t_1 bop \; t_2, t = t_1 \wedge t_2$ or $t = \neg t_1$, the only possible type for t is bool.
   If $t = if \; t_0 \; then \; t_1 \; else \; t_2$, the result follows by induction, since there is only one possible type for t_1 and t_2 (induction hypothesis), and the type of t is the same as the type of t_1 and t_2.

Finally, if $t = f_i(t_1, \ldots, t_n)$, then the result is a consequence of the fact that only rule (fn) can be used and the resulting type is uniquely determined by $\varepsilon(f_i)$.

8. Consider the SFUN program:

$$double(x) = 2 * x$$

- Show by induction that for any natural number n, $double(n)$ is equivalent to $n + n$ (i.e., show that $double(n)$ and $n + n$ produce the same value, for any natural number n). You can use either call-by-value or call-by-name semantics.
- Explain why for terms of the form $double(t)$ where t is an arithmetic expression, the call-by-value and call-by-name strategies have the same behaviour and are equally efficient.

Answer:

- By induction on n:
  Base Case: If $n = 0$ then $double(0) = 2 * 0 = 0 + 0$.
  Inductive Step: Assume $double(n) = n + n$. Then:
  $double(n + 1) = 2 * (n + 1) = 2 * n + 2 = double(n) + 2 = n + n + 2 = (n + 1) + (n + 1)$
  as required.
- Both strategies have the same behaviour because all arithmetic expressions are terminating. Moreover they are equally efficient because the function uses x, and it uses it only once.

9. Define the set $FVar(t)$ of free variables of the term t in FUN, by induction on the structure of t.

Answer:

The set of free variables of a term is defined by structural induction as follows.

$$FVar(n) = FVar(b) = \emptyset$$
$$FVar(op) = FVar(bop) = \emptyset$$
$$FVar(\neg) = FVar(\wedge) = \emptyset$$
$$FVar(id) = \{id\}$$
$$FVar(if\ t_0\ then\ t_1\ else\ t_2) = FVar(t_0) \cup FVar(t_1) \cup FVar(t_2)$$
$$FVar(let\ x = t_1\ in\ t_2) = FVar(t_1) \cup (FVar(t_2) - \{x\})$$
$$FVar(let\ fun\ f x_1 \ldots x_n = t_1\ in\ t_2) = (FVar(t_1) - \{x_1, \ldots, x_n, f\})$$
$$\cup(FVar(t_2) - \{f\})$$

10. Explain what the following FUN functions do

$$f_1\ x = \texttt{let}\ y = x * x\ \texttt{in}\ y * y$$

$$f_2\, x = \texttt{let}\ x = x * x\ \texttt{in}\ x * x$$

Show that this program is typeable in an environment Γ where

$$\Gamma(f_1) = \Gamma(f_2) = \text{int} \to \text{int}$$

Answer:

Both functions compute x^4.

It is easy to see that both equations are typeable: the left-hand sides have type int assuming x : int (we use the rule (Ap) and the assumptions $\Gamma(f_1) = \Gamma(f_2) = \text{int} \to \text{int}$), and the right-hand sides also have type int since we have x : int $\vdash x * x$: int and y : int $\vdash y * y$: int.

Selected Exercises From Chap. 7

1. Assuming that A, B, C are atomic formulas, which of the following clauses are definite clauses?

   (a) $\neg A \vee \neg B$
   (b) $A \vee B \vee \neg C$
   (c) $A \vee \neg A$
   (d) A

   Answer:

   The only clause that is not a definite clause is the second one (it has two positive literals).

4. Apply the substitution $\{X \mapsto [X, Y], Y \mapsto [X, Y]\}$ to the term $f(X, Y)$.

   Answer:

   The result of applying this substitution to the term $f(X, Y)$ is $f([X, Y], [X, Y])$, since both variables are replaced simultaneously by $[X, Y]$.

5. Lists are also predefined in Prolog. In particular, the predicate append is predefined, but in this exercise we will define a new append:

```
myappend([],Y,Y).

myappend([H|T],Y,[H|U])  :- myappend(T,Y,U).
```

What are the answers to the following goals?

```
:- myappend([1,2],[3,4,5],[1,2,3,4,5]).

:- myappend([1,2],[3,4,5],[1,2]).

:- myappend([1,2],[3,4,5],X).

:- myappend([1,2],X,[1,2,3,4,5]).

:- myappend(X,[3,4,5],[1,2,3,4,5]).

:- myappend(X,Y,[1,2,3,4,5]).

:- myappend(X,Y,Z).
```

Explain the answers.

Answer:

The answer for the first goal is `true` since the concatenation of the first two lists produces the third list.
For the second goal the answer is `false` because appending the first two lists we do not obtain the third list.
For the third, fourth and fifth goals, the answers are:

```
X = [1, 2, 3, 4, 5].

X = [3, 4, 5].

X = [1, 2].
```

The sixth goal has the answers:

```
    X = [],
    Y = [1, 2, 3, 4, 5] ;
    X = [1],
    Y = [2, 3, 4, 5] ;
    X = [1, 2],
    Y = [3, 4, 5] ;
    X = [1, 2, 3],
    Y = [4, 5] ;
    X = [1, 2, 3, 4],
    Y = [5] ;
```

```
X = [1, 2, 3, 4, 5],
Y = []
```

Finally, the last goal has an infinite number of answers. There is one solution where x is an empty list, another solution where x is a list of length one, another solution where x is a list of length two, etc. The answers computed by Prolog are:

```
X = [],
Y = Z ;
X = [_G340],
Z = [_G340|Y] ;
X = [_G340, _G346],
Z = [_G340, _G346|Y] ;

⋮
```

6. Change the order of the clauses in the previous program, and try again the previous goals. Can you explain the behaviour of the new program?

Answer:

The first six goals behave similarly, but now the last goal does not produce any answer. This is expected since we have put the clause that specifies the base case in the recursive definition at the end. Prolog attempts to find the answer using the clauses in the order given in the program, and in this case, the clause that should stop the recursion is never used.

Selected Exercises From Chap. 8

2. Recall that the notation [A, B, C] is short for [A | [B | [C | [ ]]]].

   (a) Are the terms [[1, 0], [0, 0], [0, 0]] and [X |[X, Y]] unifiable? Use the unification algorithm to answer this question, that is, try to solve the unification problem [[1, 0], [0, 0], [0, 0]] = [X |[X, Y]].
   (b) Are the terms [[1, X], Y, Y] and [X |[0, 0]] unifiable? Use the unification algorithm to answer this question, that is, try to solve the unification problem [[1, X], Y, Y] = [X |[0, 0]].

Answer:

(a) They are not unifiable because there is a clash: X = [1,0] and X =[0,0].

(b) They are not unifiable because X occurs in [1,X] (occur check).

3. Give the most general unifier (if it exists) for the following problems
   (a) `append([1,2],L,[]) = append([X|Y],Y,[]).`
   (b) `append([1,2],X,U) = append([Y|L],0,[Y|R]).`

   Answer:

   In both cases, the terms are unifiable using, respectively,

   $$\{X \mapsto 1, Y \mapsto [2], L \mapsto [2]\}$$

   and

   $$\{Y \mapsto 1, L \mapsto [2], X \mapsto 0, U \mapsto [1|R]\}.$$

4. Show that the resolvent of the clauses
   P :- $A_1, \ldots, A_n$
   and
   :- $Q_1, \ldots, Q_m$
   is also a definite clause, for any atoms $A_1, \ldots, A_n, Q_1, \ldots, Q_m$.

   Answer:

   By definition, each clause contains zero or one positive literal. Resolving eliminates one literal Q_i and replaces it by $A_1, \ldots, A_n$, with a suitable substitution (which will only modify the terms inside the literals). Therefore the resolvent is still a definite clause.

5. A Prolog program contains the following clauses:
   `sunny(mon).`

   `sunny(tue).`

   `sunny(wed).`

   `warm(mon).`

   `warm(wed).`

   (a) Write down all the responses that Prolog will give to the query

      `:- sunny(Day),warm(Day).`

      in their proper order.
   (b) Draw the SLD-tree built by Prolog for the previous query.

Answer:

The answers are: Day = mon and Day = wed.

SLD-tree:

$$\text{sunny}(Day),\text{warm}(Day)$$

$\{Day \mapsto mon\}/ \qquad | \{Day \mapsto tue\} \quad \backslash \{Day \mapsto wed\}$

warm(mon)   warm(tue)   warm(wed)

| Failure |

◇   ◇

9. Consider the following logic program to split a list into two lists.
   ```
   split([],[],[]).
   ```

   ```
   split([X],[X],[]).
   ```

   ```
   split([X,Y|L],[X|M],[Y|N]) :- split(L,M,N).
   ```

   (a) Draw the SLD-resolution tree for the query:

   ```
   :- split([0,1,2],L1,L2)
   ```

   using the computation rule that always selects the leftmost literal as the one
   resolved upon.
   (b) Indicate all the answers that Prolog finds for the query above.

   Answer:

   The tree has just one branch, which ends in a success.

   Prolog will find L1=[0,2], and L2=[1].

10. Consider the following logic program
    ```
    witness(john).
    ```

    ```
    neighbour(mary).
    ```

    ```
    hide(john).
    ```

    ```
    suspect(X) :- witness(X).
    ```

```
suspect(X)  :- neighbour(X).

charge(X)  :- suspect(X), hide(X).
```

and queries

```
:- suspect(john).

:- charge(X).
```

Draw the SLD-resolution tree for each query (using the computation rule that always selects the leftmost literal as the one resolved upon) and give the answers that Prolog will find for each query.

Answer:

For the first query, the answer is True since there is a success branch in the tree above.

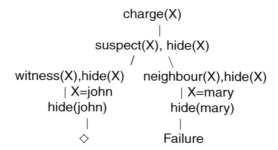

The answer for the second query is X = john.

12. Write a logic program defining a binary predicate member such that member(A, L) is true if A is an element of the list L.

What are the answers to the following queries? Draw the SLD-resolution tree for each one.

(a) :- member(1,[2,1,3]).
(b) :- member(1,[2,3,4]).
(c) :- member(1,[]).

Answer:

We can define the predicate member as follows.

```
member(X,[X|L]).

member(X,[Y|L]) :- member(X,L).
```

The first goal is true, the others are false (Failure).

The resolution tree for the last query contains just one node, the root, since it does not unify with any of the clauses of the program. We show the tree for the first query (without the substitutions since there are no variables in the query):

```
                member(1,[2,1,3])
                       |
                member(1,[1,3])
                     /   \
                  ◇      member(1,[3])
                               |
                         member(1,[])
                            Failure
```

Index

M. Fernández, *Programming Languages and Operational Semantics*,
Undergraduate Topics in Computer Science, DOI: 10.1007/978-1-4471-6368-8,
© Springer-Verlag London 2014

Printed in Great Britain
by Amazon.co.uk, Ltd.,
Marston Gate.